Lifelong Learning

a Human Agenda

Prepared by the
ASCD 1979 Yearbook Committee

Norman V. Overly,
Chairperson and Editor

Association for Supervision
and Curriculum Development
225 North Washington Street
Alexandria, Virginia 22314

Acknowledgments

Publication of this yearbook was the responsibility of Ron Brandt, Executive Editor, ASCD publications. Elsa Angell provided editing and production services with the assistance of Nancy Olson, Patsy Connors, Anne Dees, and Gwendolyn Spells. The cover and design of the volume are by Linda S. Sherman.

Contents

Foreword   *Donald R. Frost*   iv

On Approaching the 1979 Yearbook   *Norman V. Overly*   1

PART I   The Search for Goals   4

PART II   The Realities/The Obstacles   56

PART III   Coming to Terms   128

   Open Education—A Coming to Terms with
      Uncertainty   *Wilma S. Longstreet*   129

   Coming to Terms with Curriculum as a Human
      Agenda   *Virginia M. Macagnoni*   140

   Coming to Terms with the Individual as Culture
      Maker: A Pluralistic Perspective
         Carlos J. Ovando   152

   Educational Leadership—Coming to Terms with
      Responsibility   *Edna Mitchell*   161

   Coming to Terms with Monday Morning
         Norman V. Overly   170

ASCD 1979 Yearbook Committee Members   187

The Authors   187

ASCD Board of Directors   191

   Executive Council 1978-79   191

   Board Members Elected At Large   192

   Unit Representatives to the Board   192

ASCD Review Council   196

ASCD Headquarters Staff   196

Foreword

ASCD Yearbooks are the products of dedicated, creative, hardworking committees. The members take a topic approved by the executive council and develop it into a publication which will stimulate the minds of its readers. With untiring and ingenious effort, they examine what is known about the topic, postulate on the unknown, and conclude what should be our task.

Past yearbook committees are to be commended for their outstanding work, and this year's committee is no exception. After collecting and analyzing all the data, they reaffirm the concept that the human being— a person—should be the main focus of learning. And since learning is a lifelong process, all societal segments should be used as resources.

While I initially found the impressionistic approach used by the authors to be somewhat unusual, the more I read the easier it became to fall into the rhythm of the theme and pulse of the committee reflections. The interrupting and sometimes annoying but supportive tweeters and woofers provided rationale and reasons to support the thrust of the book.

A case is made that learning is truly a lifetime process, beginning when we are born and ending at death. Learning can be simply defined as acquiring knowledges and skills. Schools as institutions can provide access to knowledge and skills learning experiences, but schools are not the exclusive providers of such experiences. Therefore, it is extremely important that all resources in society be linked together to provide for learning throughout one's lifetime.

As the authors have so aptly stated, among the goals of education is a quest for human fulfillment. Yet there can be no human fulfillment unless there are both "societal fulfillment and self-fulfillment." To achieve this, the curriculum must be an open one. It must deal with the uncertainties of life as well as with the predictable and expected.

The authors have orchestrated the realities of society to support the rhythm of the theme for linking resources for lifelong learning. Now it is our turn to orchestrate realities around us to the same tune.

DONALD R. FROST, *President 1978-79*
Association for Supervision
and Curriculum Development

On Approaching the 1979 Yearbook

If you believe you learn best by being involved in the process, if you are intrigued by the ambiguity and complexity of our age, our profession, our hopes and fears, this yearbook was written with you in mind. The committee believes most readers will agree that we live in a time of much conflict and uncertainty, a time of flagging confidence and mounting problems. The search for purpose in life as well as in education continues with little evidence of resolution. At the same time we live in an atmosphere of promise and excitement, a time of new breakthroughs and opportunity for personal and social fulfillment. But how are we to proceed? What are we to think? What are we to do?

The educational community is especially hard pressed by new expectations and responsibilities coupled with calls for increased accountability and authenticity of offerings. American education has always been characterized by a responsiveness to societal pressures in its search for more adequate processes. In the present press for immediate answers, both society and the educational establishment are susceptible, more than ever, to nostrums and schemes which promise fresh or comprehensive ways of gaining a hold on the fast-evolving future. "Lifelong learning" is the latest term for the constellation of efforts designed to make education more central to the continuing human search for fulfillment. Yet the concept is too important to the quality of our future to permit it to become one more inoperative fad. For too long we have been content to respond to the beat of someone else's drum, marching after goals formulated by others. We cannot ignore the sound of the drums, but we must be more than followers. We encourage readers to become a part of the search to create their own world, to join in the learning, lifelong.

Any book about lifelong learning can only hope to deal with a portion of such an all encompassing concern. The existing literature includes specialized approaches from the perspective of the comparative educator, internationalist, adult educator, university administrator, and so on. Because of the diverse interests of ASCD readership and since it is not possible within a few pages to probe deeply into the significance of lifelong learning for all of American society, the Yearbook Committee has chosen to follow an expressionistic, literary model that permits a number of voices to speak from different perspectives as they reflect on or act out their search for purposeful learning in the past, present, and future. But as professional educators are aware, the identification of goals by individuals and groups is but one part of the process of achieving learning at any level. The realities of our diverse environments restrict and expand our options, challenge us with new ideas or lull us into complacency; most critically, they pose obstacles which seem to prevent us from breaking through to the achievement of our nobler visions.

This book does not attempt to provide answers for every questioner, seeker, or doubter. It does present a number of perspectives, and attempts to engage the reader in a consideration of the diversity of goals possible for a nation of lifelong learners. It then seeks to confront us with some of the obstacles that must be overcome if we are to become such a society. Finally, it attempts to suggest some approaches for coming to terms with an idea that should be of top priority on the human agenda. While educators have a special role to play as facilitators of learning, they have the even more urgent role to fulfill of being lifelong learners. We hope this book will stimulate the reader to reflection and action, as citizen and as professional.

We have attempted to create a learning environment or arena for you to write yourself in and create with us. If the costs were not prohibitive, we would have left space throughout the book for you to add your own illustrations and counterpoints to the expressions we have created and selected. As it is, you still have the margins. The collage of musings, vignettes, and headlines presented are intended to raise questions rather than provide answers. Some are fictional stories, some are factual reports, some are informed opinion, some are bigoted statements, but all reflect a portion of the struggle to make learning meaningful throughout life. We hope readers will consider the personal significance of each statement as well as find opportunity to pursue the meanings for society in more formal settings with students, fellow educators, and others. We have tried to avoid dogmatic prescriptions; where we have not succeeded, we hope our lapses will be further stimuli for linking yourself to the problems and promises of a life of learning.

The first two sections of the book are products of a joint writing effort, if any writing ever was. As individual contributors, we still may recognize personal words, turns of phrases, and singular contributions, especially in the Commentaries and Committee Reflections, but we also recognize that our ideas have come to reflect not a consensus, but a kind of harmonic unity—a fusion of perspectives we all share to some degree as a result of three years of intensive writing, interacting, critiquing, and rewriting. We have grown together in the process of struggling with the original theme for this yearbook: "Linking Resources for Human Fulfillment: A Design for Education Action." We have come to recognize anew the necessity and the value of each person coming to terms with his or her own setting and the interpretation of it. To this end we have endeavored to create a series of suggestions that will cause us to explore purposes, goals, contemporary realities, and obstacles arising from them that prevent the realization of human fulfillment. In the process the Committee members themselves have experienced one enriching form of lifelong learning.

A short explanation of the format we have used may be in order. Those with a grounding in literature will recognize our indebtedness to the creative spirit of John Dos Passos.[2] Those attuned to the technology of hi-fi's and sound systems will recognize the fluctuating tones of shrill—sometimes humorous, sometimes annoying—tweeters* and the under-current of lower—sometimes disturbing, sometimes solemn—woofers,* which challenge us to reflect upon the basis of our reactions as we seek the balance of understanding. The result is a yearbook in which the first two parts are expressionistic rather than logical, requiring your involvement and constant sorting, sifting, interpreting, and relating. Hopefully, they reflect something of the diversity of views in our pluralistic society and will serve to open our perspectives to the ambiguity of messages found in the broader national and global contexts to which we must respond as educators and learners.

The third section follows the traditional yearbook pattern of separate statements. Each writer attempts to come to terms with some of the barriers that prevent us from moving quickly and smoothly into an age of human fulfillment through learning.

NORMAN V. OVERLY

*Tweeters are distinguished by a light type face and this symbol:

Woofers are in a heavier type face and are preceded by this symbol:

[2] John Dos Passos. *U.S.A.* New York: The Modern Library, Random House, Inc., 1937.

PART I

The Search for Goals

"It was the best of times, it was the
worst of times, it was the age of wisdom,
it was the age of foolishness, . . ."
Charles Dickens, *A Tale of Two Cities*

Grandma's Search

My grandmother migrated to the United States as a young girl, had
13 children and worked hard every day of her 80 years. When she was
very old, I was still in junior high. Other than her very white hair and
noticeable foreign accent, there are only a few things I remember about
her. Yet, one memory has stayed with me more than any other all
these years.

I used to do my homework on a comfortable old couch with my
books strewn all about. Sometimes, she would sit down beside me and
flick through the pages of my book. She could barely read and there was
something odd about the way she turned the pages. It was almost as
though she were caressing them. It was almost as
though she were caressing them.

Every now and then, her gaze would come to rest on a diagram
such as those used in projective geometry and she would obviously be
trying to fathom its meaning. Once in a while she would ask me about

4

something, but my explanations were never very satisfying to her. I suppose, in a way, I was a little bothered by her asking me questions that were so difficult to answer. One evening, frustrated more than usual by my inadequate responses, she turned to me and said: "You must learn better! You must study more! The world is so hard to understand and these books help you. These pages can help you to feel more comfortable with the world. When the radio talks about the atom bombs and you understand about atoms, it makes you feel so much better than if you don't understand them. I know because I am so ignorant and I want so much to understand what is happening all around me."

At the time, I thought she really didn't understand the things young people need. Who cared about atoms or dumb geometric diagrams? There were things bothering me like my friend who was pregnant and didn't know what to do and my wanting to learn to dance in case I was asked at the first school party I ever attended.

To this day, I question what education should be about. Somewhere among the goals of education is the quest for human fulfillment. But where do dancing and atoms and dumb geometric diagrams fit in our struggle for fulfillment?

Committee Reflections on Learning

THE LEARNING DREAM

Pemican and succotash,
Leather thongs chewed to a fine consistency—
Skills past, still passing from age to age.
From the long houses, igloos and pueblos
Rose dreams of families, communities of families, nations
Confronting the elements, rubbing shoulders with friend and foe.

The bearers of Good News and powerful arms,
Of Ten Commandments and restrictive convenants
Came with confusing aims, bound to each other against the unknown,
*   yet knowing; believing, yet searching; stumbling, yet certain*
*   of their vision.*

Teachers became the taught
In the cruel winters of Cape Cod,
The mosquito swamps of the South,
The parching heat of desert sands,
The howling winds of Rocky Mountain blizzards.

Dreams arrived in many guises—
Strident Roger Williams,
The stiff-backed order of Puritan social control,

The flaming assurance of Spanish monarchy and church,
Indentured servants and slaves—
All nurturing hopes for survival and urgently creating
New Realities
In the face of a native tribal order—quietly watching.

Family hearth or Dame School,
Philadelphia dock, slave auction block,
Each contributed to the fulfillment of hopes—
Dreams of advancement and adventure, dreams of despair,
    dreams changed and forged from necessity.

Prosperity and time clothed reality in myth for some;
For others, the dream struggled to emerge from the nightmare
Of days in bondage to cruel masters, coal dust, endless rows
    of vegetables
And the relentless rhythm of assembly lines and steel rails.
Slowly hopes frayed,
Nudged and buffeted by the will to survive.

But still they learned.
Still the dreams remained in cloistered memory and communal liturgy.
In frontier seminaries and village grammar schools,
In the universities of Europe,
In academies and synagogue schools,
    In fields and slave quarter cells,
They labored and learned,
Learned to labor and become a part of a bigger dream.

The people affirmed, decided, ruled.
The people became US.
Brawling frontiersmen found common cause with powdered landlord.
A new covenant, a social pledge was made—
Grounded in a search for the common good.
All men created equal—the noblest dream!
But in the process majority imposed, power counted,
    knowledge gave power.
Order courted new order, crushing dreams.

Nightmare brushed against paradise.
The new dream bled into a new reality—darkness for the Jew,
The Black, the possessors of accents 'foreign,'
Unwanted, unclaimed, uncertified.
But still we came—or could not leave—
Came not knowing or, knowing, unable to risk more.

Caught in an eddy, we met the tide with
  our own tide—
Persistent hopes from east and west, south and north
Slipped into the vortex and challenged it.

We learned and we taught.
From Mexico, Italy, Ireland;
China, Scandinavia, Japan;
Germany, Russia, Holland—
Pieces of the world
People of the world
Dreaming polyglot dreams,
Nourished in deepest anguish.
Though mauled and maimed, we broke forth with stronger
  dreams,
Deferred, but practiced, in the long watch of sleepless nights.

We learned in labor hall and sanctuary,
In storefront and Carnegie Library,
In ethnic club and ghetto confrontation.
We learned we have much to learn.
We learned realizing dreams are hard.
We learned the struggle is life long.

SUNDAY EVENING NEWS BRIEF

. . . **brought to you by the makers of Klorets for sweeter taste and the United Association of School Leaders** . . . **MISUSED DATA BANK INVADES RIGHT TO PRIVACY** . . . GOVERNMENTAL STUDY SHOWS 18-25 YEAR OLDS FACE GLOOMY EMPLOYMENT FUTURE . . . **Minorities Face Increased Unemployment** . . . **WOMEN AND YOUTH, LAST HIRED, FIRST FIRED** . . . CAREER EDUCATION EXPENDITURE QUESTIONED . . . Will it create more jobs? . . . **Teacher Fired — Admits Homosexuality** . . . **ALTERNATIVES TO TRADITIONAL FAMILY LIFE INCREASING according to a recently completed university study** . . . AMISH STILL SEE EDUCATION AS THREAT TO THEIR CULTURE

Saul Bellow Wins 1976 Nobel Award

Saul Bellow, chronicler of the condition of the modern world, has won international respect and admiration for his sensitive portrayal of the rootlessness and fear of failure endemic in modern life. The implications of his analyses are far reaching in the search for human fulfillment.

John and Mary Freeman Escape

Ten years ago, the Freemans left their comfortable home in the suburbs and set up their tent in the wilds of a forest preserve. They were determined to escape the tensions and artifices of modern life and face, as their ancestors had before them, the rigors of the wilderness and the challenge of a hard but honest life. They hoped to be free of the bureaucratic messes and compounding dishonesties that typify experiences in the modern world.

The Freemans have succeeded in building a very comfortable home by using the most rudimentary tools and only the materials they could glean from the woods. All their food is also gathered from the woods.

Although their two children do not know how to read, they have an extraordinary knowledge of plant and wildlife and can find their way in the densest forest by using the stars and sun to guide them. The Freemans express great happiness and no desire to return to their old, "modern" ways.

A MAGNIFICENT TWINKLE

Immensity starts in The Eye
Millions, trillions, zillions,
Maybe more, miles away.
Planets, stars, meteors
Among the mysterious masses of creation.
Black holes and radiation belts
Pulling and tugging, shaping the universe
*   and I*
*   started in The Eye.*
Me—an expression of mystery.
Strobe flashing in the vastness.
A magnificent twinkle!!

SUNDAY FEATURE 1990

It was not too long ago that computers were still based on sets of switches that could be programmed as either on or off. All directions given to the computer were limited to the arrangement of these switches. The creative qualities of the human brain went unrivalled.

In an exciting new development, all this has changed. Nuclear Magnetic Resonance (NMR) has revolutionized the basic quality of computer thought. The slight frequency differences in the magnetic fields of nuclei, detectable in most molecular combinations, have been used for decades to identify the atomic components of almost any substance. In the late 70's, a scientist by the name of Raymond Damadian[1] adapted NMR's to the early detection of cancer cells. Now, it has become possible to record, on infinitesimal chips, the differences in magnetic fields of nuclei which occur when the brain is engaged actively in thought. Several minutes of brain activity can be packed into one chip. At first, the interfacing of these chips with the more traditional parts of the computer posed real difficulties to scientists. These difficulties have now been overcome and we stand at the threshold of an electronic revolution unlike anything ever experienced before.

Although we still do not fully understand how human thought processes work, we have succeeded in harnessing these processes within a computer structure. In some limited ways, we can combine the creative, flexible qualities of human thought with the speed and reliability that has come to be associated with computers.

Helen Keller's Search for Fulfillment

Deaf and blind from birth, Helen Keller spent the early part of her childhood unable to express her inner being in terms that might be shared with others, or to receive from others insights into the nature of her existence. She was a child surrounded by objects she could touch but not name; she stumbled across similarities which she had the potential to recognize but not the means to express; she could fondle and know affection, but the idea of love was something she had to create alone.

That she broke through the barriers and claimed her humanness has touched a chord of understanding in several generations. The denial of human fulfillment was, in her case, so primordial to the nature of our

---

[1] Raymond Damadian. "Field Focusing Nuclear Magnetic Resonance (F.O.N.A.R.): Visualization of a Tumor in a Fine Animal." *Science* 94: 1430-2; December 24, 1976.

existence that we can all share with her the excruciating frustration of that denial.

We live, however, in a time when the circumstances of the world around us have become extremely complex and distant from our original needs for survival. The unfolding of ourselves into this world is necessarily so strange, so confusing, so unpredictable, that the nature of human fulfillment has itself become a perplexity.

Of course, to be capable of listening, speaking, reading, writing is still basic to the individual's interaction with the world. Once, these abilities might have been thought sufficient in helping each of us to achieve fuller insights into the meanings of human life and to move toward a determination of how that life is best led. But once, we were unaware of quantum black holes that engulf anything which happens along into apparent nothingness. Once, the possible annihilation of the world was a capacity attributed only to God, as was the mutation of genes and the determination of when pregnancy would begin. Once, deciding how best to lead our lives lay within the range of our senses or the immediate extension of them via relatively simple tools. Having a "good" job was a survival need that occupied much of the time we spent finding ourselves in the context of our world. Once, we felt sure about the basics.

Seeing is Not Enough

Although the New York State Legislature enacted "The Pure Water Program" in 1964, a two-year study of the Hudson River waters, completed in 1977, concluded that much of the improvement made was in appearance only.

The waterway looked and smelled cleaner, but its deadliness had, if anything, increased. The state program emphasized the elimination of "traditional" pollutants such as "suspended solids" and "coliform bacteria," while it allowed such hazardous substances as benzene, polychlorinated bi-

phenyls (PCB's), xylene, cyclohexane, etc., to be dumped into the river waters.

Usual water treatments are ineffective against these manufactured, toxic chemicals. Communities taking their drinking water from the Hudson may ingest significant levels of chloroform, bromodichloromethane, dibromochloromethane, and carbon tetrachloride, none of which were ever intended for human consumption. The level of chemical toxins has been so high that most kinds of commercial fishing along the Hudson have been banned since February, 1976.

Committee Reflections on Human Fulfillment

The complexity of our present circumstances seems to have left many of us out of touch with our world almost as effectively as if we had been born deaf and blind. It is not simply that our senses have failed us—they are still adequate to the daily unfolding of our lives—but in order for us to be capable of dealing with the destiny of humanness that is now within the grasp of humankind, we must be in command of skills quite distant from those we use in our day-to-day world. These are skills far less comprehensible in terms of human drama than those so valiantly fought for by Helen Keller. Indeed, they are almost boring! Nevertheless, if a handful of intellectually specialized elite are not to take over the directions of human destiny, we must become competent in such skills as developing and using computer languages; programming and manipulating an array of mechanical devices that enable us to explore the universe as well as our own intimate biology; and applying a range of rational systems from information theory to statistical analyses.

Just a short time ago, skills such as those mentioned might have been irrelevant to human fulfillment. Now, they are basic if we are to keep in touch with the realities of our present circumstances and the power that humankind can wield. But are they enough to assure human fulfillment? The complexity of life mounts as our goals become more and more obscure. Several generations have already been born into an environment of continual change and an exponential increase in what is taken to be common knowledge. The urgent question is where are we headed?

It is not, however, that the young are immediately aware of the extraordinary influence that technology and burgeoning knowledge have upon their lives. Like Helen Keller, their learning is filled with the development of their senses. As soon as they are born they begin to learn. They do not need a formalized system of education to decode the experiences of their daily lives. However, some of their most important experiences cannot be fully comprehended without the ability to abstract insights from events often not observable via the natural human senses.

For example, on a spring day, the Hudson River may appear lovely and even clean to the naked eye while chemicals pollute the waters with dangers both predictable and unpredictable. It is difficult to measure the import of such dangers when the river still looks as it used to look in one's childhood. To cope adequately with such phenomena, ability to deal with statistical and chemical evidence and ability to think abstractly about complex cause-event sequences are bare essentials. It is because what children learn on a daily basis is so very remote from such skills that the question of how education should help us all to fulfill our human potential is so perplexing. At a very general level, it can be asserted that education ought to prepare us to deal with and achieve control over the circumstances of our times. But which circumstances?

    To wander without purpose in an aura of failure can only lead to the deepest despair. We are people in despair. Somehow, we must again become creators of and participants in our reality. We must become the makers of our history and our culture.

Rico's Quest

The French Revolution is an example of the ultimate in human protest, Mr. Greenspan intoned to this class.

That's a lot of b-u-l-l, man! Rico whispered as he buried his head in the crook of his arm. Damn the French Revolution! he thought. What would Greenspan look like in powdered wig being carted through the streets of New York? Off with his head! I wonder if it'd hurt? Nothing could hurt like my gut right now. God, I'm hungry! How much more can I take of this?

He glanced at his new watch just as the bell finally rang, then casually swung his wrist in an arc that would catch the eye of Barb, current Numero Uno. They touched, headed for the street and the familiar brownstone stoop that served as headquarters for after-school meetings in the absence of a drive-in. A set of wheels sure would be nice. If he only knew how to drive. Eddie had ripped off a car from some visitor to the Big Apple. Eddie's a real operator. He really knows. They'd been out for a ride, but Eddie wouldn't let him take the wheel. What chance did he have of ever peeling rubber down Chestnut Avenue? He couldn't even afford the rubber. He smiled at his own joke and wondered what the Jock would say about that in phys. ed.! I could teach the Jock a thing or two, he mumbled.

What you say? Barb asked.

Nothin! I think I'd like to be a quarterback on the Jets. Rico Namath, Yeh!

You sure can pass to me, Rico.

Rico had seen some passes in the steamy farm shack his family left behind 12 years ago. He'd like to go back, see his old house. More than that, he'd like to see his dad. He didn't know why. Those were bad memories. The Big Apple had gone rotten fast. There was never anything good to eat, not enough room to sleep. Everybody had money but them—and some of their neighbors. The scenes kept getting worse until the old man just cut out. Maybe he's back in Puerto Rico. Maybe he's gone to Alaska. Big money in Alaska! He could stand the cold. Maybe he's driving trucks out West. That'd be the life. Trucks or motorcycles. Anything to get away from this ugly neighborhood and this stinking school.

S: Hey, Mr. Gutierrez, why did you decide to become a biology teacher and end up working in this rotten high school? Nothing good ever happens here.

T: You know, my being here is no accident. I want to be here. Years ago I discovered how difficult it is for people like us to overcome all the obstacles that keep us from reaching our dreams. I had a teacher in high school who had been to Puerto Rico and could see something good in us instead of all the bad. One day he told me: "Gutierrez, I think you have a fine head. And you seem to be interested in science." And he said if I wanted to go to college he would help me get there. So I went to college and majored in biology and became a teacher. I suppose because of what old Mr. Johnson did for me, I decided to come back to a "rotten" school — like you call it — to see what I could do.

A Commentary on Determining the Basics

There should be no mistaking the general commitment of American educators to the education of all youth nor of society to effective public education. However, within the plurality of American society there is no single acceptable articulation of these commitments. To be educated means different things to different people. The old model of the liberally educated person is no longer adequate or widely understood. John Gardner has called the fostering of individual fulfillment and the nurturing of free, rational and responsible men and women "the great basic goals" of American education.[2] This is a noble vision that will receive wide support but it suggests a multiplicity of aims and an area of potential conflict between personal desires and national aims. One response to the conflict has been recurring calls throughout our history for a return to the basics as common ground for all citizens.

The concern for the "basics" may be one of the rare instances in the history of American public education when the ideals of most educators and parents have matched. If the results of Gallup polls and Phi Delta Kappa goal development exercises[3] are to be believed, there

[2] John W. Gardner. *Goals for Americans, The Report of the President's Commission on National Goals.* New York: American Assembly, Columbia University, 1960. p. 100.

[3] Phi Delta Kappa. *Workshop Packet for Educational Goals and Objectives.* Bloomington, Indiana: Phi Delta Kappa, Inc., N.D.; and *The Gallup Polls of Attitudes Toward Education, 1969-1973.* Bloomington, Indiana: Phi Delta Kappa, Inc., 1974.

is more agreement about the primacy of the basics than about any other educational concern. In addition, the practices of educators and the pattern of common curricula described in studies by Goodlad,[4] Jackson,[5] and many others suggest that more attention is given to the basics as typically defined, than to any other aspect of curriculum. If these data are accurate, then what is all the fuss about?

As James L. Jarrett[6] has pointed out, we all want to define basics in our own way, but the meaning of "basic education" is not self-evident. The basics may be expected to include not only the three R's (a too narrow and stultifying limitation) but also language, grammar, science, history, geography and other nineteenth-century traditions presented in the traditional way without recourse to contemporary computer programming, environmental studies or other relevant content, materials, or application. Tradition may be strong enough to permit the inclusion of art, music, and physical education, but these at best have halfhearted support. More commonly championed is the concern for discipline and control of both body and mind. In addition, a fair segment of our population includes preparation in whatever may be considered fundamental for seeking, finding, and keeping jobs as part of their idea of the basics.

The traditional preoccupation with narrowly perceived basics results in students being less inclined than ever to go to school, to enjoy school, and to be stimulated by it. As a result, increased attention must be given to maintaining motivation, establishing a broader array of goals, and creating supportive learning environments which will reinforce the natural desire and enthusiasm of youth for learning.

MONDAY MIDDAY NEWS BRIEF

DESPITE POTENTIAL DANGERS DNA RESEARCH CONTINUES . . . **Our scientists are taking every precaution to guarantee the safety** . . . ENERGY PROGRAM LACKS PUBLIC SUPPORT . . . Indecision continues to mark the President's efforts . . . **CRIME LABELED MAJOR SOCIAL DISEASE BY EMINENT AUTHORITY** . . . Looters called misfits in a free society . . . HOUSE ETHICS COMMITTEE FIRES ITS COUN-

---

[4] John Goodlad et al. *Looking Behind the Classroom Door.* Worthington, Ohio: Charles A. Jones Publishing Co., 1970. p. 120.

[5] Philip W. Jackson. *Life in Classrooms.* New York: Holt, Rinehart and Winston, 1968.

[6] James L. Jarrett. "I'm for Basics, But Let Me Define Them." *Phi Delta Kappan* 59[4]: 235-39; December 1977.

SEL . . . A misfit says the chairman . . . **Oil Glut Creates Credibility Gap**

Case Study of a Small Town (1956-1976)

Some folks just viewed the death of the town as a natural part of the life cycle. "There is a time to live and a time to die," some said sagely. But Tom and Anne looked with rage at the impact of human neglect and indifference on their town. Sandy Cove had been a quiet seaside town on the coast of Oregon. Only a few years ago the blue waters sparkled as the waves rolled in against the rocky coast. Seagulls circled overhead, and otters played and swam just off shore. The economy of Sandy Cove was based on logging from the coastal forests, fishing and some small farming operations. Change had come slowly at first; only a few people had spoken out against what was happening. It seemed in the beginning that it was only a summer problem. Just a seasonal swamping by the tourists.

Then Sandy Cove was discovered by the traveling caravans of vacationers. The beautiful clear coastline was assaulted by a spreading wave of buildings and people. Mobile-home parks, marinas, fast food chain restaurants, motels, and chockablock condominiums descended on the shore. Narrow ribbons of asphalt widened to broad, fast motorways with complex loops for convenient on and off ramps. Thousands of people with leisure time on their hands were welcomed by other new business people eager to turn a dollar quickly. Some of the oldtimers objected to the change, but no one spoke of zoning or planning. Growth produced growth. The summer people began taking over; before long, many were remaining year-round. Factories appeared and even more people came. Sand dunes were leveled for building; inlets were filled with dirt and debris to provide a foundation for sea-view lots; the river and waters became the dumping grounds for factory waste and human excrement. The shoreline was destroyed as a habitat for marine life. Plankton, the basic source of food for fish, absorbed the poisonous wastes dumped in the water and passed these toxins on to the fish and through them to the people of Sandy Cove.

A mysterious epidemic of encephalitis struck the town. It was traced to a virus found in the local fish. The panic produced was not immediate, but at first only an uneasy undercurrent of dismay and fear. One by one the motels closed and restaurants stood empty. The factories began to shut down. Those based on wood products found the supply of raw materials disappearing. Those based on the fishing industry could no longer sell their products because of the threat of contamination.

It took only 20 years from start to finish. Tom and Anne were childhood friends, ten years old and in the fourth grade together, when the first motels began to go up. By the time they were 15 the sky was filled with the smoke from factory stacks. When they married at 20, Tom resisted working in the factory. He was one of a small group of citizens who tried to organize the town to save its coastline. There was talk, of course, but no strong action.

When their son was nine years old, Tom and Anne made the decision to leave Sandy Cove, hoping to find a safe and healthy place to start again. Perhaps it was still possible to restore the coastal area and make it again habitable for humans as well as other forms of life. But to choose that uncertain course would commit their son to a lifetime of work redressing the wrongs of only two decades. As much as they loved the land and the sea, they loved their son more. Now Anne and Tom were giving up, too.

An Open Letter

Mr. Editor, We Disagree

The New York Times lead editorial last Thursday, March 24, called on the Carter administration to act "to safeguard the earth against the menace of plutonium" by stopping work on the breeder reactor and prohibiting nuclear fuel reprocessing. We disagree.

We can't turn the clock back. Plutonium has been produced for many years. It is being produced now by 60 nuclear power generators in the United States and 118 in 18 other countries. Spent fuel rods containing plutonium as well as unburned uranium are accumulating in reactor storage pools all over the world. . . .

There is far more danger of nuclear proliferation from the existence of numerous small reprocessing facilities scattered around the world than from large, perhaps multinational, centers operating under international controls. We believe the only practical way to reduce the proliferation threat from nuclear power programs is to have spent fuel returned to the supplier nations in exchange for low-enriched uranium. To avoid large accumulations of spent fuel and heavy energy and foreign exchange drains, the supplier countries would recycle the recovered products in their own reactors.[7]

Mr. Raymond C. Baxter, President
Allied-General Nuclear Services

[7] Excerpted from a paid advertisement in: *The New York Times*, March 31, 1977. p. 32.

NEWS FEATURE 1995

One of the best-kept secrets in the long history of the National Science Foundation broke this past week. It is only through the persistent efforts of reporter Angela Thurman of the Reston Picayune that the full story has been printed.

In 1991, the National Science Foundation funded a project which proposed to incorporate a Nuclear Magnetic Resonance Chip Computer into the fuel combustion engine of a lightweight jeep. The objective was to achieve the flexible regulation of the engine's operations so that fine adjustments to changing driving conditions could be made by the engine. If the engine could make split-second adjustments, not only would the fuel savings be considerable, but general wear and tear on engine parts could be significantly reduced.

The project was successful beyond all expectations. During the first trial run of the jeep, the NMRC computer was able to initiate engine adjustments according to road conditions. During the second run, undertaken in arctic-like conditions, the engine unexpectedly initiated not only the planned adjustments but the speed and direction that the jeep would follow. The jeep escaped the control of the driver and turned back toward the warmth of the hangar, where it had been stored. When the driver tried to turn off the ignition, the NMRC computer refused to allow the engine to be shut down, turning the key back to ignition almost as soon as it was turned off. Apparently by accident, one of the test observers was hit by the jeep and suffered a broken hip. That was when the driver decided to puncture the jeep's fuel tank. With its energy source exhausted, the jeep and its NMRC computer ceased to function, to everyone's relief.

If nothing else was learned from the project, it was realized that giving harnessed human thought processes (NMR chips) mobility could comport significant dangers. Human thought augmented by interfacings with computer capability may be so far superior to natural human thought as to threaten our control over computers. We must understand more fully the nature of human intelligence in order to know what may happen to that intelligence when transferred into an NMR chip.

Committee Reflections on Technology

We seem to be pawns in an inevitable, worldwide tragedy, written into our destiny by technology. We go on mass producing and selling, far and wide, nuclear weapons that promise the earth's demise, and then wonder if we are not mad. We go on increasing our consumption of the earth's fuel supplies even though we know that something must be done to modify our consumption if we are to avert disaster. We pollute the very environment that supports our survival, and then insanely talk, admittedly in dispassionate ways, about the economic trade-offs of having more jobs in exchange for somewhat less breathable air. It is almost as if the technological-industrial complexes had taken on a will of their own and had escaped even the control of their own executives, who, after all, must share with the rest of humanity the tragic results of mindless technological progress. Technology seems to be telling us how to live whether we like it or not, and too many of us have either given up and fallen into apathy, allowing the tide to take us where it will, or retreated completely into a posture of doing away with all technology.

While technology seems to be pushing us toward tragedy, it has, however, helped us to escape many of the tragedies that were once a normal part of life. The simplistic rejection of technology ignores the major contributions that technology has made to a better quality of human life. Because we have poorly managed the incredible powers proffered us by our technological-industrial complexes and have slowly relinquished our control over them does not diminish the magnificence of the gains they have helped us make. The explosion of knowledge is not just a prosaic phrase of twentieth century writers, but a true representation of significantly richer insights into the structure of existence. The inordinate over-consumption of material goods by Americans, while perhaps a source of shame, is also tangible evidence that technology can achieve a level of production sufficient to the basic needs of humankind. To retreat from the successes of technology would not only be folly but inhumane. It would be inhumane to return to older, so-called "organic" methods of farming and condemn millions, perhaps billions, of people to starvation. It would be inhumane to deny the benefits of medical progress to the millions who would otherwise die of such diseases as smallpox and infantile paralysis. It would be inhumane to allow the ravages of winters and insufficient food supplies to so occupy our efforts as to permit only a small elite the energy and time to explore more fully the meaning of being human.

For those of us neither willing to retreat nor to wallow in senseless apathy, the question is one of regaining control, of learning how, once again, to direct the technology that is, after all, no more than the sum of our rational efforts to gain command of the circumstances surrounding our lives. That sum is considerable for we have spent centuries and hosts of brilliant minds producing the knowledge that now seems on the verge of taking us over. We were so set on acquiring knowledge and its practical applications that we failed to develop ways of managing what we had produced. In the resulting value gap, a hypothetical economic model known as "free enterprise" has operated as though it were a sufficient basis for making far-reaching value laden decisions affecting the nature of our lives, not merely economically, but socially, politically, intellectually, and personally. We have allowed companies which have achieved commercial success via their mass-produced technologies to extend their economic power over many other aspects of American life. The big grow bigger; the little become alienated. If democracy is to survive at all, technology must be brought within the reach of the people and free enterprise must be placed in the total context of respect for the individual rights of all humankind.

Technology has given us everything. Dial-a-prayer, Dial-a-joke, Drive-in mortuaries. Who knows what's to come? Dial-a-Ph.D.? Dial-a-patriot? Dial-a-physical? Dial-a-terrorist?

TUESDAY EVENING NEWS BRIEF

. . . **brought to you by Preparation-O for immediate relief** . . . PEACE EFFORTS COST 2500 ENGINEERS THEIR JOBS . . . **FORCED RETIREMENT DECLARED UNCONSTITUTIONAL** . . . PCB'S CONTAMINATE MOTHER'S MILK . . . Health officials announced today that all nursing mothers should report to their family doctor for tests . . . **Millions of Americans Move Toward Simpler Life Style** . . . RIGHT TO REFUSE MEDICATION AND LIFE SUPPORT MACHINES CONTESTED BY DOCTOR'S ASSOCIATION . . . **STERILIZATION OF BLACK TEENAGERS REPORTED** . . . Records Reveal Government Authorization . . . **RELIGIOUS CULT PROLIFERATION PERPLEXES COURTS** . . .

A Commentary on Human Fulfillment

One's capacity to relate to the past, present, and long-term future is the unique characteristic of human existence. The fact that we can look back and see ourselves as we were in the past and project ourselves in self-conscious imagination into the future for weeks, months or years makes intelligent growth and change possible.[8]

[8] William Walsh, editor. *Counseling Children and Adolescents*. Berkeley, California: McCutchan Publishing Corporation, 1975. p. 213.

While learning has always been a natural and essential trait of humanity, we wonder about the relationship between learning and self-fulfillment, between self-fulfillment and human fulfillment as these occur for the broader social collectivity. Is learning related to self-fulfillment? To what extent is self-fulfillment related to human fulfillment? Can one achieve human fulfillment in a social collectivity without achieving self-fulfillment? These questions are difficult to answer. Defining fulfillment is a monumental task.

Are fulfillment and purposiveness related? The "gnawing emptiness, longing, frustration and displaced anger" which can take over a person when his potential is not fulfilled would seem to be the same kind of reaction that also characterizes a sense of lack of purpose.[9] Fulfillment seems to encompass both the achievement of purpose and of potential, and yet not all purposes nor all potential securely relate to fulfillment. There is necessary interaction between these and the tenor of the times. Every historical period sets images of successful fulfillment against which each of us can feel as well as estimate our own fulfillment.

The concept of fulfillment hinges on an array of purposes and potential derived from personal values, emotions, aspirations, intellectual processes, skills and cultural settings. For different individuals, self-fulfillment may mean status, money, power, a beautiful life, a career, or a balance between ego and altruistic motives.

The human being, however, does not stand alone but is also fulfilled as a member of a larger social group. In this sense, fulfillment may depend on the achievement of cultural pluralism and political democracy, or making public facilities such as hospitals, utilities, and schools available to all.

To consider fulfillment in terms of society as a whole raises more questions than answers. On one hand, the individual frequently interprets society's demands to be too prescriptive and oppressive. Conversely, society often perceives the individual as not contributing to the greater good of all—of lacking purposes that contribute to society as a whole. There is an abrasive but nevertheless intimate relationship between the purposes and potential of the individual and those of her society, which confounds any precise definition of fulfillment. True human fulfillment may well be in the achievement of a balance between the demands of the individual and the demands of society. It is through society that a person's identity emerges, but only if the powers exerted by society over the individual do not oppress her autonomy and ability to create and modify the values of her society. One must be able to deal with societal concerns and demands effectively so that the needs of one's own self-fulfillment may also be honored.

    [9] Edward T. Hall. *Beyond Culture*. New York: Anchor Press, Doubleday & Company, Inc., 1976. p. 4.

Human Fulfillment is:
    a steak on every barbeque;
    two cars in every garage;
a C.B. in every car;
2½ baths in every house;
a boat and trailer in every back yard;
an R.V. with T.V. in every driveway;
a college degree for every child.

HAPPINESS AND THE "AMERICAN DREAM" [10]

Question: "Generally speaking, how happy would you say you are—very happy, fairly happy, or not too happy?"

	AMONG WOMEN ONLY				AMONG MEN ONLY			
	Very happy	Fairly happy	Not too happy	Can't say	Very happy	Fairly happy	Not too happy	Can't say
UNITED STATES	43%	47%	10%	*	37%	54%	8%	1%
Canada	38	57	5	*	35	60	4	1
Western Europe	19	62	17	2	21	58	19	2

---

* less than one percent.

Western European results include interviewing completed in France, Italy, the United Kingdom, West Germany, Netherlands, Spain, Belgium, Denmark, Switzerland, Finland, Sweden, Norway, Portugal, Greece, Austria, Iceland, and Luxembourg.

Question: "Thinking about how your life is going now, do you think you would be happier if things could be changed about your life?"

(Those who said "yes" were asked the following question) "Would you like many things about your life changed or just a few things?"

	AMONG WOMEN ONLY			AMONG MEN ONLY		
	Yes	No	Don't know	Yes	No	Don't know
UNITED STATES	58%	38%	4%	63%	34%	3%
Western Europe	58	35	7	63	33	4
Canada	54	44	2	54	43	3
	Many	Few	Undecided	Many	Few	Undecided
Western Europe	11%	45%	2%	14%	48%	1%
UNITED STATES	6	51	1	10	52	1
Canada	6	46	2	8	45	1

[10] The Gallup Opinion Index, Report 128, March 1976. p. 23.

IDEAL LIFESTYLE [11]

Question: "Let's talk about the ideal life for you personally. Which one of the alternatives on this card do you feel would provide the most interesting and satisfying life for you personally?" (Respondents were handed a card with five alternative life-styles.)

AMONG WOMEN

	Married, children, full-time job	Married, NO children, full-time job	Married, children, NO full-time job	Married, NO children, NO full-time job	Single, full-time job	Un-decided
NATIONAL	32%	6%	44%	3%	9%	6
RACE						
White	32	5	46	3	8	6
Non-White	39	15	25	3	16	2
EDUCATION						
College	37	11	34	3	10	5
High School	31	3	49	3	9	5
Grade School	32	6	42	5	7	8
REGION						
East	38	5	39	4	9	5
Midwest	29	5	51	2	8	5
South	32	5	46	2	6	9
West	30	6	40	6	15	3
AGE						
Total Under 30	40	6	37	1	14	2
18-24 years	45	8	31	1	15	*
25-29 years	30	4	48	*	12	6
30-49 years	36	4	48	2	4	6
50 & older	24	6	46	6	10	8
INCOME						
$20,000 & over	41	9	37	2	6	5
$15,000-$19,999	38	7	41	3	4	7
$10,000-$14,999	30	4	54	3	5	4
$ 7,000-$ 9,999	24	3	50	2	15	6
$ 5,000-$ 6,999	35	2	39	11	11	2
$ 3,000-$ 4,999	31	6	44	2	8	9
Under $3,000	27	11	34	2	19	7
POLITICS						
Republican	29	4	54	3	5	5
Democrat	32	6	41	3	13	5
Independent	37	6	41	3	6	7
RELIGION						
Protestant	30	5	49	3	8	5
Catholic	36	5	40	4	9	6
OCCUPATION						
Professional & Business	35	8	40	3	7	7
Clerical & Sales	38	9	33	*	16	4
Manual Workers	35	4	46	3	8	4
Non-Labor Force	27	4	48	4	8	9
CITY SIZE						
1,000,000 & over	34	5	38	3	15	5
500,000-999,999	29	13	38	3	10	7
50,000-499,999	35	3	45	3	8	6
2,500-49,999	39	6	39	3	9	4
Under 2,500,	26	5	53	4	6	6
MARITAL STATUS						
Married	32	5	52	3	3	5
Single	39	12	16	4	27	2
Have children	35	4	49	2	6	4
Have no children	29	7	39	4	13	8

* less than one percent.
[11] *Ibid.*, p. 30.

Self-Evaluation Questionnaire

Please mark an "X" in the appropriate box.

	Yes	No	Unable to answer
1. Can you define human fulfillment?	☐	☐	☐
1.1 Lifelong learning?	☐	☐	☐
1.2 Intentionality?	☐	☐	☐
2. Can public education support any of these?	☐	☐	☐
2.1 Should it do so?	☐	☐	☐
2.2 Would you be willing to pay for it?	☐	☐	☐
3. Do you feel better now that your eyes have skimmed these questions?	☐	☐	☐
3.1 Did the questions turn you off?	☐	☐	☐
3.2 Would you do away with questionnaires?	☐	☐	☐

N.B. IF YOU ADD TO THIS QUESTIONNAIRE, YOU MUST ALSO ADD YOUR OWN BOXES.

A Commentary on the Intra-Generational Crisis of Identity

We have talked so long about the difficulties arising from the "generation gap"—especially about the difficulties several generations have found in communicating with their children—that we have overlooked a more disconcerting phenomenon, one that risks tearing our individual integrity to pieces. Today technological change has come to mean that the experiences of our own youth—that we came to know, love and believe in as children—are no longer relevant to our adulthood; the ways we grow up with are not the ways we can live with as adults; the images of reality that we came to depend on as youngsters are not the images we can validly hold as adults. Most of us still cling to the image of good family life that was idealized for us in childhood even though it seems that kind of supportive family structure is disappearing. We still cling to the work ethic and the dignity it gives people, even though our technology strains toward the elimination of work and we know there are not enough jobs to go around. We are caught in an *"intra-generational crisis of identity."*[12]

Somehow, we must relate the images of our youth to the way we live as adults. We need to bring our youthful experiences together with the experiences of adulthood in an ongoing conscious stream and not as disparate bits and pieces. There can be no human fulfillment unless we are together within ourselves.

[12] John J. Jelinek, editor. *Improving the Human Condition: A Curricular Response to Human Realities.* Washington, D.C.: Association for Supervision and Curriculum Development, 1978. p. 229.

HUMAN FULFILLMENT = Individual Fulfillment ⇄ Societal Fulfillment

The goals of schooling can never be fully clarified until the nature of the interactions between the individual and society have been clarified. This is a necessary prior step. Yet, even while we grope, we must go on deciding. Even while our goals are not clear, we must go on.

Committee Reflections on Living With Others

We cannot approach human fulfillment until we learn to talk to each other about

— individuals seeking fulfillment
— the intra-generational crisis of identity
— communities seeking fulfillment
— persistent human problems.

Learning to live with and among others, with mutual respect, understanding, and constructive compromise is more necessary now than ever before in human history. In a world with distances between human beings shrinking as a result of communication and transportation technology and population growth, the confrontation of human differences reaches proportions previously unknown. Such differences encompass the interface of nations, of rich and poor across and within national boundaries, differences in cultures and ethnic groups, differences between sexes, between age groups, and between subsets of communities. Barriers to understanding and communication abound in the face of differences in appearance, cultural practices, values, life-styles, aspirations and expectations.

Learning to live with others, maintaining a quality of interpersonal relationships which accommodates to differences while at the same time nurturing human and societal fulfillment, is essential for human survival. This issue has been stated so many times in so many ways we recognize it as a truism. Yet, it remains an overriding concern for all who reflect on the human condition.

The experience of each person includes lessons in human interaction. That is a fundamental aspect of growing up. Yet, these lessons seem not enough to overcome the difficulties in communication so typical of our times. Perhaps, with deliberate attention, learning experiences can be planned to provide opportunity for the development of constructive modes of human interaction. The question is whether the schools can be the vehicles of such attention. Can they intend to teach communication while not imposing particular styles of interaction or a single value position on any individual or group of human beings? Individual personalities and needs differ; all human beings living in a pluralistic world need to recognize the range of human behaviors and understand one another better. We urge the schools to do this. We are not sure they can.

WEDNESDAY EVENING NEWS

School Bond Issue Defeated Again

OPTION PLAN SCHOOLS OFFERED CITY WIDE

As part of a plan to meet mandated integration guidelines, the City School Board began a campaign to sell parents on the merits of alternative school offerings, K-12.

UNIVERSITY ENROLLMENT STABILIZING

PROJECTIONS OF TEACHER SUPPLY AND DEMAND GLOOMY

A recent HEW publication on the education profession concludes with ". . . the teacher surplus is likely to continue and even if the assumptions leading to the lowest projections of teacher supply materialize, there will be about half as many more persons available as openings."

ENERGY CRISIS HITS MIDWEST

Schools Receive Lowest Priority

Schools face an immediate 50 percent cutback in electricity. A spokesperson for the State Regulatory Commission said schools and churches must meet the most stringent requirements as they are not essential to economic stability.

NEWS FEATURE 1978

How do Americans feel about education? What do they expect? What do they attain? Consider:

• A study of young adults four years out of high school revealed that their high school aspirations for education have far exceeded their actual educational attainment. Despite this disparity educational aspirations *remained* high. In fact, it was found that the sample was even *more* strongly oriented toward further education after having been out of high school for four years.[13]

• Research conducted among black and white rural youth in 1972 concluded that individuals' aspirations for how much education they *wanted* far exceeded their reality-based predictions of how much education they actually *expected* to attain. Moreover, blacks were more likely than whites to perceive structural factors such as lack of opportunities and lack of aid as hindering the attainment of their goals.[14]

• Currently, there are 50 million Americans enrolled in institutions of education, from kindergarten to university.

• College textbooks in the U.S. are being revised down to the ninth grade reading level. As the Australian publisher Rupert Murdock commented, "I think it is time for the U.S. to be as much concerned about its inner defenses—the inner defenses of literacy—as it has been in its great generosity in helping to educate the so-called Third World."[15]

• Most Americans tend to work at jobs for which they were not specifically trained by an institution of formal education.

• As higher education alters its content and structure in order to lure the new "student" (the adult part-time) some anticipate that post secondary education may, in essence, become a new component of the leisure industry.[16]

• While the Carnegie Commission on Higher Education has found the percentage of persons engaged in adult education is increasing yearly, it has also reported that: (1) "the average duration of a sustained learning effort is considerably less than one year"; (2) the most frequently given reason for studying is to learn something about hobbies or recreation. Vocational subjects and general education ranked second and third after recreation. Home and family life, personal development, and particularly, public affairs were much less frequently mentioned.[17]

---

[13] J. E. Dunkelberger and Cheryl A. Sink. "Alternative Educational Attainment Mechanisms in Early Adulthood." Paper presented at the annual meeting of the Rural Sociological Society, August 23, 1975, San Francisco, California; and J. E. Dunkelberger et al. "Educational Aspirations and Attainment of Southern Rural Youth." Paper presented at the Rural Sociology Section of the annual meeting of the Agricultural Scientists, February 1974, Memphis, Tennessee.

[14] John K. Thomas and Arthur G. Cosby. "Early Achievement Patterns of Southern Males: Racial Profiles of Status Attainment and Mobility Attitudes." Paper presented at the Rural Sociology Section of SAAS meetings, New Orleans, Louisiana.

[15] *Los Angeles Times*, May 29, 1977.

[16] Sally Helgesen. "Students of the Subjective." Harpers 254 [1525]: 26-33; June 1977.

[17] Carnegie Commission on Higher Education. *Toward a Learning Society: Alternative Channels to Life*. New York: McGraw-Hill Book Company, 1973. pp. 28-29.

• On a survey of "self-initiated" adult learners, only 3.5 percent cited a formal school setting as the learning site most suitable to their moods.[18]

"I only took the regular course."

"What was that?" inquired Alice.

"Reeling and Writhing, of course, to begin with," the mock turtle replied, "and then the different branches of Arithmetic — Ambition, Distraction, Uglification, and Derision."

Lewis Carroll, *Alice's Adventures in Wonderland*

Schools Reeling – Teachers Alienated

American education is reeling from attacks which have mounted in intensity over the past decade, coming from all sides. Accusations are leveled at the schools for the decline in academic standards. Students and the public at large express growing disaffection with learning opportunities offered in the schools. Serious financial problems cripple every program of reform. Growing disillusionment and hostility reflect widespread alienation of the schools from the society which they serve.

High School Irrelevant – Why Go? Many Ask

A recent study conducted by John Flanagan, former head of the American Institutes for Research (AIR) in Palo Alto, California, states that interviews with a cross-sectional sample of 1,100 adults over 20 years old revealed that they felt their formal education was irrelevant to their later lives. Robert Gagne, Florida State University, suggested that the evidence from these interviews leads to the conclusion that a high school education has little if any useful purpose. Flanagan believes that the interviews point up a glaring deficiency in education, a failure to help students develop goals for their lives.[19] Individuals desire and need a sense of direction for continuous intentional learning.

---

[18] William Pierce. "Lifelong Education—into the Nation's Third Century." Columbus, Ohio: Center for Vocational Education, the Ohio State University, 1976.

[19] John Flanagan. *An Empirical Study to Aid in Formulating Educational Goals.* AIR—42000—675. Palo Alto, California: American Institutes for Research, June, 1975.

84 Year Old Receives M.A. in History

Since the age of 69, Nissim Malabel, a retired California advertising salesman, has dedicated his life to receiving a "modern education." On June 10, 1977, at the age of 84, he received a master's degree in history. His goal is to join a university faculty in southern France.

When Malabel first applied for admission to college, his application was rejected because he couldn't produce his school transcripts from Turkey. They had been destroyed in the aftermath of World War I. So, in order to satisfy "requirements," he completed an adult high school diploma and only then entered the university.

Malabel has paid for his education principally from his savings, but he firmly believes that tuition should be eliminated for older people in order to allow more of them to enroll. His message to people who marvel at his dedication and vitality: "You have to recognize the 'goodness' of education."[20]

Learning: Fun With Technology

While educators wrestle with the problems of technology run rampant in the world, students are having the time of their lives learning through playing with the new playthings of a technological age. Sixth graders in Odense, Minnesota, have changed the process of education by using videotape as the medium for learning fundamental skills. They are teaching one another basic steps in problem solving by recording on videotape the processes they used in exploring a mathematics problem. The class is also using videotape as a way to collect information, organize it for presentation, and present it clearly and creatively. Since many of the children have video playback and recording equipment at home, they are often able to prepare their assignments as homework. One innovative youngster, planning a winter vacation trip with his parents, presented two weeks of his anticipated class participation and recitation on videotape to his teacher. The current controversy in this case is over whether or not to count him present for the average daily attendance figure.

Further use of technology includes the calculators that invade classrooms throughout the nation. While children and teachers may have been relieved of the "math blahs," fear is raised in the hearts of parents who are concerned that their children will never be able to do basic arithmetic without a calculator in hand. "Not so," say the educators. "Children not only learn more about mathematics with the new tools, but have more fun doing it!"

[20] Mark Forester. "The Old Man and the Degree." In: *Los Angeles Times*, May 25, 1977.

What was that about school being fun? Math, fun? Even with calculators? No way, Baby! Math is math, no matter what buttons you push. It wasn't meant to be easy, and sure isn't supposed to be fun! At least, not for most kids. Maybe the time will come when we'll all use pocket calculators just the way we wear watches. No school teaches the basics anymore, like how to tell time without a watch! I mean, really tell time. The same thing may happen with arithmetic someday, but right now those kids better learn math in their heads, not their fingers!

It's easy enough for dewey-eyed educators to talk about learning for fun, or for the joy of learning. But when it's your kid who's winged his way through school and can't fill out an application form, you wouldn't talk about fun — you'd talk about learning!

Committee Reflections on the Responsibility of Schools

Even though the primary responsibility of the school is to promote learning, the school is not the exclusive provider of learning experiences. Societies have survived without schools. Education and learning are not synonymous with schooling; it has even been suggested that schools inhibit education. However, access to knowledge and skills would be severely limited if schools were not readily available.

The school is the institution supported by society to ensure that its young are (a) introduced to major concepts drawn from a vast and expanding reservoir of human knowledge, (b) equipped with skills essential for coping with those concepts, (c) provided with opportunity and guidance in developing critical thinking and problem-solving skills, (d) encouraged to develop processes for valuing and decision making relating to their roles as human beings within a society, and (e) exposed to esthetic experiences in art, music, and dance which enhance their capacity for enjoyment of life and sharing in the cultural experiences of humankind. These items do not comprise an all-inclusive list but they are suggestive of the content and processes which are vested in the school by society as fundamental responsibilities. Fulfilling these social needs with processes responsive to individual aspirations and capacities is a task too important to be left completely to informal channels.

Learning in school is rarely associated with fun or pleasure. Unfortunately, schooling is more frequently associated with getting grades, getting by, getting out, getting into college, getting a job, getting . . . getting . . . getting . . .

School is not a place to be, but is a way to get somewhere else . . . often into another school. If school learning is linked to extrinsic

**rewards, it should not be surprising that learning for personal pleasure
. . . learning to quietly satisfy a burning curiosity . . . learning for the
satisfaction of learning . . . happens more often outside than inside
the classroom.**

A Commentary on the Role of Education

While the key function of traditional, formal, public education still
is to transmit the cherished attitudes, values, knowledge, and skills of
the dominant classes, an emerging imperative is recognition of the need
to free *all* people from internal and external oppression. This changing
perspective, while unsettling, will enable people to achieve a sense of
control over their lives—to resist, instead of weakly acquiescing to individual, group, institutional, or cultural pressures. Obviously, the ability
to exercise freedom hinges on an array of social, cultural, economic, and
political factors. If public education is to fulfill its commitment to freeing
all of society, education must provide multiple options rooted in prob-
lem-posing contexts. For it is from the exercise of free choice based on
understanding of the conflicting forces in society that satisfaction within
life is achieved.

Experience has taught us that for learning to be meaningful, it must
be rooted in the needs and interests of the learner. The cultural context
of the learner must be recognized as central to the curriculum. Only in
this fashion will education generate excitement and have meaning in
terms of the human experience. As Morphet and Jesser note,

> . . . If schools do not work great change in their ability to adjust instruc-
> tion to learning styles and potentials of highly-variant students we are headed
> for mammoth, and perhaps disastrous wastage. The basic rationale of instruc-
> tional programs is still that of expecting all students to conform to, and hence
> learn from, a monolithic scheme. That scheme is modified from time to time
> and from place to place. It becomes increasingly apparent, however, that the
> approaching rationale is to adjust instruction to the needs of the learner.[21]

In a post-industrial, yet extensively underdeveloped, world characterized by affluence and a complex knowledge base but also by oppressive poverty, education which will enable us to survive the turn of
the century will have to be carefully planned. Such education should
take into account the "post-figurative"[22] and "future shock" characteristics of modern society. Given this reality the skills of acquiring, processing, and recycling knowledge will become crucial to an individual's
sense of well-being. In order to move away from being a society of people

---

[21] Edgar L. Morphet and David L. Jesser. *Designing Education for the Future
(No. 4): Cooperative Planning for Education in 1980.* New York: Citation Press, 1968.
p. 28.

[22] A term coined by Margaret Mead to indicate situations in which the older
generation learns from the younger. Margaret Mead. *Culture and Commitment.* Garden
City, New York: Natural History Press/Doubleday and Co., 1970. p. 1.

caught in an intra-generational crisis of identity, four objectives will have to become educational imperatives rather than educational options: learning to learn, relating meaningfully with others, being able to make rational decisions about myriad life options,[23] and being able to identify information that offers new power for living.

The four objectives cited above directly imply the potential ability which all humans can exercise as creators of their history and culture. As such, they can provide a setting in which persons are crucially aware of the possibility of changing their world if they are not satisfied with the status quo. To maximize social, economic, and cultural development, knowledge must not be acquired in sterile, prepackaged units but rather must be flexibly bound with carefully delineated values.[24]

Never in recorded history have all members of a society become literate without the specific intention of developing literacy.

Superintendent Love Unveils "Three-Way Learning Contract"

The city of Oakland, California, responded sharply when the Superintendent of Public Schools distributed a much talked about but little understood draft of a Three-Way Learning Contract. The Superintendent set one day as a "Festival of Learning" to enable parents and students to visit schools and sign the contract. Administrator and teacher organizations alike raised complaints. In the interest of public service the local paper published the entire document as follows:

FOR THE STUDENT

Academic Achievement

1. I will know grade level expectations for specific subjects.
2. I will know my own achievement levels.
3. I will have in class the necessary tools for learning. (Books and other assigned materials.)
4. I will complete assigned work neatly, accurately, and on time.
5. I will use the library and other resources to help me.

Interest and Motivation

1. I will do the best possible work at all times.
2. I will be constant in my efforts to improve any weakness in my skills.
3. I will take advantage of every opportunity to learn.

[23] Alvin Toffler. *Learning for Tomorrow: The Role of the Future in Education.* New York: Vintage Books, 1974. passim.

[24] Joseph P. Farrel. "Educational Systems and National Development." In: Thomas J. LaBelle. *Education and Development: Latin America and the Caribbean.* Los Angeles: UCLA Press, 1972. p. 224.

Attendance
1. I will go to classes . . .

Citizenship
1. I will know and follow rules . . .
2. I will respect the rights of others at all times.
3. I will exhibit a positive attitude to-ward learning at all times.
4. I will pay attention in class and be respectful of others.

Homework
1. I will set aside time after school each day . . .

FOR THE PARENT/GUARDIAN

Academic Achievement
1. I will know the grade level expectations for my child.
2. I will know the achievement levels of my child.
3. I will review . . .

Interest and Motivation
1. I will encourage and support . . .

Attendance
1. I will assume responsibility . . .

Citizenship
1. I will know and support district and classroom rules . . .

Homework
1. I will provide a quiet time and place for study without T.V. . . .

FOR THE TEACHER

Academic Achievement
1. I will know and use grade-level expectations in teaching.
2. I will interpret grade-level . . .

Interest and Motivation
1. I will encourage the student . . .

Attendance
1. I will motivate good attendance . . .

Citizenship
1. I will assume responsibility . . .
3. I will enforce all rules fairly and firmly. . . .

Homework
1. I will provide homework . . .[25]

Are these goals or a contract for guilt? Who ever does the best possible work at all times, let alone a child!

A Teacher's Lament

Yesterday, I was at another one of those in-service workshops required by our contract. I wouldn't mind them so much if only they would deal with the problems I have in the real world. This time, it was a drawn-out sermon on how teachers should help kids to find themselves—you know, fulfill their potential. If a kid socks you in the jaw, it's all right to punish him, but then you're supposed to make the most of his physical prowess. What am I supposed to do—put a prizefighting ring in my classroom?

[25] *The Montclarion,* Oakland, California, September 28, 1977. p. 6.

How am I to help each kid work out his or her own special way of being? I have 31 kids in my class. Sure, I know they have different capacities for learning and different interests, but I don't know how to cater to all those differences and still teach the things they all ought to know when they leave my class. Hasn't anybody heard of account-ability? Besides, it seems to me that we're all stuck in this world together and that fulfillment has got to mean more than just catering to a bunch of spoiled brats with individual potential. I mean there's human fulfill-ment and potential that operates in the group as a whole, isn't there? Without society working as well as it does, we would all of us be strug-gling individually not to starve to death, like a bunch of primitive cave dwellers. Shouldn't kids learn how to fulfill themselves as members of society? They have got a lot to be grateful to society for. Don't you think they need to fulfill themselves as members of society?

Maybe we should try to do both—I mean self-fulfillment and societal fulfillment, but I've got to admit I'm not sure how that can be done.

The trouble is they expect us teachers to do everything—be mothers and fathers to the kids, help them prepare for good jobs, teach them how to get along with each other, encourage their individuality and on and on. I'm going in so many directions, I'm not going anywhere.

Grandma and the Typewriter

Mrs. Schreiber's son was a very odd-looking man of 35. He was quite bald except for a few thin strings of hair that swirled around the crown of his head. His features were thin and sharp and could have belonged to a banker except his eyes would jump from spot to spot as though they were on a roller coaster and trying to get off before the ride was over. In contrast, he spoke very slowly, sputtering short, simple sentences and stopping after each sentence with pride, waiting for others to applaud. Mrs. Schreiber always said, "Good, good, son. Go on."

When he was a child of three, horse-drawn carriages were still com-peting with the automobile, and, as his mother told the story, he stepped out from behind their very first car into the path of a speeding carriage. He lay between life and death for weeks and was never quite normal again.

Still, he had attended school for a while, a long time before I ever knew him. It must have been a good experience for he aways talked about when he would go back to school as though that were to be tomorrow.

I must admit I did not like being near him and tried hard to fade into the background of our small apartment whenever he was around.

He always seemed just a little dirty, and I could never get used to the sputters that would hit my face and arms with frequency whenever he spoke. Though I am ashamed now of the feelings I had then, I find I still shudder in disgust when I recall the few times he crowded close to me and tried to talk.

But my grandmother had a special feeling for him. She really took him seriously. She would often say that from the minds of such simple people she could learn better about life than from geniuses: "Who could understand geniuses, anyway?" and she would smile and touch Mrs. Schreiber's hand in a warm, rubbing pat.

My Grandma was truly a blessing for Mrs. Schreiber's son. They shared in common an enthusiasm for school that seemed unreal to me. No matter what the topic started out to be, eventually my Grandma would say, "When you go back to school, you will learn all about that." Still, I never said anything for fear I would be drawn into one of their odd conversations.

It was, however, inevitable, the day my Grandmother gave me my very first typewriter. I knew even then it must have taken every spare penny she had. It was my first step toward being a journalist. I was so thrilled that I even invited Mrs. Schreiber's son to come and see my typewriter.

"C. . . ca . . can . . . can I . . . can I t . . try?" he sputtered.

"Sure," I said, a little hesitant inside and certainly sorry I had said anything. He sat down and held both hands high above the typewriter, palms down, fingers extended, almost like a plane hovering before it lands. He began to blink wildly, his eyes jumping all over the room until they finally came to Grandma.

"Hhh . . . . how? How? How?" My Grandma didn't know how. She had never worked in an office and rarely had any business in offices that might have had typewriters. She had, of course, seen them in movies, but the day she gave me my typewriter was the first time in her more than 70 years she had had any personal experience with such a machine.

"How? P . . pl . . please . . hhow?" His hands still hovered above the typewriter. My Grandma seemed lost. She wanted to teach him, but she was afraid to try it herself, and I suppose she knew how I felt about poor Mrs. Schreiber's son.

"I don't know how. Don't worry. When we go back to school, there will be someone who knows how. We will learn together, when we go back to school." His eyes stopped blinking and his hands dropped to his lap. I really felt a little sorry for him, but it was the sadness in my Grandma's smile that made me say, "What do you need school for? School isn't a magic place where you suddenly start learning. Sometimes, you can learn much better at home. I know how to type. I can show you. You don't need school." And I proceeded to show both of them how the paper was put into the typewriter, how the margins were set, and, of course, how to hit the keys.

Grandma and Mrs. Schreiber's son took turns at the typewriter. The best he could do was hit a few of the keys and then stop with great pride waiting for the praise my Grandmother would give him. But within an hour, my Grandmother could slowly type a sentence, and she was both overjoyed and in awe of her accomplishment.

As Mrs. Schreiber's son left for home, he gave Grandma a big hug, somewhat like a little boy might have, and said, "I . . I . . I like t . . type . . typewri . . writers. I like t . . to l . . learn. I wan to l . . learn a . . all . . . . all m . . my l . . life!"

"Me, too," she said, patting his back. When he was gone, she just stood for a moment, thinking. "He is right. It's nice . . . it's a good feeling to learn all life long. And you are right, too. School is not the only way. Maybe, there are better ways to learn when you are old like me. But when you are young and everything is so mixed up—and changing—and new—and you have nobody around that understands all these new things, what would you do without school?"

Rico — Decision Maker

Mr. Armstrong had given Rico a week to make up his mind. Some choice! Make peace with Miss Silverman, or the streets. "What can I do in either case," he mumbled to himself. He had never felt more alone. He was aware of the calls of his friends as he shuffled along, but he did not hear them. He was trying to buy a few extra minutes, as if that would make the decision easier or more sensible. But it wasn't going to be easy and it didn't make sense. How had he gotten himself in this jam?

He wasn't sure that *he* had gotten himself into anything. He didn't ask to be born. He didn't ask to be Puerto Rican. He didn't ask to be poor. He didn't ask to be brought to New York's East Side. He didn't ask for much, really. But someone was always dumping on him. "Speak 'purely,' " his English teacher said. Miss Silverman was forever on him to watch his language. "Why doesn't she watch hers!" he shouted in frustration. "Just because I mix English and Spanish you'd think it was a federal case. I get fed up with everything having to be their way. Why not mine? Now Mr. Armstrong says I can have it my way! But how can I? They'd think I was nuts at home. I wonder how pu-u-ure she is anyway." He exaggerated the vowel sound a la Silverman, as had become his habit. "Well, I learned! One more golden rule! Don't make fun of Miss Silverman—at least not twice a period."

He caught a glimpse of Freddie, Juan, and Tony lounging on the hulk of a stripped Buick in the next block. There was the choice in rawest terms! Miss Silverman or a stripped Buick! He'd be no better off than Tony or all the rest. What could he do? A stock boy, maybe? Not with his school record and the tightness of the job market. Anyway, Ma wouldn't let him quit. He'd have to be kicked out. And he'd been through that scene before. He had to finish school and get a *good* job. But Freddie claimed to have finished school. What did it get him? He couldn't read more than an automobile manual. He couldn't figure charges on a pawn ticket. He was always getting ripped off by somebody.

Miss Silverman said she was trying to help. "She sure has a funny idea of what helps," he thought. "English, English, English. Doesn't she know there's more to living than English?"

A lot had happened since he arrived in New York. He had learned a lot. He wondered about going to school at the "Y" or maybe getting into one of the special government training programs. And then, there was always the Army or Navy. But he didn't like any of the choices. He could learn some things but he needed to "get it together." "Why doesn't somebody help me decide!"

"When it's all on the line, I don't have a choice," shrugged Rico to himself. "And Mr. Armstrong knows it! I have to stay. The odds are long, but they are all I can get."

A Commentary on Expanding the View of Learning

Americans have been remarkably well socialized into admiring and desiring the "paraphernalia" dispensed by their educational institutions. Credentials and certificates have become ends of education while the substance of what is studied has become increasingly irrelevant for the lives we must lead. Efforts to achieve a learning society able to cope, in an ongoing way, with multiplying social complexities have been submerged in the bureaucratic traditions of an established institution. While our means of communication and our need to communicate better with each other continue to increase, educational institutions barely take note, allowing the young to sleep through endless hours of English classes that never go beyond the parsing of sterile sentences or a disjointed series of topics pursued superficially. While diversified modes of collecting and storing information become more central to our daily lives, students spend four or five years of precious learning time practicing the addition and subtraction of fractions. All that seems to count is endurance, for in the end they all receive a diploma. We allow them to expend their time in pursuit of a credential, ignoring the effect of such waste on their futures. But we can no longer afford to be blind to this conspicuous waste of human resources. We must be responsible for each other. If we are to develop a learning society we need to intervene in our personal and corporate reality creatively and responsibly. We need to go beyond pursuit of the "paraphernalia" of literacy to pursuit of meaningful learning in terms of human fulfillment that is lifelong. The intent of learning must be clarified.

Granted we are all learners in myriad ways from the moment of conception until the last moment of consciousness. But in large measure we do not reflect on the significance of our learning or even recognize that we are almost continuously engaged in learning at varying levels and with varying intensity. In fact, for humans learning is nearly synonymous with living. When we cease to learn we begin to atrophy and the process of becoming is short-circuited or otherwise thwarted, diminishing life itself. However, the expanded vision of learning is seldom recognized because of society's emphasis on formal education and the too-easy equation of education with schooling and schooling with learning. As a result, the typical perception of education is of schooling as something to be endured or completed; since schooling is erroneously equated with learning, learning also becomes something to be completed and done with.

Another impediment to the idea of extending learning throughout life is the idea that for learning to be significant or meaningful it must be encapsulated and certified by a recognized institution. Thus, learning to garden, be a mechanic, play the piano, appreciate art or history or literature, repair televisions, build a home, cook gourmet meals, or become a homemaker are viewed as legitimate, valuable learning if pursued in a formal institutional setting. But if pursued independently, informally, or outside the confines of institutional structures recognized as legitimate educational entrepreneurs, such learning is perceived to be of less importance, even to the point of being overlooked in self-reports of one's "education."

Any effort to extend the idea of learning to a lifelong enterprise and realize a learning society must take into consideration the limitations imposed by tradition as well as by the vested interests of structures that benefit from the maintenance of restrictive covenants. When organizations or government agencies control the legitimation of most significant learning, individuals are encouraged to limit their concern for learning to those receiving social recognition. We fail to reflect on the deeper personal significance of learning. We need to approach opportunities for learning with greater openness and with greater consideration of the role *our* learning activity, irrespective of location or aegis, is to play in the realization of *our* humanity.

    " . . . the evolutionary vigor of mankind can wither away although it is surrounded by mountains of coal, oceans of petroleum and limitless stocks of corn; it can do so as surely as in a desert of ice, if man should lose his impulse, or worse, develop a distaste for ever-increased growth 'in complexity and consciousness.' "[26]

THURSDAY MIDDAY NEWS BRIEF

G.E. INITIATES MANAGEMENT TRAINING PROGRAM . . . **MUNICIPAL LIBRARY SETS UP HUMAN RESOURCES NETWORK** Hotline established to encourage community to share talents with others. **Joyce Conden, Director of the Lifelong Learning Council asked that** . . . PREVENTIVE MEDICINE PROGRAMS SPONSORED THROUGH OPEN EDUCATION EXCHANGE . . . Doctors at City Hospital have agreed to participate in a new project through the local television station. Programs on preventive medicine and screening of basic diagnostic techniques will be coupled with neighborhood clinics which will handle routine examinations on a regular basis. Paramedics will be hired to staff the clinics with doctors available on call and for referral . . . BOOKMOBILE PURCHASED BY CITY . . . **PLANNED PARENTHOOD SPONSORS LAMAZE CLASS** Natural childbirth is on the upswing according to a report released by the local office of Planned Parenthood. Lamaze is just one of many approaches to family involvement in . . . **League of Women Voters Slates Seminars**

History Through Grandma's Eyes

My Grandma was almost always very energetic no matter what she did. Even when she was sitting, supposedly relaxing, there was a sense of alertness about her that was uncanny—downright disconcerting for a 13 year old like myself. Still, I had come to expect her display of energy and that, I suppose, is why I so vividly remember the day I came home to find her sitting listlessly at the kitchen table.

[26] Teilhard de Chardin. *The Future of Man.* New York: Harper & Row, Publishers, 1964. p. 205.

She was not crying, just wrapped in something distant that I could not fathom. On any normal day, my Grandma would have given me a thick piece of rye bread spread heavy with chicken fat. That day, she just asked me if school had gone all right. It was always the same question and it had become boring to me. Usually, I would respond with as little information as possible. But I felt the need to see the energy back in her eyes and I responded with a lengthy description of my day. She became even more distant. Finally, I had to ask: "What's the matter, Grams? Why are you so sad?" I almost never asked my Grandma anything about herself and my questions must have startled her. Her eyes blinked quickly several times and she looked at me as though she had just become aware of my presence.

"Today, Jan Polsky died. You never knew Jan Polsky, but he was my last friend from the old country."

I sought to comfort her: "But there are still many people here that love you . . . "

"You don't understand. Jan was the last person who knew me when I was young like you are young now. He knew me when there was not a wrinkle in my face and my hair was black—so black . . . "

It was hard to think of my grandma with black hair. For as long as I could remember, it had been white. I mean really white! She must have read my thoughts.

"You find it so difficult to think of my hair as black? Maybe you don't even believe me. Sometimes, I doubt myself." She paused and held her breath deep down inside her like she was mulling it over along with her memories.

"Now, there is no one left to say it is true. All my past, it's . . . it's like make believe, like something we made up. Jan and I, we could talk about the boat to America—we could tell each other it was true . . . how we wore all our clothes on our backs." She looked at me just ever so defiant. "Yes . . . I had seven dresses, two slips and pants—all long— all on my back. You could poke me with your elbow and I would not feel anything I was so fat with clothes. We never took anything off on the boat. There was nowhere to put clothes and if we took them off maybe someone would steal them. Jan, he had a good memory. He could remember everything like yesterday."

"Grams," I said, "I believe you. I believe you just as much as that guy who wrote my history book. Only he doesn't have people like you in *his* history. He doesn't have people who talk. His people are born in some year, fight a war in another year and die in still another year. There must be a million years and I've got to memorize them all."

My words irked her. She snapped back into her usual vigor and went into one of her "education-is-good-for-you" tirades: "You must learn history. It is important to know what happened and when. You were born in America and you should know how America happened. It is not so important to know what happened to me." Her voice began to drift a little. "Maybe, if I could write—really write, not just my name and things like that—I would write it all for you so when I am gone, maybe you would still believe. But I am not important history. You must study important history."

Still, the thought persisted. Why wasn't there a place for the history of grandmas. Would there be any place for my history when no one would be left to tell me it was true?

    There is a need to be reassured that our contributions have merit beyond the limits of personal satisfaction. Credentials, no matter the cost, are a necessary component of personal security as well as societal and institutional survival.

The Price of a Ph.D.

As recently as February, 1978,[27] $25,000 could get you an immediate Ph.D. from New College in San Francisco. In an effort to raise operating capital the college president came up with one of higher education's most direct examples of entrepreneurship. An advertisement appeared in *The New York Times* announcing that "an established recognized college, raising funds for program development, will consider awarding Honorary Doctorate to creditable donor of $25,000 or more." While other institutions may not advertise their financial gain from the granting of honorary degrees, the practice is not new, but this was more audacious than most.

Administrators of more than one educational institution are facing increasingly difficult moral dilemmas brought on by fiscal difficulties. Rising costs for capital investments and day-to-day operations are straining the solvency of many institutions. But new educational enterprises, no matter how noble their mission, are confronted by the spectre of losing everything unless unusual steps are taken to stabilize their financial foundation. A faculty member at New College summarized his rationale for support of the selling of Ph.D.'s as follows: "It's a trade-off. We are trying to keep an institution alive so work can go on that is humanly valuable! I have more serious reservations about the corporate behavior of the University of California, or Stanford or MIT on how they secure their funds. This place needs cash. Short of breaking the law, how the hell do you get it?"

[27] Based on an article appearing in: *San Francisco Sunday Examiner & Chronicle,* March 5, 1978. John Jacobs. "Ph.D. in Life—$25,000 a Sheepskin." Section A. pp. 1, 6, and 7.

In his view major college degrees are not cheapened by Defense Department grants to the universities for weapons research or by a university's investments in South Africa.

Carol

She was nearing the end of her first pregnancy with the anticipation and excitement building within her nearly matching the physical distension that cradled her hopes. It was time to leave for the Lamaze class. Carol felt unusually anxious and pregnant. She wanted the child just as she had wanted to marry Mike and she wanted to be happy and fulfilled. Even though this was the peak of her experience as a woman so far, she wondered if she was expecting too much.

During the past eight months she had alternated between elation and apprehension on more than one occasion. She didn't fear the delivery. In fact she didn't fear anything except the uncertainty about what this new role would mean in terms of her many dreams for herself and Mike. She hadn't minded working to help him pay for his degree. In large measure she felt closer to him, an important part of his being. But his being was moving further and further from her in terms of formal education and what she saw herself in the process of becoming. She had filled her lonely hours, "personal time for you," Mike called them, with a series of short courses in the continuing education programs at several universities in the Chicago area. She found time for the Red Cross and helped with a number of civic projects. Certainly her days were full, but they weren't very satisfying.

Mike kept encouraging her to make new friends, to take advantage of this and that, until she thought she would explode. She was tired of being force-fed like a goose. It always seemed as if someone else was deciding things for her or that she was following what she thought were society's expectations.

She was no different from Mike with his compulsion to keep the crabgrass out of the lawn so as not to irritate the neighbors. She chided Mike about the fetish and he in turn ribbed her about how bright she was with her newfound competence in quilting, naming the Wives of Henry VIII, and ceramics.

"At least I'm not spending all my time at bridge," she would retort, when the ribbing became a bit pointed. Somehow her mother's resolution of the conflict between personal desire and social expectation didn't work for Carol. Nothing seemed to work. She just kept going, expecting tomorrow to take care of itself. But there was always a sense of uncertainty.

"Let's go," she called. "I don't want to miss the last lesson."

And Mike

Mike quickly buttoned his shirt, slipped into a pair of loafers and nervously turned to brush a stray hair. It was time for the Lamaze class. The commuter had been late getting back to Winnetka and Carol was unusually testy and expectant. He smiled at his little pun and it broadened into a wide grin of relaxed good will. Even the routine of the office and scramble for survival in the ad agency had become bearable with the anticipation of their firstborn.

It had been five years since they married. The first few months had passed quickly with a minimum of strain and adjustment. They were really together. Decisions were jointly made. Each basked in the reflection of the other's little successes and happinesses. But at some point between the first and third years the luster began to dim. Mike couldn't put his finger on it. They tried to talk about it—when they had time. He had gone back to school to get his MBA. The financial crunch had made it seem wise for Carol to postpone getting pregnant so she stayed on the pill.

The stress of job and classes every other night caused minor friction to mount to the point that each considered moving out for a while. It didn't seem serious but it was frustrating. Their interests were diverging as his work took him into areas of business and finance that she neither understood nor wanted to know about. Added to this strain was her desire to have a child. Mike, too, *wanted* a child but going off the pill didn't seem to be enough. They consulted doctors, had tests, and followed advice from all quarters.

He remembered the sense of euphoria they both experienced nearly eight months ago when she quietly told him the news over dinner. They had babbled and dreamed and planned long into the night, each afraid to trust the news.

She had announced that they would take classes in natural childbirth and he had acquiesced. Suddenly what had seemed so simple had become complex. New fears tugged at him. The meaning of fatherhood and being a husband looked different. He hadn't thought of needing to be educated to be a father. Now he wasn't sure even special classes were preparation enough.

He closed the door and headed for the car. "The last lesson," he whispered to himself. "Wanna bet?"

 Individual Fulfillment is a Luxury of Affluent Societies.

College Student Fulfillment for a Week:

Sun.	Mon.	Tues.	Wed.	Thurs.	Fri.	Sat.	Special Reminder
Sleep	Spanish Exam	6:30 Tennis	Classes) a.m. }	6:30 Tennis	Classes) a.m. }	Debate	Don't schedule so much next week!
Lunch with Debbie	Tutor? Jr. High}	Class Report Due	Study	Class	Get the car fixed	Trip	
Library Research Paper	Class}	Study in Library	Class Bio-Exam	Interview Career Center	Class 1:00-3:00		Fit in music practice
Study for Spanish exam	Co-op Board Meeting	Food Service Job 4:00	JOB 4-7	JOB 4-7	Soccer Game 4:00	↓	
Write to Dad & Mom	Write Report	Work on Debate	Practice Music 8:00-10:00	Laundry ?	7:00 Pizza Poker	Date? (maybe)	or give it up!

But I need time to think. I don't want all my seconds filled.

Committee Reflections on Marketing Education

The educational establishment has evolved without a clear sense of direction. On the one hand the public schools have emerged as an instrument of government attempting to meet the needs of a popular democracy struggling to manifest the concepts of freedom and individual dignity in a just society. At the same time religious groups, political and social activists and individual entrepreneurs have built competing educational institutions to meet their own ends. The pressures of an expanding population and struggling, competitive economic system have molded and warped societal and individual perceptions in such a manner as to bring into conflict the nobler dreams of a benevolent social system and the day-to-day realities of economic and political survival. In the process, educational institutions have become more than the societal channel for transmission of the majority culture. They have taken on the task of maintaining the corporate dreams and creating a supporting ambiance for a particular economic position.

Common access to education at all levels has become part of the national dream and has insinuated the aims of *educational institutions* and *their* survival into the overall need structure of society. Thus, schools must survive, not only as institutions to maintain and foster the economic and social order but as employers and contributors to economic and

social stability. Both forms of stability are realized by continuing traditions and meeting expectations about the form and content of education
which is rooted in the past. As a result, major efforts and resources are
expended on maintenance of irrelevant and outmoded programs and
practices without primary regard for their educational significance in the
present. This is as true for universities as for grade schools.

The *form* of education most highly valued by society has increasingly
become the university degree. Universities have responded to the popular
market, even to the detriment of learning. Individuals who make it on
their own, without benefit of formal education, are increasingly rare.
Horatio Algers have little standing in today's society and less hope of
success. Those individuals who would prefer not to attend college are
bombarded by commercials expounding the values of education as well
as by family pleadings and the lure of employment opportunities.

Viewed from another perspective, the commingling of business,
politics, and education has led institutions of higher education into the
market place where they have become hucksters bent on following the
business paradigms to their limits, creating markets for their wares that
will meet the transient markets of a rapidly changing social scene.

But beyond the maze of courses, degree programs, extension offerings
and adult education courses that the public schools, colleges, and universities may offer, lies a welter of opportunities for formal and informal
learning sponsored by social clubs, philanthropic organizations, religious
groups, fraternities and sororities, governmental agencies and sundry
other promotors. The opportunities run the gamut from fly casting and
bread making to theological discussion groups and self-awareness training. How can one hope to select meaningfully from such a smorgasbord?

Rather than educational institutions and other entrepreneurs addressing themselves first to the task of fulfilling societal and individual
needs and goals, they are caught up in a marketing passion play intent
on the survival of pharisaic tradition irrespective of the human cost.

THURSDAY EVENING NEWS

LABOR UNION DAY CARE CENTER UNDER FIRE

New Air Fares Increase Number of Overseas Travel Seminars

Competition for overseas travelers has reached fever pitch in corporate headquarters of all major
carriers. Educators may receive the
most benefit if ads for summer
travel are an indication.

FARMER'S FLY-IN SCHOOL UPDATES FARM TECHNOLOGY

The poor dirt farmer of Mississippi wouldn't recognize his corporate brothers who flew into Wichita over the weekend to attend a

jointly sponsored meeting of major manufacturers of farm equipment and area agribusiness heads.

SESAME STREET VALUE CHALLENGED BY EDUCATORS

The debate over the value of Sesame Street as a readiness experience for preschool children is coming under closer scrutiny as a result of study by a group of researchers at Pittsburgh.

NONFORMAL EDUCATION GAINS MOMENTUM

A Legislator's Query

Perhaps there is no one institution of learning, regardless of the qualities we try to build into it, that could handle the many needs of children growing up in a world with so many unknowns. Certainly it makes little sense to continue doing what we have been doing in American education, which is repeating the same studies, from the Revolution to adding fractions, over and over again while students persist in forgetting what they have memorized and while what they have memorized continues to move further and further away from the realities of adulthood. The cost is too high, the benefits too few. We need lifelong learning. This means not only major revisions in what we conceive to be the avenues of education, but also new sources of support. Can the schools as they exist now handle the requirements of a modern education?

A Superintendent's Response

Yes, they can! If they recognize the limits of the learning experience provided within their walls; if they can accept the validity of nonschool learning; and if they can become organic links coordinating and unifying learning opportunities within and beyond the school.

Hyde Park Interlude

"To hell with schooling. You're just trying to protect your own territory and stay in the act. All this concern for human fulfillment is a crock. Restructure the system and you don't have to worry about maintaining discipline, morale, and payrolls."

"What are you taking after the schools for? You're wanting to change the whole of society. Once you deinstitutionalize society you'd find the schools would be deinstitutionalized. What we're all about is echoing the values of the dominant culture."

"Then it's a conspiracy of the majority and vested interests."

FUSS AND BOTHER[28]

Ostinato #1

Ostinato #2 Fuss and bo-ther, Fuss and bo-ther,

com - mo - tion, con - fu -sion, dis - tur-bing, too
noi - sy, too sil - ly, bad man-ners, com-

Soli (1) Soli (2)

The chil-dren can not come here, The chil -dren must not be here.

(All)

This is no place for kids & dogs; this is no place for games

and frogs. The chil-dren must not be here. Fuss and bo-ther!

A Commentary on the Dilemma of Goals in American Education

In the United States democracy and education have had a long and mutually supportive relationship. While the value of education is widely recognized, as the society has become more complex there is less unanimity as to its function, especially in the case of formal schooling. From the beginning of modern American history education has played a series of roles. As a people we have never fully committed ourselves to a single goal for education, rather the particular times and demands for group cohesiveness has greatly influenced formal education and most particularly public education to the extent that in perspective we may identify different but overlapping claims. The fact that public education has played such an important role in the development of our collective conception of education creates special problems for us as we try to determine its function. Historically we have experienced periods in which the predominant purposes of education were religious. The salvation of the individual's soul, as well as the well-being of the collected community, was perceived to be inextricably entwined with one's ability to read holy writ and with the preparation of an educated clergy. Later, the creation of a free and literate society served as the cornerstone of the democratic experiment that gave birth to the United States. The nation's

[28] Jane Ellefson. "Fuss and Bother." Lincoln, Nebraska: First Plymouth Church, U.C.C., February 1976.

founders supported Jefferson's dictum that a nation cannot remain free if its citizens are ignorant. Independence was followed by increased efforts to better equip a diverse population for political and social responsibility. Successively, the waves of immigrants, the rising demands of industrialism, and technologically induced changes created special needs and challenges that served to define the function of education in terms of a growing economy; this was coupled with an increased societal dependence on credentials and formal certification of education for job placement. The result was the primacy of economics as a force in determining educational purposes.

While the nation lacks a central governmental voice to set policy and determine a single function for education, the public and professional disposition has frequently been set forth by national committees and commissions such as the Commission on the Reorganization of Secondary Education and the Committee of Fifteen, the Harvard Committee and the Educational Policies Commission and, more recently, national pollsters such as Gallup and Harris. The committee approach has been basically reactive and has left formal education vulnerable to charges of lack of leadership and susceptible to the pressures of the moment. In this atmosphere of imprecise focus, it is to be expected that the public would ask what education is trying to do or to complain because it isn't doing everything.

In truth, American education serves many functions. What is lacking is any clear sense of united direction or philosophical commitment. At certain points in our history commitments have arisen but typically they have been induced by external threats. The most obvious example of common commitment is visible during times of war. In such instances public education takes on a central purpose with greater clarity than at any other time because society as a whole sets aside diversions and focuses on a single objective. At other times of crisis, we have been able to rally large segments of our population or special-interest groups around banners raised against racism, integration, homosexuality, pollution, declining reading scores, or all manner of parochially perceived evil. In these instances, formal education frequently does respond acceptably in the eyes of the critics.

It is regrettable that American education seems to find its unity of purpose only in response to crises and negative stimulation. Goals that will endure and contribute to human fulfillment need to grow from periods of reflection and calm. Obviously, leadership for determining the function of education may come from many sources. But in a democracy, it must come from the people.

The problem is twofold: how is the will of the people to be heard, and accurately interpreted? And once determined, how are the necessary socioeconomic and political support structures to be marshaled? Education serves as a catalyst in the transformation of societies. Note for instance what Castro, Mao, and Nyerere have done in their societies with structural and ideological support for informal as well as nonformal approaches to education.[29] The question is, with how much intentionality should the catalysts operate; how clear, how firm should the goals be?

Education, in the best of conditions, cannot function as a panacea for all personal and collective ills. It will function most efficiently when there is common commitment and clear intent. In a democracy it is neither desirable nor possible to have education function as an assembly line. The primary function must be an untidy process of helping the society as a whole and individuals within society to strike a balance between personal and group aims and needs while at the same time maintaining an atmosphere in which there is freedom to function and skills equal to the task. But public education cannot do this alone. It is but one institution engaged in developing the broad outline of an improved quality of life for a free people.

FRIDAY MORNING NEWS
NO NEWS IS GOOD NEWS
Ruth the "Zoomer"

Ruth jerked her head abruptly to bring the classroom back into focus. She had nearly fallen asleep even though her favorite professor was talking about her favorite poet, William Blake. She glanced at her wristwatch. Only 15 more minutes to go! If she could just keep herself awake! She quietly tensed the muscles of her legs, stretched her toes, crossed and uncrossed her legs. Anything to stay awake. The class was interesting, but she was exhausted. She had been up with the baby most of the night and up again at six-thirty to get the two oldest children off to school and take the two younger ones to the childcare center. She had pushed herself to the edge of her physical strength to be on time for her nine o'clock class, but here she was falling asleep almost as soon as she sat down. English was her major and this particular class was a high point.

"For a 26-year-old single mother of four, all under the age of nine, to go back to college probably is madness," she thought. "Maybe that's my attraction to Blake. Why don't I just stay home and live off the welfare checks." She wondered whether she'd get a job with a degree, anyway. Jobs were hard to find. She recalled the battle with her caseworker.

"What can you do with an English major?" she'd been challenged. "You need vocational skills with all those children to support." Childcare funds seem to be only for women who will be immediately employ-

[29] Magnus Haavelsrud. *Education for Peace: Reflection and Action.* London: IPC Business Press Limited, 1976. pp. 69-77. Elaborates on interrelated societal and education issues.

able after completing their program of post high school education. "English doesn't seem to fit the social worker's idea of my needs." Sometimes she thought her caseworker was right. But still she wouldn't stop. Her success as an English student had given her a feeling of confidence and hope she had never known before. The world of words and ideas could not be abandoned, not yet anyway.

Being poor was embittering, especially when the kids were sick. Being female and alone was frustrating and imprisoning with the constant demands of the kids. She *couldn't* give up the children, but she hoped she wouldn't have to give up the college education either.

As she glanced around the class, filled with young undergraduate women, she saw a few others her own age or older. These were known as the Resumers—"Zoomers," they called themselves. A very special group of women they were, returning to college or just starting to college after some interruption in their lives. They gave strength to each other. Ruth felt better as she looked around the class.

Class was ending now; she would have an hour in the library before the next class and then home. These hours of separateness and renewal were so short, and yet Ruth felt herself growing. She was more than "Mommy." She could think, and write, and speak. There was much more to learn and share. Some of it she would show the children some day.

George's Wife . . .

When I opened the door, George was standing there, his face twisted with tension.

"What is it man? Come on in!" I said, reaching out to put my hand on his shoulder.

"She's left me and the kids," he blurted out as he slumped into a chair by my kitchen table. He cradled his head in his hands, his whole body torn with sobbing for a moment; then the anger and control returned.

"What is the matter with her? What is going wrong with the whole world?" he asked, accusing more than questioning. "I have worked day and night to support them, to earn enough money to keep us going. We were doing fine, and things would have been even better. All I asked of her was that she stay home and take care of the kids. She was lucky that I wanted her to be a wife. She didn't have the problems some women do who have to work and take care of the house at the same time! I told her no wife of mine was going to take courses in a beauty college. Imagine what would happen to the kids if she was combing and setting hair all day, coming home tired at night."

"Maybe she'll come back," I said reassuringly. "What are you doing about the kids?"

"My mother will keep them awhile," he responded, suddenly seeming very drained with no more anger. "I guess she just got tired of being cooped up in that apartment with the kids all the time. That stupid woman! All I wanted her to do was stay home and take care of the kids! Didn't she know I got tired of working at a crummy factory. That's a trap, too! She'll soon see that it's not that exciting to be out there trying to make a living. But, it will be too late. The kids and I don't need her if she doesn't want to do her real job, and do it right!"

Committee Reflections on the Need for Lifelong Learning

Ruth's desire to study English represents one type of human longing for learning. We hear the voices of so many others, Rico, the Teacher, Grandma, Mike, the Superintendent, Carol . . . a collage of humans struggling, needing learning to help them through the struggle.

Insofar as learning is a key to human fulfillment, we need to respond. As educators we must become involved with the struggle and the longings. Individual fulfillment is a process, not an end product. How can we foster the process lifelong?

Glaring headlines highlight the personal and societal crises with which we continuously live and grapple. The issues represented by the media are reflections of the inextricable interaction of political, economic, and personal pressures. They indicated the growing sense of urgency for the fuller development of human potential and power, of human fulfillment as individuals and as members of a diverse society.

The question of improving education goes well beyond simply modifying schools. It confronts us with the need to reconceptualize education, its importance and role in our everyday lives. If we wish to view education as a way of engaging ourselves in the processes of fulfillment, then we must break away from the constraints of traditional conceptions of education and schooling. We must focus on the centrality of learning as involvement in the processes of lifelong fulfillment. Education should be empowering.

A national commitment to the concept of lifelong learning seems essential if society is ever to realize its potential for fulfillment through an improving quality of human life. It is insufficient to depend on the happenstance of situations, socioeconomic status, or the sporadic philanthropy of power brokers and legislatures.

Admittedly, the extension of intentional learning to the whole of society and to the whole of life comports risks for the traditional structures of society and the power brokers. With the extension of access to knowledge there inevitably will be great discomfort and dislocation. Even so, opportunities for human fulfillment that lie in a realization of life-long learning lead us on.

A Commentary on Lifelong Learning — Needed Clarifications

Lifelong learning—appearing on the surface to be a simple, nearly self-explanatory term—is a concept of surprising complexity, which describes the involvement of an individual in one aspect of natural human activity from birth to death. However, a cursory review of the current dialogue reveals that lifelong education, lifelong learning, adult education, continuing education, permanent education, recurrent education, and at least two dozen other terms are used synonymously or associatively, resulting in distortion and misrepresentation of the distinct qualities inherent in lifelong learning. It is imperative that we cut through the verbal jungle, if a national commitment to human fulfillment through learning is to be achieved.

Webster defines "lifelong" as "lasting for all one's life." Literally, lifelong means beginning at birth (or sooner in the eyes of some) and lasting until death.

Learning is defined as "the acquiring of knowledge or skills." Although this definition may not be an all-inclusive one, by omission it does suggest one very important characteristic of learning: it is not place specific. Learning is a process which takes place in informal and formal settings, day and night, planned and unplanned. While there are many conflicting views about what learning is and exactly how it occurs, two generally accepted premises are that nearly all humans are capable of some learning and learning is a continuous process beginning with a surge of responses and accommodations to one's environment soon after conception and continuing until death.

When learning is combined with lifelong, the inherent ability of individuals to be involved in the process throughout life is affirmed. It suggests that learning is not restricted to any particular age group, is not limited to any one particular place, nor is it dependent upon public recognition, certification, or credentials.

There is a major difference between learning and education. Both refer to acquiring knowledge and skills, but only education suggests a general restriction of this acquisition to formal schooling or training. This basic distinction between learning and education has even greater significance if we consider how these terms are applied. Education is characterized by two underlying assumptions. First, in the United States, until relatively recent times, education has referred almost exclusively to schooling—an individual's learning or education level was determined by the number of years he or she had participated in formal schooling. The normal pattern was K-12, possibly followed by two to six years of college or professional training. This pattern has been altered somewhat in recent years. Preprimary and primary education programs have been added at one end, and adult or continuing education programs have extended the other end. Thus, education has taken on a wider meaning in terms of participation years. However, learning and education have continued to be equated with formal schooling, especially in the minds of the general public. Exceptions can be found; for example, non-traditional programs and external degrees are gaining more attention today. But even these are encumbered by direction and supervision from formal educational systems. Consequently, they reflect certain formal instructional patterns such as a set number of required hours and success-ful completion of a written examination.

A second assumption, closely tied to the practice of equating learn-ing, education, and schooling, is that of equating learning and education with formal instruction and training. Formal means many things. Tradi-tionally, it means what Freire calls "the banking concept"[30]—the process of teachers teaching and students receiving, memorizing, and storing bits of knowledge. One has only to visit a few classrooms to find that this concept is still prevalent, even though some exceptions can be found. More and more schools are implementing out-of-school programs and on-the-job training programs. But, even these programs are designed and implemented under the close, watchful eye of a formal education system. This control is not inherently bad, but the tendency is to fall into the traditional formats. Furthermore, these "informal" programs are viewed as extensions of the formal instruction and not usually as substi-tutes or alternative modes of instruction. Consequently, formal instruc-tion in the traditional subject areas, by qualified teachers, has often become a required addition or prerequisite to the "informal" programs.

An additional confusion arises from using similar terms such as adult education and continuing education as though they were synonyms for lifelong learning. To a considerable extent, the problems surround-ing efforts to clarify the concept are tied to a historical practice of equating lifelong learning with adult level learning. Adult education is but one of many important aspects of lifelong learning. It is not even synonymous with adult learning. Adult learning involves more than formal schooling situations characteristic of most adult education pro-grams. Lifelong learning is a more inclusive and complex concept than any of the many terms that would appear to be synonymous.

A Teacher's Musing

Definitions are fine, but they always seem to be way out in the mid-dle of the universe somewhere. I took a course in ham radio operating last year. Is it or isn't it an example of a program for lifelong learning?

[30] Paulo Freire. *Pedagogy of the Oppressed*. New York: Herder & Herder, Inc., 1971. p. 58.

I can just hear the so-called "experts" responding "It is, and it isn't. It fits, and it doesn't."

Nuts. They keep on cranking out these new terms, a dozen a year, and I spend all kinds of time trying to understand what they mean; but even when I do understand, I usually have trouble coming up with real-world examples. A definition is like a perfect vision of something that can only exist in this world imperfectly. Well, if it can only exist in this world imperfectly, what difference does it make whether we call it continuing education, adult education, or lifelong education?

What it all boils down to is we want to find ways to keep people studying even after they've stopped going to school. We want learning to continue to be planned—an intentional undertaking, not just the haphazard way adults usually learn. Intentionality, that the real name of the game!

A Professor Responds

Lifelong learning *is* an ideal; intentionality *is* an essential part of that ideal. Each one of us has to work at a translation of the ideal in terms of the real conditions we have come to know. In education we seem to always find ourselves debating from opposite ends—from the individual-personal perspective and from the social-governmental perspective—even though we recognize that both perspectives coexist in reality and function interactively. If only we understood the interaction more fully! If only we were sure how the intentionality of the individual ought to relate to the intentionality of society. If only we would use intentionality to resolve the so-called "intra" generational crisis. Our present state of knowledge about humanness and human fulfillment is circumstantial and far from secure. Our ideals must be put into context not because the acontextual abstraction isn't intellectually more desirable, but because that is the state of our present understanding. More to the point, every time we put together a practical example of some idealistic term we are doing all that can be done for now. Perhaps tomorrow we will do better. Perhaps we will achieve the perfect formula for lifelong learning that can be applied regardless of the specific conditions.

As for now, we can do nothing but continue to subordinate perfection to the workings of what is practical. What we do may seem relative to the workings of what is practical. What we do may seem relative to the circumstances; and yet, we bear within us the belief, however unsubstantiated, that there are perfect criteria and that these perfect criteria can be worked toward so that a more perfect human fulfillment can be achieved. That we continue to produce new terms and new definitions is a reflection of our continuing search for perfection.

"Little by little I began to divine the all-embracing, pan-human significance of the bloody experiment taking place in Russia's boundless land; her boundless soul. My mind began to tolerate and accept the revolutionary slogans which formerly had seemed so extremely naive and utopian to me. As I gazed at the famished faces, sunken cheeks, and clenched fists, I began to have a presentiment of man's divine privilege: by believing in a myth, desiring it, imbruing it with blood, sweat and tears (tears alone are not sufficient, nor is blood, nor sweat), man transforms that myth into reality.

I was terrified. For the first time I saw how creative man's intervention is, and how great his responsibility. We are to blame if reality does not take the form we desire. Whatever we have not desired with sufficient strength, that we call nonexistent. Desire it, imbrue it with your blood, your sweat, your tears, and it will take on a body. Reality is nothing more than the chimera subjected to our desire and our suffering." [31]

Committee Reflections: These Are Our Goals

That education can be a lifelong process is by no means a new idea. It is an idea, however, that has taken on a new sense of urgency. The mindlessness of our technological-industrial complexes has fostered among us a terrible sense of impotence that only an intentional, lifelong effort to continue learning and understanding can help to overcome.

In our efforts to achieve a learning society, we must recognize that neither control of technology nor democratic participation in the course of society nor a shared sense of human fulfillment can be achieved by our citizenry unless we become:

1. knowledgeable of our social, cultural, political and personal situations;

2. aware of our alternatives;

3. able to undertake independent inquiry;

4. capable of making appropriate choices with the power to carry them out;

5. committed to the exercise of justice.

Unless citizens are informed and cognizant, their participation is a game of charades, no more than a popularity survey based on haphazardly formed images having little to do with reality or with the results of any coherent inquiry. Unless individuals are in command of those skills which will enable them to direct the quality of their personal and social lives, there can be no human fulfillment.

Lifelong education should not be viewed only as a potpourri of

<hr />

[31] Nikos Kazantzakis. *Report to Greco.* P. A. Bien, translator. New York: Simon & Schuster, Inc., 1965. p. 391.

courses offered by local school districts to adults to help them fill their leisure time in ways that are personally interesting or to retool their work skills so as to better suit the needs of industry. To cater to the personally felt needs and interests of individuals is, of course, one desirable goal of lifelong education which might help us shut out the impositions of technology, but it avoids the massive problems confronting us as we broach the 1980's. We cannot hope to regain control over our destinies, if lifelong education is translated *only* into leisure-related activities.

A lifelong curriculum needs to be imbued with intentionality well beyond anything ever undertaken by the traditional public school. In light of the enormous sway held by business and industry over the directions of formal schooling, it is probable that the public school is the most poorly suited vehicle for the task before us. If the public schools are to be vehicles for lifelong learning, then they must be radically reconceptualized.

It is important to recognize that when we speak of planning and development of a lifelong curriculum that "planning" does not mean that what would be included would be locked into a set of specifically detailed contents. The nature of planning can be open-ended and flexible as well as closed and flexible. Nor should a lifelong curriculum exclude personal interests and needs, although a reassessment of these considerations in the total curriculum must be pursued continually. *A lifelong curricular plan should mean the overt establishment of our intentions, as individual members of a democratic society, to deal with as broad a spectrum of the personal and social consequences of modern life as we can conceive in an effort to reassert our control over the directions of our lives.* Since too many people at all stages of life lack some or all of the necessary human and material resources to take advantage of formal instruction, the system must be opened so that lifelong learning is recognized as the birthright of all.

An optimal lifelong learning environment is one that provides not only goals but also means to carry out those experiences that enable persons to maximally develop themselves vis-a-vis their society.

There is evidence that school environments separate individuals from their life space. Environments such as mobile libraries, banks, museums, garages, streets, empty lots, cemeteries, empty churches, are rarely orchestrated into the learning experiences of the population.

Contextualizing the learning experiences to the needs, interests, perceptions, aspirations, and abilities of the learners is an absolute necessity. This means that the learning environment must have woven into it the heterogeneity of the population manifested in ethnicity, age, sex, class, race, ideology, rural-urban differences. We believe that there are no learning panaceas for all contexts but only dynamic learning interactions.

The Committee

PART II
The Realities/The Obstacles

"... it was the epoch of belief, it was the
epoch of incredulity, ..."
Charles Dickens, *A Tale of Two Cities*

The Realities surround us—hound us with their urgency. Hunger, strife, fear, ignorance, injustice, and on and on! No single act or societal plan will ensure the realization of the ideal fulfillment of human potential —but if only we can succeed in becoming better....

The Committee

THE MOUNTAIN AND THE RIVER

In my country there is a mountain.
In my country there is a river.

Come with me.

Night climbs up to the mountain.
Hunger goes down to the river.

Come with me.

56

Who are those who suffer?
I do not know, but they call to me.

Come with me.

I do not know, but they are mine
and they say to me: "We suffer."

Come with me.

And they say to me: "Your people,
your luckless people,
between the mountain and the river,
with hunger and grief,
they do not want to struggle alone,
they are waiting for you, friend."

Oh you, the one I love,
little one, red grain
of wheat,

the struggle will be hard,
life will be hard,
but you will come with me.

                                        Pablo Neruda[1]

Dependence

In the late 70's, the United States was dependent upon imports for more than 25 percent of each of twelve critical raw materials used in key industries; nearly 33 percent of American corporate profits resulted from multinational corporation investments and production. The implications of industrial data for the past decade are clear— American industry is dependent upon imports and exports to keep its economy functioning smoothly. In turn, the rest of the world looks to the United States for economic stability.

The Gap

Some time ago, Barbara Ward called attention to the growing gap between rich nations and poor nations.[2] The Poor People's March

---

[1] Pablo Neruda. *The Captain's Verses.* Donald D. Walsh, translator. New York: New Directions Publishing Corporation, 1975. Copyright © 1972 by Pablo Neruda and Donald D. Walsh. Reprinted by permission of New Directions.

[2] Barbara Ward. *The Rich Nations and the Poor Nations.* New York: W. W. Norton & Company, Inc., 1962.

on Washington dramatized the im-mediacy of that gap within the United States itself. Sporadic explo-sions of the pent-up fury of the American "underclass" are a stac-cato punctuation in the subcon-sious lullabye of national affluence. The gross statistics of affluence hide the depth of the despair, the alone-ness, the helplessness. The Ameri-can poor are one with the poor of the world, but with a difference. "The poverty in the black and Puerto Rican neighborhoods on the West Side of Chicago is worse than any poverty"[3] seen in West Africa. In the eyes of many sociologists, the major distinguishing features of American poverty are the break-down of the family structure and the loss of any sense of community. For large segments of the popula-tion in American urban centers, the sense of alienation is total. Money, food, and jobs are only part of the answer.

How does a 29-year-old ex-junkie find hope? Where can a 10-year-old child turn when deserted by her father and with her mother in jail for prostitution? Who will take responsibility for the 80-year-old immigrant grandmother suffering from a stroke in New York while her family resides in California? How can the classroom teacher raise the achievement level of chil-dren from such settings?

They Raved, But They Were Not Mad

"When radio hits oral, nonliterate peoples, it intensifies excitability. Villagers who once had no knowledge of what was happening in some distant capital now receive that news daily in a form which makes it appear both urgent and relevant. But they cannot reply. Therefore, they become at once more excited and more frustrated because nobody seems to be listening to them."[4]

Committee Reflections on Global Interdependence

Marshall McLuhan has not created our Global Village, he only named it. With the naming has come a sense of familiarity that leads us to accept the condition without understanding the implications. We fail to grasp the urgency of social changes caused by the increasing global interdependence.

A minor fluctuation in the price of gold in London has an immediate impact on transactions in Tokyo. A rebel incursion in central Africa affects purchasing policies in corporate board rooms from Moscow to New York. Whether technological advance, national calamity, or political

---

[3] *Time* 110 (9) ; August 29, 1977.

[4] Edmund Carpenter. *Oh, What a Blow That Phantom Gave Me!* New York: Holt, Rinehart and Winston, Inc., 1972. p. 178.

manipulation, action in one area is followed by responses of increasingly complex subtlety and significance in many other areas.

The international marketplace creates demands for new products leading to trade imbalances while the demands of consumption prematurely push developing nations into advanced levels of technological development. At the same time agriculture in developing countries continues at a subsistence level, with most nations incapable of producing their own food. On a worldwide scale, hunger, malnutrition, and starvation result from the inequitable use and distribution of resources. The problems are not simple. Each area of concern, whether urban growth and deterioration, war and conflict, environmental pollution, population explosion, resource shortage, or income disparity, is inextricably related to other problems in all parts of the world.

While interdependence is a favorite topic of discussion among the world's well educated, the people it may affect most dramatically are the illiterate poor. It is they who are dependent on international trade for their very survival and at the same time victimized by the creations of consumerism. While bellies go empty at night, the transistor radio has become the indispensable symbol of social achievement.

Nevertheless, our interdependence is not a new phenomenon. From its inception the United States has been shaped by the interdependent relationships of many cultural and national forces. In addition, the growth of technology and industry has had a major impact on the tightening of our common bonds. But a recent factor in the acceleration of interdependence has been the increased destructive capabilities of armament technology and the resultant threat to human security. The superpowers have trapped themselves and the rest of the world in a death-defying race for nuclear superiority that holds the whole of humanity hostage. We either live together or we die together.[5]

The chasms between cultures and nations can never be returned to their prior conditions. While the desire for isolation or going-it-alone continues to emerge in the wake of complex relationships, no one is inclined to couple that longing with a renunciation of rights to critical resources in fuels, minerals, foodstuffs, or freedom of association. We already participate in a global culture whether we are willing to affirm it or not. Indeed, given the extent and depth of our involvement with each other, the old saw that "Either we hang together or we will hang separately!" takes on new urgency.

Most of the world's population lives in villages. A transnational perspective is an abstraction that must seem very distant for these village dwellers who are involved in a con-

[5] Edwin O. Reischauer. *Toward the 21st Century: Education for a Changing World.* New York: Alfred A. Knopf, Inc., 1973. p. 31.

tinual struggle for minimum necessities. These are the people labeled, "in need of development" by the intellectual elite. These are the people who have been labeled by Western change agents as distrustful, evasive, uncooperative, fatalistic, hostile to polity, lacking in empathy. The poor of the world have been perceived as objects to be acted upon rather than as co-inhabitors of a global ecosystem. They have been treated as passive entities rather than as dynamic human beings.

I work in a school as a custodian and I hear all about the latest fads in education. This year, global education is "in." One of the younger teachers is really hooked on it. There are pictures and maps all over the room and the kids are studying about what jet flight is doing to the world. I guess that is all right, but it really doesn't help these kids to understand what life is really like. Me, I come to work every day—eight hours cleaning, one hour eating, two hours on the freeway and a few hours to be with my family. My home, the three floors of this building, the 30 miles of freeway—these are my life. Sure I like to hear about other places like Ethiopia and Tokyo, but I need to know my own territory better. How do I get along better with the people around me and maybe even manage to get a merit raise. You know, I've never even been on a jet.

NEWS FEATURE 1977

Trying to Make Sense of It

"Is it possible to make sense of what is going on in the world, to set oneself for the future? Of course we cannot predict the sudden storms of history. But history is more than storms; it is also a great Gulf Stream, carrying us along its broad currents. Here are a few dead reckonings on the directions in which I think that stream is moving, and a few reflections on what we must anticipate as we go with its currents.

"1. We cannot expect social contentment from economic growth. This strikes me as one of the few important lessons we can learn from the past half century. There was a time, not so long ago, when statesmen and scholars alike believed that economic growth brought social well-being in its train—that the cure for social and political disaffection, for riots and radicalism, was simply more income.

"I no longer think we can indulge in that lulling belief. We have had a half century of unprecedented economic improvement, both here and abroad. No doubt that growth has alleviated much misery and has staved off much unrest. But I do not think anyone can say that it has brought a general sense of well-being, contentment, good will, gratitude. This has very sobering implications for capitalist societies, which have always assumed that wealth alone would bring stability, morale, commitment to the system.

"2. Western industrial societies are moving both toward planning and toward the market. Looking back over the past 50 years, it is clear that all Western societies have moved in the direction of economic planning. It is also clear that planning is more cumbersome, infuriating, inefficient, and bureaucratic than most planners had anticipated. It is not surprising, then, that we now hear a clamor to remedy the problems of planning by returning to the mechanism of the market, with its self-firing stimulus of individual betterment and its winnowing force of competition.

"What the enthusiasts for market 'solutions' overlook is that the market brings its own difficulties. Unemployment, economic instability, social neglect, the exercise of intolerable private power are all by-products of the market process. They are why planning arose in the first place, and why it will arise again if the scope of the market is broadened. Thus, planning generates a need for the market, and the market generates a need for planning. Between this Syclla and Charybdis all Western economies must make their way.

"3. The deepest subversive threat to capitalism is the acquisitive drive on which it depends. Acquisitiveness is the form of social behavior nurtured and encouraged by capitalist society. Under the name of the Profit Motive it is regarded as the very *élan vital* of the system. Considered as Bettering Our Condition (as Adam Smith put it), acquisitiveness is the socially approved motive for all citizens, workers and capitalists alike.

"Yet for all the esteem in which acquisitiveness is held, we have always recognized that it is a dangerous form of social behavior.[6]

Have I heard that before???
"Master, what good must I do to gain eternal life?"
". . . go, sell your possessions, and give to the poor, and then you will have riches in heaven."

Matt. 19:15.

Committee Reflection on GNP vs. GNH

Where minimum needs are guaranteed, development can come to mean growth in "gross national happiness" rather than in gross national product exclusively. Development need not be equated with the unreasoned production and consumption of material goods; nor does mate-

[6] Robert L. Heilbroner. *The New York Times.* October 10, 1977.

rial development need to be equated with the "good life." While technology and economic prosperity are necessary, development must be conceptualized as growth in the ability to live a fuller, more dignified life. Rather than think of development quantitatively, much more emphasis should be placed on its qualitative aspect. Development can mean providing the opportunity for all individuals and nations to realize their potential.

Can there be an abundance for all? And if so, abundance of what? Perhaps two of the greatest contemporary ironies of Spaceship Earth are (a) that technological development is seen as the key to the material well-being of the world's growing population and (b) that technological development is threatening to destroy the natural resources which are ultimate sources of this well-being.

A Commentary on Global Values

Not only are there global violence, global industry, global communication systems, and global conflict, but there are also emerging global values. With increased frequency, businesses of many nations are investing in the American economy. Even the more traditional and controlled societies of Asia, Africa, and the Middle East are sending large numbers of students to the United States to continue their studies. In the case of students from oil-rich nations and other affluent societies, it is not uncommon for them to arrive with their young families fresh from the isolation of very different and very conservative cultures. The result is an increasing confrontation of cultures with differing value structures. The points at which the disparate values meet form part of the growing edge of a rapidly emerging system of global values. The press of time, the explosive change of circumstances, and the increase of knowledge leave little space for savoring and developing individual accommodations to the new as Grandma did.

To be sure, the emerging global values are not pure, intentional distillations of carefully formulated positions. Rather, they are apt to be hybrids created from the frequently abrasive encounters of basically incompatible economic, social, religious, and political systems. At the same time, some cultures accommodate competing principles and tenets in a new syncretism with global appeal.

Religious dogma and sectarianism, characteristically exported by Americans, have recently been imported to the United States. Zen, Tao, Muhammed, Buddha, and the Hindu gods have joined Moses and Jesus as familiar, challenging, and sometimes threatening models of religious and ethical values contemplated by American youth. When increased global interaction is coupled with internal breakdown in tradition and lessening of formal adherence to authoritarian moral and ethical prescriptions, the setting becomes charged like a volatile gas, surging against its container. Large segments of society are engaged in the testing of the container of traditional values, searching for a values structure that will be sufficient for tomorrow. While not articulated clearly, the outlines of global values systems are becoming visible; they vie for consideration.

Grandma's Wealth

My grandma was as poverty stricken a migrant as any that came to the United States. She remained very poor for the first half of her 80 years and then she became wealthy. Admittedly, her income never rose far above the U.S. Government's official poverty line, but she felt wealthy. She owned a car and she had a bathtub with hot and cold running water inside her house.

Even when she was very old, she played like a child with her bathtub. She took two, sometimes three baths a day and after each, she would scrub and polish the tub and stand back in pride for several minutes admiring her possession.

As a young teenager, I used to think her performance a little weird. Why would anyone stare in admiration at a bathtub? How materialistic, I used to think. But perspectives change. Perhaps for me, born into and accustomed to technological facilities of all kinds, wanting a new car every year or three bathrooms in my home reflects materialistic gluttony. But for my grandma, having a bath every day had been an unreachable ideal that had unexpectedly become reality. She relished her tub, every day she lived, with an inner satisfaction that I wish I could know. She never thought of turning her tub in for a better one. She never even thought of adding a shower, though she could have. She enjoyed her dream turned reality beyond any measure I can express, and felt no need to set new goals of wealth for herself.

Though I know I am monetarily better off than she ever was, I feel poor. I always want something else. There's always a new little gadget to acquire even though I have collected so many things that I feel beleaguered by their mounting presence in my home. Still I go on acquiring. It all seems so senseless. In a way, I blame technology; in a way, I blame the education I received as a child; in a way, I blame my own weakness. Most of all, I want to regain control over my own senseless consumption that reeks of the lowest kinds of materialism. There was a wonderful idealism in my grandma's reverence for a bathtub that I have never known. And there is an awful selfishness in my consumption that I wish I did not know.

SUNDAY NEWS BRIEF

"SMALL IS BEAUTIFUL": IDEA GROWS THAT BIG BUSI-NESS MAY NOT BE BEST . . . **NATIONAL ENERGY PROGRAM FAILING . . . Action to date has had little effect on the American consumption of natural fuels. Unless more stringent conservation measures are taken the world will face a massive depression of economic growth** . . . WESTERN STATES FACE 16 PERCENT CUTBACK IN ELECTRICAL POWER . . . **GNP IN U.S. INCREASES;** Business leaders heartened . . . **TEST TUBE BABY BORN** . . . DEEPEST SECRETS OF LIFE BEING CLASSIFIED . . . 5,375 "Message Units" have been found in DNA of Virus PH1 X-174. The propriety of DNA research has finally become a topic of concern for Congress . . . **GENETIC DECODERS READING THE MESSAGES OF DNA . . .**

Young girl: Please, Sir—I don't want my genes read today!
Genetic Scientist: Better read than dead.

NEWSFLASH 2006

We interrupt this program for an important announcement. Word has just reached this station that the central computing center for New York State's largest electric light and power company has been taken over by a band of terrorists calling themselves the PAFS, "The People's Army for a Fair Society." Exactly what demands the PAFS are making is not yet known . . . Their control of the computing center is, however, a severe threat to the well-being of this state's population. In recent years, most of the working controls for power production have been converted to microchips interfaced with the central processing unit located at the center. Any large scale destruction of these would put the lights out for millions of homes and businesses for several months at least . . . Although solar energy heating units have been widely installed, electricity and gas are still the major sources for the state's heating. Should the terrorists decide to cut off or destroy the CPU and its microchips, millions would be without heat in the midst of this very cold winter. The emergency is real and we advise everyone to obtain some kind of thermal blanket designed for sub-freezing temperatures. A provision of matches, cooking fuel, flashlights and battery-operated radios will also be useful should the terrorists carry out their threat . . . At this point, we can only hope that the People's Army for a Fair Society will be fair to the people—to the thousands of elderly who may not be able to move from their homes—to the youngsters who may not even know what the word "politics" means —and to the rest of us who feel that we are being bullied into someone else's "fair society" . . . Please do not call this station for further information. You know all we know. As soon as we have anything new to communicate, rest assured we will do so. In the meantime, let's listen to the soothing sounds of Arnie and his Synthesizers Ten.

Committee Reflections on Remote Control

Is there a point of complexity beyond which technology no longer serves human needs? Illich has noted that the beautiful aspect of an old sewing machine was that a person equipped with a small screwdriver and some household oil could make the necessary adjustments to correct any malfunctioning. A bicycle is still one of the few machines with which the owner can interact in an uncomplicated fashion. On the other hand, a modern television threateningly warns its owner: "Caution, high voltage inside. Only qualified personnel should disassemble. This unit is fully transistorized and contains no tubes or user-serviceable components." Not only does the complexity of television technology discourage an owner from making "home repairs," but the remoteness of the source of broadcasting leaves the consumer vulnerable to program decisions made largely by the industry. The concept of "remote control" for television has a double meaning.

TV Entertainment

The Los Angeles Times reports that the number of hours children watch T.V. has dropped significantly. Analysis of the data suggests T.V. games are replacing some viewing. Parent groups interested in making inroads in the programming of violence on television applaud the general decrease in viewing time, but data to date do not indicate any more enlightened discrimination in selection of programs that are watched. This is not a case of less being better. Those such as Bill Moyers who would bring quality programming to the major networks are finding it hard to do so. Enlightened documentaries just do not sell enough beer and bras.

 The perfect Christmas gift for Nielsen households would be a collection of T.V. electronic games. Anyone for Atari?

Editorial

Watching a Man Die

The world has had an opportunity to watch a man die on television. The film footage of high wire performer Karl Wallenda's fall was incredible. Some saw it more than once, while others refused to watch. "How could they show something like that?" was asked. Should this footage have been shown?

Some regarded Karl Wallenda as a man who "needed more." Such people were quick to assert that there are individuals who can't survive on the things that make normal people happy. Normal people can sit on a front porch and breathe the spring air and see the sunset and listen to the birds and be moved and be content. Others just must have more than that. Their juices simply won't begin to flow unless they have challenges and take risks normal people wouldn't dare to take.

When spectators camped all night to see Karl Wallenda walk Tallulah Gorge, most of them knew they would never do something like that.

They fulfilled their fantasies whenever Wallenda walked.

But shed no tears for the old man on the high wire. He dared fate and he confronted death nearly every day of his life. He got away with it his three score ten and more. A man like that deserves, when the time finally comes, to die seeking his fulfillment.

Parents' Lament

Ironically, just two weeks before the death of Karl Wallenda, our family sat together to watch the special made-for-T.V. production of the story of the Great Wallendas. Our seven and eight year olds were spellbound by the daring and intensity of commitment portrayed on the screen. As has become a pattern, they asked, "Is it real?" "Did they really walk on a wire while balancing people on their shoulders?" When told it had really happened but this was only make-believe, they looked confused. Other questions tumbled out. How do they do it? Aren't they scared? No, they wouldn't be scared because it's only make-believe. But how do you know it's make-believe?

As the tragedy which snuffed out the lives of two men and paralyzed another unfolded, the children continued to explore the significance of the human ability to create the semblance of reality without the risks. Similar discussions had preceded this one when news reports carried pictures of terrorist and war-wrought carnage. But the answers are hard to find and the kids are never satisfied. In a sense, television has come to be the technical myth maker that turns real events into fairy stories. As much drama is created when a puppy is lost as when the Wallendas fall from a high wire. My wife and I can't help wondering what this is doing to our kids' reality. Should we forbid their watching?

Wilma: My T.V. is on the blink. The shop said it will be two weeks before it will be repaired.
Edna: My goodness! What will you do for a babysitter?

SUPER BOWL SUNDAY

"They sure mess up my Sunday afternoon. I'd like to watch T.V. but there's nothing but sports, sports, old crime movies and more sports. Super Bowl Sunday! Why is it I'm not one of the 85 million Americans stuck on this national pastime? Am I weird? Everytime there's a T.V. show *I* like, it gets canceled. Tomorrow at work everyone will be talking Super Bowl. If you're going to be "with it" you've got to watch. What else is there to do on a Sunday afternoon, anyway.

"Oh well, I guess I'll just turn it on for a little while."

Committee Reflections on Television

The media, especially television, fill large portions of our children's lives. In the process, the development of rational powers in our young is undermined. Exciting, tension-packed events of life and death are squeezed between soap commercials. Not only are the thought processes of our children caught up in serial images that seldom explore underlying causes or ultimate consequences, but children also become habituated to numerous dramatic "highs" within relatively brief periods so that times of quiet when reflective thought could develop are, instead, insufferable periods of boredom.

Although the evidence is not readily available, the signs that we are being drugged by media-like tension and excitement are evident. For example, we elect our public officials on the basis of media-managed images and saturate the airways with violence while demanding law and order on the street.

At a time when rational powers have given us insights into new kinds of control over the destiny of this universe, it is ironic that our respect for rational abilities seems to be declining steadily. Many of our young do not consider the exercise of rational powers to be important. The scientists—miracle workers of television mythology—and even the great detectives who never bleed when beaten up will work it all out, seemingly. They will tell us what to think. Why worry?

 Adult Fulfillment: Having your T.V. set attached to a home video recorder so you won't miss any favorite programs.

Double Adult Fulfillment: Having a video recorder and a remote control channel changer.

MONDAY EVENING NEWS BRIEF

COUNTY WELFARE COST UP . . . NEW YORK TIMES FINDS BANKS LACK ETHICAL STANDARDS . . . **G.M. AGREES TO OUT-OF-COURT SETTLEMENT IN ENGINE SWITCH CASE** . . . GRADE INFLATION CHALLENGED AS UNETHICAL . . . YOUTH VIOLENCE, CRIME INCREASING SHARPLY IN U.S. According to a recently completed governmental study, persons under 18 are responsible for nearly half of all serious offenses in the U.S. In 1975, the city of Detroit set a curfew of 10 p.m. for all youngsters aged 16 or under because of the numerous serious crimes committed by this age group . . . In 1976, one third of all murders committed in the city of Chicago were committed by people who were under 21 years of age. The overall number of murders in the United States reached an all-time high in the decade of the 70's. The small decline in serious crimes that has been observed is attributed to a decline in the youth population . . . In 1977, New York City experienced a near-total power outage. Looting was rampant and thousands of people were arrested while breaking store windows, stealing merchandise, or trying to sell their stolen merchandise on the street to passersby. The New York City courts were brought nearly to a standstill . . . In 1978, demands for stiffer punishment continued to crescendo. Violence must be met with violence and the certainty of punishment. More and more public figures are adding their voices to the crescendo. "Enough introspection and blaming society!" has become the refrain.

Committee Reflections on Violence

Not only are we afraid to walk out on the streets, we are even suspicious of our most "respectable" citizens—of the big oil executives who give and take bribes, of politicians who do likewise. Theirs is a subtler violence, but it wounds as well. Can a society survive with the continual exercise of threats? Does there not need to be some agreement among people about what is an acceptable way of acting and interacting? When lawyers, presidents, and street kids are all out for their own self-interests and willing to ignore the law, can society continue to exist?

In an age of abundance, when even the poorest live better than their forebears, can all this violence and crime—this lack of morality—be attributed solely to the unequal distribution of society's benefits? There must be more far-reaching as well as intimate causes for what is happening. The question is whether, as a society, we can survive long enough to learn.

Musings Circa 2010 A.D.

At 90, I've had a lot of chances to look back. Nothing much has changed. After more than a decade of this century my heat and light are being threatened again. I've been blackmailed so often in the past 50 years, that I just can't seem to muster the energy to care. It just seems I've lived my whole life in an age of blackmail.

I remember back in the 60's when the first airline hijackings took place and we all got so upset. The airlines established checkpoints to search everyone, and we all went for it as a way of protecting ourselves. But economic blackmail was harder to handle. The strikes just got worse and worse. One year the garbage was piled so high in our street that everyone in the neighborhood agreed to help transport it to the city dump. That was when the striking garbage men attacked us with stones and clubs. Were we glad when the police arrested us, even if we hadn't started the battle! We were not a fighting group of people. But jail was better than a bloody head.

Another year, the farmers got together to keep their produce off the market. They just weren't getting a fair price. As time passed and a real food shortage developed, we sure were glad when a national emergency was declared and the president sent in the military to force the release of foodstuffs. But soldiers don't make very good farmers.

Looking back, it all seems like an orgy of self-centered individuals drunk on their own righteousness. "If you don't give me what I want, then I will deny you food . . . life . . . sanitation . . . whatever."

The blackmail of the century, I suppose, took place when those terrorists threatened to explode an atomic device inside a New York subway tunnel. Thank God for the scientist (I wish I could remember her name) who had invented a machine that could detect the location of atomic weaponry, just in case some terrorist group might try such a crazy stunt.

The blackmailing just goes on and on. What else is there to give up or do? We live in protected compounds now. Everyone is thoroughly searched. No one remains unidentified anymore. We all had our social security numbers magnetically imprinted on our skulls. In a way we are in a new kind of feudalism. All of us look to our compound leaders for protection. In return for their competence as computer experts we give our loyalty and a part of our work.

It is not a bad life for a 90 year old. Still, I wonder if the young people today know what it's like to have the whole world to wander about in?

We should have considered the implications of rampant blackmail and the political uses of violence better than we did. As I think back over it all, my views really did not keep up with the technological changes in violence. Keeping up was the key. Why didn't we? It took only a handful of people to build and hide an atom bomb that could destroy the lives of millions of people. Civic violence became too easy to engage in. Any half-wit could program society's destruction. But I really didn't understand this in the 60's when all sorts of groups were taking over everything from buildings to airlines to prisons to universities and making all sorts of threats.

Oh, well. Inside this compound, even the PAFS can't get to me. We have our own independent power system. It would mean reduced energy, but enough so that we would have heat and I could go on reading. I may be 90, but my eyes are as good as the day I was born.

A Commentary on the Conflict in Freedom

We are a people troubled. We are a people caught in a struggle to know more fully the meaning of freedom. On the one hand we have moved rapidly in the development and extension of personal freedom. On the other hand we have lost our sense of social cohesion. Individual rights are regularly affirmed by the courts, the popular press, and an expanding materialistic culture that makes it seem as if everything is immediately at hand but for the asking or a slight fee. Through the pop culture media of music, drugs, and personal awareness training, the message is carried that the individual is free. The historic political doctrine of the inviolability of individual conscience has become the equivalent of anyone's beliefs are as good as anyone else's. The personal judgment of each individual has become the standard for action. The result is the essence of anarchy. Everyone reigns supreme.

In the midst of this commitment to individualism, education has begun to talk of the development of greater decision-making competencies and skills in interpersonal relationships while avoiding overt consideration of basic norms or standards to which individuals may turn for guidance in moments of uncertainty.

Without standards, everything is up for grabs, all-at-once. The old standbys of family relationships, religious associations, and nationalistic identifications are no longer fulfilling. We have demythologized and debunked all our fairy tales, and yet a part of us longs to believe in the land of make-believe. Not only do we long to believe, we will believe. In what will we believe? We experiment with LSD and other mind "expanding" drugs, studies of ESP, glossolalia, Zen and yoga, weekly sessions with a psychiatrist, and mass movements of religious cults.

While being challenged to decide and to act on the basis of rational decisions, our angst in the face of the decision-making process rises. We seek the support of others. It is threatening to stand alone, even long enough to become sensitive to the problem, to face the self in a responsible way. At every turn we elect the comfort of groups that have not given themselves sufficiently to in-depth consideration of the problem. Thus we occupy ourselves with the trivial and insignificant. New demagogues are accepted as providers of assurance as we venture into uncharted areas.

We have failed to recognize that the essence of freedom is based on group values and respect for commonly accepted criteria. Without consensus, however tenuous, individualism becomes anarchy which negates freedom. We have lost our vision of the community as balancing force to personalism carried to extremes. Humankind has a dual orientation— born to be free as an individual and free in relationship to others. As a society we cannot continue to avoid consideration of the structures and values of freedom.

Mac's Farm

Mac had struggled through the depression, wet summers, dry summers, severe winters and other acts of God but he never understood why he had to fight big government, too. He fought for a time. He used a variety of tactics. He tried marketing his own crops and dairy products from a roadside stand. And gradually, reluctantly, he met the regulations requiring separate milking parlors, detached milk houses and protected grain storage areas. In time he joined the local co-op. Now he asked himself why. He had broken his back for 60 years and now having to sell the farm . . .

"Five years ago I bought a new tractor with attachments for $25,000. Today the same tractor costs $47,000. Five years ago corn brought $2.35 a bushel. Today it will only bring $1.79 if you're lucky. How can the government expect you to stay in business?

"The neighbors wonder how I can give up a piece of land that was homesteaded by my great-grandfather. Well, I'll tell'em how I can do it. I've been dipping into my savings for over ten years to keep a dream alive. What chance has a little guy got against a bunch of bureaucrats in Washington? They send out their extension agents and inspectors to tramp around and tell you what to do so that you don't have a chance to do your own thing at all. My dad and granddad knew how to make things go. I would too if the government would just stay out of the way.

"First they pass a regulation to use a new crop spray. Then they change their minds because it's dangerous for livestock. Why don't they make up their minds? Why should I be stuck with unusable chemicals and dying cattle? I get fined for failure to comply with their regulations, but what happens when government makes a mistake?

"If big government just wouldn't interfere, I could still make a go of it. I'm sure my sons would have stuck with me if there'd been any future in it—but instead, they got out. I don't know how anyone is going to do it any better. I'd like to see the Secretary of Agriculture make a go of it on 140 acres."

HONESTY IN LABELING

We Bring America What It Wants!
(Advertisement paid for by U.S. business and industry.)

Committee Reflections on Individualism and Democracy

Individualism and democracy are antithetical. Individualism, left to its own natural development, leads to the dominance of the strong over the weak. The attributes that comprise strength may vary from culture to culture, but the dominance of a few unconstrained individuals over the many is an inevitable result. In order to have individualism, democracy must be modified; in order to have democracy, individualism must be constrained.

In other words, there is a tremendous gain in vitality and creativity to be derived from the exercise of individualism; at the same time, there is also tremendous danger to the continued existence of American democracy. If individualism is carried to an extreme it means anarchy. No form of government can survive anarchy. The paramount problem of

American society is allowing individuals to be free while constraining their individualism. This cannot be achieved without people wanting to foster each other's individuality and constrain their own. Herein lies the essence of "equal opportunity." It can not depend on law alone.

Steven's Dilemma

I had barely arrived at my office when I received word that there had been an urgent call from my ten-year-old son, Steven. I hastened to return the call to find out what was happening. Steve sobbed into the phone, "I was kicked out of class for talking back to the teacher." He reported that he had questioned one of her statements and she accused him of "smarting off." "While I was standing in the hall outside the class, the principal walked by and ordered me to his office." Steven was very upset because he felt he had been mistreated and no one would listen to him. After some consoling words quieted him, I hung up. Then I called the principal to get his perceptions.

The principal explained that it was his observation that Steven has a highly developed sense of fairness which creates occasional problems for him. "For example," he said, "whenever he is disciplined, he wants to know why others don't suffer the same consequences for similar infractions of the rules. He has to understand," the principal continued, "that life is not fair and rules are rules!"

Italian Reflection

It was post-war Italy in the early 60's and really a wonderful period in Italian history, full of hope, expansion and construction, all couched in the midst of sweet rolling hills and hazy skies. I was working for a newspaper then, interviewing people about their participation in World War II: Had they been supporters of Mussolini? Had they joined the anti-fascists toward the end of the war? What about the treatment of the Jews—had they gone along with the way their German allies had conducted the concentration camps?

They were all sensitive questions asked all too bluntly by an outsider who hoped the shock of the questions would uncover a bit more of the truth. Most responded vaguely, perhaps no longer sure themselves of what they had believed. But one elderly lady, with stringy white hair tied in a bun at the back of her head and lips like toothpicks in the midst of an angular face, showed the anger and emotion at my questions that others may have tried to hide, if for no other reason than to be good hosts.

"You see this house?" she said in her slightly broken English. I looked around at the dimly lit, three-room apartment and nodded lightly, afraid to say anything lest she stop. "You see this bed?" and she pointed to what was more like a cot standing quite high above the lacquered wood floors. "When they hunted Jews, I hid my Jewish friends under there." She paused an instant to catch her breath, but she obviously was not finished. "And when they hunted the anti-fascists, I hid some of them under there. And when the fascists were hunted and afraid for their lives, I hid them under there!"

She leaned back satisfied that she had said her piece. I said nothing, hoping she would go on. She took my silence as a sign of bewilderment. "You ask why? Why, because they were all human beings. No human being should be hunted because of what he is or what he believes!"

"But, wasn't that risking your own life?"

"It was worth the risk for me, and for many Italians. You ask us the wrong questions. You ask us how we survived the war. We did what we could to live well. You don't ask us what we believed deep down—so you don't know what we really did so that we could stand proud before God. You will never understand nothing of us until you understand what we believe."

So many years have passed since that interview. I have long since returned to the United States. I have participated in our many struggles as a nation from the race riots to Watergate and I have come to realize how fortunate that little angry old lady was, for she was sure of what she believed. I am not at all sure.

 "There is so little tragedy in life. Tragedy depends on significant relationships. Instead our society is floundering in bathos and a sense of ennui—soap operas, nostalgic comedies, light beer, and low calorie potato chips reflect the superficiality of our passion. We bestir ourselves only enough to become voyeurs of our culture rather than creators. We are products of our consumerism."[7]

A Commentary on Stages of Morality

In his longitudinal study of the development of moral thinking, Lawrence Kohlberg has posited a series of steps or stages through which children's moral development progresses. His research indicates that development may stop at any level, while each stage includes core values of

[7] George E. Arnstein. "Bad Apples in Academe." *American Education* 10 (7) :14; September 1974.

the prior level. As one progresses through the stages, moral positions are articulated in a "more universal, differentiated, and integrated form."[8] The ultimate moral maturity is a principled sense of justice.

If Kohlberg's levels of moral sophistication are accepted as a defensible explanation of moral development, the work of Turiel[9] takes on significance. In a series of carefully replicated studies he demonstrated that while children understand moral messages below their level of development, they are not apt to comprehend messages more than one stage above their level. This suggests that educators and parents must exercise caution in the moral messages they communicate if they are to be of assistance to the young.

Few curricula treat moral development directly. Moral education is largely a part of the unstudied or hidden curriculum in most schools, a by-product with as much chance of being mis-education as positive education.

The transformation of the hidden curriculum into a moral atmosphere is not a matter of one or another educational technique or ideology or means, but a matter of the moral energy of the educator, of his communicated belief that his school or classroom has a human purpose. To get his message across, he may use permissiveness or he may use discipline, but the effective moral educator has a believable human message.[10]

It is too easy for us to fall back on a law and order level of moral action. Perhaps this is the level at which the majority is most comfortable. But humankind deserves more opportunities to rise above this basically defensive posture.

TUESDAY EVENING NEWS BRIEF

DIVORCE RATE CLIMBS: PERCENTAGE OF WORKING MOTHERS INCREASES . . . TEENAGE PROSTITUTION IS UP . . . Authorities from all major cities, meeting in Washington, report that they are baffled by the sudden rise in the number of young people, male as well as female, involved in the night life of their cities . . . **WOMEN'S RIGHTS DEBATE CONTINUES** . . . State legislators in over a dozen states are being lobbied

[8] Lawrence Kohlberg. "The Moral Atmosphere of the School." In: Norman V. Overly, editor. *The Unstudied Curriculum.* Washington, D.C.: Association for Supervision and Curriculum Development, 1970. p. 116.

[9] E. Turiel. "Developmental Processes in the Child's Moral Thinking." In: P. Mussen, J. Heavenrich, and J. Langer, editors. *Directions in Developmental Psychology.* New York: Holt, Rinehart, and Winston, Inc., 1969.

[10] Kohlberg, *op. cit.,* p. 121.

heavily by foes of women's liberation . . . PSYCHIATRIST RE-PORTS HIGH ANXIETY AMONG MIDDLE AGED . . . GREY PANTHERS' LEADER VISITS CITY . . . **SOCIAL INSTITUTIONS UNDERGOING SIGNIFICANT CHANGE** . . . According to the U.S. Census Bureau, the largest jump in divorce rates ever recorded occurred between 1970 and 1976. For every 1,000 married persons in the United States, there were 75 divorced persons in 1975. In 1970, there were only 47 divorced persons per 1,000. The percentage of unmarried women between the ages of 20-24 rose from 36 percent in 1970 to 43 percent in 1976. Furthermore, unmarried women between the ages of 25-29 made up 15 percent of the total population. The decline in the birthrate is the most startling of all: 42 percent of the married women in the 20-24 age bracket do not have children, up from 24 percent in 1960. The U.S. Census Bureau also reported significant declines in nursery and elementary school enrollments, while college enrollments increased by 34 percent during the first six years of the 70's. College enrollment among women between 25 and 34 doubled in comparison to the 1970 figure. Nearly 11 percent of the total population is over 65 years of age and that percentage is expected to increase.

An Intra-generational Crisis: On Being a Housewife

"My son lied about it on his college application. My husband mutters it under his breath when asked. And I had grown reluctant to mention it myself.

"The problem is my occupation. But the statistics on women that have come out since the Houston conference have given me a new outlook. I have ceased thinking of myself as obsolete and begun to see myself as I really am—an endangered species. Like the whooping crane and the snow leopard, I deserve attentive nurturing and perhaps a distinctive metal tag on my foot. Because I'm one of the last of the dying breed of human females designated, 'Occupation: Housewife.'

"I know it's nothing to crow about. I realize that when people discuss their professions at parties I am more of a pariah than a hooker or a loan shark is. I have been castigated, humiliated, and scorned. In an age of do-your-own-thing, it's clear no one meant me. I've been told (patiently and a little louder than necessary, as one does with a child) that I am an anachronism (except that they avoid such a big word). I have been made to feel so outmoded that I wouldn't be surprised to discover that, like a carton of yogurt, I have an expiration date stamped on my bottom.

"I once treasured a small hope that history might vindicate me. After all, nursing was once just such a shameful occupation, suitable for only the lowest women. But I abandoned any thought that my occupation would ever become fashionable again, just as I had to stop counting on full-figured women coming back in style. I'm a hundred years too late on both counts.

"Now, however, thanks to all these new statistics, I see a brighter future for myself. Today, fewer than 16 percent of American families have a full-time housewife-mother. Comparing that with previous figures, at the rate it's going I calculate I am less than eight years away from being the last housewife in the country! And then I intend to be impossible.

"I shall demand enormous fees to go on talk shows, and will charge for my autograph. Anthropologists will study my feeding and nesting habits through field glasses and keep notebooks detailing my every move. That is, if no one gets the bright idea that I'm so unique that I must be put behind sealed glass like the Book of Kells. In any event, I can expect to be a celebrity and to be pampered. I cannot, though, expect to get even.

"There's no getting even for years of being regarded as stupid or lazy, or both. For years of being considered unproductive (unless you count five children, which no one does). For years of being viewed as a parasite, living off a man (except by my husband whose opinion doesn't seem to matter). For years of fetching other women's children after they'd thrown up in the lunchroom, because I have nothing better to do, or probably there is nothing I do better, while their mothers have 'careers.' (Is clerking in a drug store a bona fide career?) For years of caring for five children and a big house and constantly being asked when I'm going to work.

"I come from a long line of women, most of them more Edith Bunker than Betty Friedan, who never knew they were unfulfilled. I can't testify that they were happy, but they were cheerful. And if they lacked 'meaningful relationships,' they cherished relations who meant something.

They took pride in a clean, comfortable home and satisfaction in serving a good meal because no one had explained to them that the only work worth doing is that for which you get paid.

"They enjoyed rearing their children because no one ever told them that little children belonged in church basements and their mothers belonged somewhere else. They lived, very frugally, on their husband's paychecks because they didn't realize that it's more important to have a bigger house and a second car than it is to rear your own children. And they were so incredibly ignorant that they died never suspecting they'd been failures.

"That won't be true for me. I don't yet perceive myself as a failure, but it's not for want of being told I am.

"The other day, years of condescension prompted me to fib in order to test a theory. At a party where most of the guests were business associates of my husband, a Ms. Putdown asked me who I was. I told her I was Jack Hekker's wife. That had a galvanizing effect on her. She took my hand and asked if that was all I thought of myself—just someone's wife? I wasn't going to let her in on the five children but when she persisted I mentioned them but told her that they weren't mine, that they belonged to my dead sister. And then I basked in the glow of her warm approval.

"It's an absolute truth that whereas you are considered ignorant to stay home to rear your children, it is quite heroic to do so for someone else's children. Being a housekeeper is acceptable (even to the Social Security office) as long as it's not your house you're keeping. And treating your husband with attentive devotion is altogether correct as long as he's not your husband.

"Sometimes I feel like Alice in Wonderland. But lately, mostly, I feel like an endangered species."[11]

Linda: Supermom

The story was a familiar one, but to Linda it was unexpected and painfully new. It was her divorce. The stereotype of the career woman in-midst-of-marriage-crack-up was no longer a remote characterization. It was the scenario being played out in her life—now!

A male professor warned her, more than ten years ago, when she started back to graduate school, that she would sacrifice both her marriage and her career if she tried to balance them simultaneously or combine them. Combine them! What a joke that seemed now; a combination with *some* chemical explosion!

[11] Terry Martin Hekker. "The Satisfaction of Housewifery and Motherhood in an 'Age of Do-Your-Own-Thing.'" *The New York Times.* December 20, 1977. p. 43.

And yet, at the time, it seemed possible. What had happened? She and Tony had two children, she was teaching, he was a successful young executive on his way up the corporate ladder. He seemed genuinely supportive when she told him she wanted to begin graduate work on a degree in counseling. They both agreed that home and family were their first priorities, and work and graduate study were secondary. But somehow, things began to get twisted. Priorities were shifted ever so subtly. It appeared to Linda that Tony must have been talking about *her* priorities, not his, although it had not sounded that way in the beginning. The housework and childcare responsibilities didn't change for her as the graduate load increased. Instead, she doubled her energies as a Supermom to counteract her fear of neglecting her husband and children. The more she gave, the more they accepted and expected. At the same time, she was being recognized by her colleagues and her professors as one who could assume responsibility and leadership. These first small successes were fun to share with Tony, but gradually it became clear that her achievements annoyed or threatened him. He exhibited only casual interest when she shared with him her first published paper.

The small hurts were buried, the small successes in her career were minimized and weighted with guilt, as she compensated with a flurry of extra service at home. A low point of indecision and loneliness occurred when she was invited to give an opening address for a professional meeting at the same time as Tony's annual company party. Tony actually expected her to go with him and turn down the first opportunity she had to share professionally the results of her two year research project. It was a difficult decision to make and it represented a turning point in their lives. She gave the speech. The die was cast. Tony sullenly accepted the changes in her life. They stopped discussing her work. The bitterness between them grew, and their lives began to diverge.

The children were between them, both holding them together and dividing them in ways hard to identify. Now the end of the marriage had come. They accepted it as the only humane alternative. Tony wanted a different type of wife; Linda wanted a different type of life. She was entering a new and rewarding period in her career; she now had the children to care for without Tony's psychological support or physical presence. It would be difficult. She had always dreamed of being a successful wife and mother. She had not planned to have any other career. It had all happened in small and unexpected increments, but it was all part of her too; she could not deny this fulfillment of herself. She had not found complete satisfaction in housework and mothering, although she enjoyed that part of her life. If only she could have been different, less restless, less curious, more easily satisfied. If only Tony could have been different, less threatened, more helpful, more sharing in her life. If . . . if . . . if. But, she would not live with regret. She could not reject her own growth and her need for a life with its own meaning.

Committee Reflections on A Model: Intragenerational Crisis

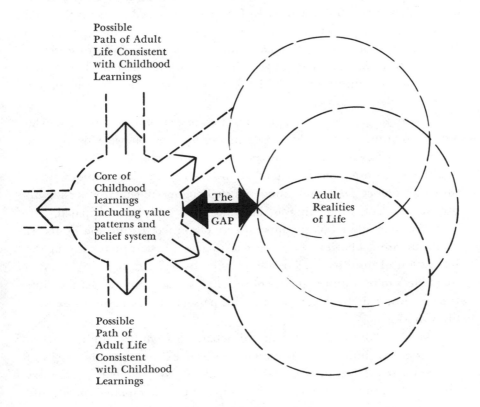

A MODEL: INTRA-GENERATIONAL CRISES OF IDENTITY
*THIS IS A PICTURE OF THE GAP WE MUST BRIDGE
IN OUR SEARCH FOR FULFILLMENT*

Dave's Mid-Life Christmas Card

The Christmas card arrived with a copy of Dave's most recent epistle to the scattered flock. Each year for the ten years since his separation from Ellen, I had come to expect this annual disclosure of his search for meaning in life.

Dave's roots were in the solid middle-class phalanx of society. Upper middle was really more accurate in terms of family income, educational level, social expectation and sense of identity. He entered college in the early 50's and found himself in one liberal cause after another. Ultimately, his deep social sense merged with his basic religious identification and he went off to seminary to save the church from itself. It was an uneasy calling, but one he pursued with imagination.

His life had been an expression of "now" and relevance. He *was* the wave of the future. New ideas for the revitalization of the church and the stimulation of youth in the service of the church flowed from his pen and intruded in every discussion he entered. And then the young began to listen and the church began to act (if only on occasion). When the action came, it was not always to Dave's liking or by his design. The action seemed to lack direction. A leader needs followers, but instead of followers, challengers arose.

His most critical challenge came in the personhood of Ellen who agreed in principle with his positions but insisted on working out the details in her own way. Her success in her work and his failure to pass qualifying examinations for the Ph.D. in International Economics was the ultimate conflict. He found economics challenging, but totally outside his humanistic bent. Academia was the opposite of what he anticipated. Personal freedom and scholarly pursuit were permitted, within the limits set by his advisor. The institution of teaching was little different from the institution of ministering. He was plagued by a desire to bring his personal ideas to bear on the inertia of social ideas and practices. At the same time, he worried about how to bring his personal behavior into line with his own ideas.

At 40 he found himself divorced, separated from his children, alienated from his church, and grubbing a meager existence on the docks of San Francisco. He read Archibald MacLeish's *J.B.* frequently, felt sorry for himself, wondered about the meaning of life, contemplated suicide and generally found the absence of any relevance in this or his earlier life slightly amusing. Participation in the life of the collected community of God was a central tenet of his faith, and yet for eight years he had not been inside a church—nor had he missed it. A supportive home and happy marriage was another value of high priority in his pantheon of virtues, and yet there was a strange sense of personal well-being in having shed Ellen and the children that overcame his sense of guilt. "A man should use his natural talents to their fullest in the service of humankind"—he had been taught that while very young and he believed it! Yet, being a clerk in a longshoremen's office did not go far toward stewardship of his talents. "It is a strange dilemma," he reflected, "this search for meaning in the past and present value structure."

On Being Real

Do you know the little book *The Velveteen Rabbit* by Margery Williams? This comes from the chapter "The Skin Horse and the Rabbit":

"Real isn't how you are made," said the Skin Horse.

"It's a thing that happens to you. When a child loves you, then you become Real."

"Does it hurt?" asked the Rabbit.

"Sometimes," said the Skin Horse, for he was always truthful.

"When you are Real, you don't mind being hurt."

"Does it happen all at once, like being wound up," he asked, "or bit by bit?"

"It doesn't happen all at once," said the Skin Horse. "You become. It takes a long time. That's why it doesn't often happen to people who break easily, or have sharp edges, or who have to be carefully kept. Generally, by the time you are Real, most of your hair has been loved off, and your eyes drop out, and you get loose in the joints and very shabby. But these things don't matter at all, because once you are Real, you can't be ugly, except to people who don't understand."[12]

Committee Reflections on Creating Reality

Fulfillment requires that individuals, as members of groups, institutions, and cultures, understand their values and functions as creators of and participants in their reality. This blend of reflection and action, called "praxis" by Paulo Freire, is the birthright not only of the elite but also of those immersed in the culture of "silence."[13]

To be a creator and participant one must be able to see—to see what, to see how. The media have already inalterably and dramatically changed the nature of the human senses:

People still experience the need to translate images into observed reality. When they travel, they want to see the Eiffel Tower or Grand Canyon exactly as they saw them first on posters.

Today's images are often self-sufficient. We now have ads that give more satisfaction than their products. Conceivably there doesn't even have to be a product. Sometimes when we try to purchase a product advertised on TV, we're told, "It's not yet in distribution," which probably means not yet in existence since consumer interest is often tested prior to production. . . .

"Oh, what a beautiful baby!" exclaimed a neighbor.

"That's nothing," replied the mother. "You should see his photograph!"[14]

Who creates reality? Is the meaning derived from that reality illusory? How do we know? Does it matter? Does it matter if statistics indicate

[12] Margery Williams. *The Velveteen Rabbit*. New York: George H. Doran Company, 1922. pp. 3-4.

[13] Paulo Freire. *Pedagogy of the Oppressed*. London: Herder and Herder, 1970. p. 76.

[14] Carpenter, *op. cit.*, pp. 6-7.

that blacks in the U.S., especially the youth, are worse off today than they were ten years ago? Does it matter if a leading newspaper says, "This development is the single most volatile factor' in potential urban unrest and holds explosive implications for the future stability of the entire society"?[15]

Does it matter that social science research indicates that racial and class prejudice are widespread among 1976 high school students, despite the civil rights movement?[16] How do societies engender and nourish inhumanity? In a large-scale technologically enmeshed world, how can "belonging" and a sense of success, as opposed to "rootlessness" and a sense of failure, be attained without the psychological destruction of "us" by "them"?

A Commentary on the Social Utility of Core Values

There can be little question but that a system of core values underlies every civilization. We have, nevertheless, moved away from open affirmation of common values with many embracing relativism as a value base and others holding to absolutism. We are caught as a society between extreme positions that belie core values.

Within American culture, the Western philosophic and religious traditions originally provided the core values. Simply stated, among these would be:

—do to others as you wish others to do to you (Golden Rule);
—human life is sacred;
—the individual has a right to freedom and self-expression;
—the individual has a responsibility to be a contributing member to the group.

Through time the values have been absolute in substance but relative to the context of their interpretation. We have failed to recognize the significance of our core values as the warp and woof of our social fabric. They are there, undergirding us, but seldom addressed directly or acted upon intentionally.

We even claim not to teach values in our schools lest we offend the rights of individuals to decide for themselves. But we fail to ask where the constructs come from which permit us to decide. The danger is not in our failure to teach values or in our recognition of core values, but rather in our teaching, unaware, of seemingly innocuous relativity that stands for nothing under the banner of individual freedom and social independence.

[15] Heubert Hill. "Blacks Still Lag in Jobs, Income." *Los Angeles Times.* March 7, 1976. Part IX. p. 1.
[16] Harriet Stix. "Gentleman's Agreement Among Young." *Los Angeles Times.* January 25, 1976. Part IV. p. 1.

Our responses to situations begging for moral decision making are couched in the cliches of yesterday's answers. We uneasily practice ad hoc values that will not support an integrated system strong enough to hold us together.

From the rationality of humankind have sprung the marvels of industry and technology in response to basic needs and desires. But as technology has met the needs and satisfied the primal drives for human survival, new needs have been created to keep the technological and economic institutions alive. Thus, agencies and institutions developed to serve humankind have come to master us and create values patterned after institutional images rather than human images. Profit has become a priority value. The economic system no longer profits merely by meeting survival needs. Instead, needs are manufactured to maintain the system and we are manipulated and controlled to the point that we agree that the greater good is larger profits and more consumer goods. It is as if we have a tiger by the tail and can not let it go.

Decisions at all levels of government tend to be made on the basis of financial costs rather than the costs in human life. We have become obsessed with short-term gain and blind to long-term consequences. We have suffered the diminishing of our humaneness and are on the verge of surrendering our democratic freedoms in order to maintain a makeshift economic structure now elevated to a position of value dominance—profits before all else! In the language of our heritage we are willing to trade our birthright for a bowl of porridge.

ROUND AND ROUND AND ROUND

Mr. Lewis:
Young lady, if I were your father, I think I could not help but be hurt. Still, I understand how you feel about all that talk on core values. I wonder how my own situation would apply. Sure, I'm 70, but I look, feel and act like a man of 50. The doctors tell me I'm in great physical condition. Nevertheless, I've been put out to pasture —forced to retire—told I am too old to handle my job, which involves sitting at a desk all day. I told them to give me a test and check whether my mind was able, but they didn't care about my mind—just that I was 70, and it was time to get rid of me. How is that for doing unto others?

Jeannie:
I can't hack all that
stuff about core values. It
just doesn't make sense in the
real world. I'm the one that's pregnant!
I'm the one that's got to tell my mom and
dad. And they'll be upset, I'm sure of that. But
why should they be? I didn't hurt anybody. All
I did was love. Talk about doing unto others!
I want to be loved. I want to love. And if I'm
going to have a baby, I can love it—or
maybe let it be loved by someone else.
Or, maybe, have an aborton. . . . How
is that for doing unto others?" Is
the baby inside of me really a
baby?

Ron:
It isn't that I
don't understand your problem, mister, but at least you've
got some money coming in. Look at
me. I'm 18 and I can't get a job anywhere. Everyone thinks I ought to get out
and earn a living but no one tells me where to
find a job. What's so wonderful about work, anyway? Why can't they just give you enough
money to live on? I mean, if there are too
few jobs around, why should having a
job be so important—as if it were a
core value. What core value does
working represent anyway?

Committee Reflections on Valuing and Curriculum Development

Valuing is inescapable in any effort at curriculum development. Even if we take the position that all historical periods or all ethnic groups have the right to establish their own standards for good and less good, we are teaching a value—that of relativity. It would be like saying to our young, slavery is evil today, but in the past it was not so evil because people held different standards. Curriculum must deal with values and must be cognizant of the values being expressed via the structures and approaches to knowledge it chooses.[17]

[17] James Macdonald, Bernice Wolfson, and Esther Zaret. *Reschooling Society: A Conceptual Model.* Washington, D.C.: Association for Supervision and Curriculum Development, 1973.

We have not been developing curriculum within the context of the twentieth century. We have allowed the scholastic traditions of the past to suffocate every moment of curricular renewal that has occurred. The back-to-basics movement is but one more stifling blow to a relevant curriculum. Can anyone today deny the central importance of computer technology for the knowledgeable person? Can anyone claim that knowing how to interpret the labels on consumer goods is less important than knowing the parts of the amoeba? Can anyone seriously believe that divorce is not a major sociological trait of our society today? Yet, where are these dealt with in our subject-laden curricula? If our youngsters are lucky, they may have a teacher who will bring in a few labels off commonly purchased goods and help them interpret the significance of the food they consume to their bodies and their environment—but only by chance and only if they are lucky.

The point here, however, is that curriculum must reflect a new conception of its fundamental processes. Instead of merely adapting existing knowledge to schooling so that it may be better absorbed by students, curriculum development must involve the creative structuring and restructuring of knowledge. It must also mean bringing into the curriculum decisions about how such knowledge shall be approached. Shall students work as inquirers? Shall they exercise skills to help them fit in? Shall they be divergent and unorthodox?

Clearly, such curricular decisions require a continuous study of our values as individuals and as a society. What does any particular organization of knowledge say to students? Should it be said? What else might be said?

Breaking through, whether for lifelong learning or for a brief period of childhood preparation in public schools, must involve a profound reconceptualization of what it is we are doing when we engage in developing curriculum. Developing curriculum needs to be recognized as a set of decisions about the structures of knowledge to be utilized, the approaches to knowledge to be employed and the values sustained by such structures.

The New Third World: California 1990

According to an article in the *Los Angeles Times* ethnic minorities may comprise the majority population of California before 1990.[18] This projection is based on the assumption that the current rapid growth rate of minority ethnic population will persist. In the seven years following the 1970 U.S. Census, the Third World population of California grew by more than 4 million to an estimated 8,336,000 (34 percent of the total population). These figures do not include approximately 1.2 million undocumented alien workers.

[18] Based on a report by Bill Sievert. "California May Be America's First 'Third World' State." *Los Angeles Times.* December 11, 1977. Part VI. p. 3.

The significance of the population projections are not clear nor are the interpretations placed on them by various state officials. While Rupert Francisco, director of the study, sees the shift in population balance as a boon for the Third World group. Troy Duster, associate professor of sociology at the University of California-Berkeley, cautions that present patterns of "white flight" in the face of minority advancement may turn to "white fight." The public response in support of Bakke, who asked the Supreme Court to rule on the constitutionality of special university admissions criteria for minorities, is an example of the backlash which has already begun.

George Singh, a counselor with Centro Legal de la Raza in Oakland, suggests that the key to preparing members of the Third World to function effectively as a majority is education. "Unless we get our kids through school the state will have problems coming up with enough doctors, lawyers, and professional people to meet its needs." Meeting such rapidly changing educational needs will call for restructuring the educational system as well as modifying societal expectations.

Roundtable on the Hidden Curriculum

Parent: We shouldn't be talking about a hidden curriculum, but about many hidden curricula some of which are at cross purposes, working against each other. For example, students learn the rhetoric of democratic government and that all men are created equal, but they learn these words in classes where teachers are often authoritarian and children are stigmatized by special labels which set them apart as unequal. Or they learn in classes where grouping and tracking are rigidly based on artificial measures of intelligence, and where "bright is best" and "slow is bad."

Student: The hidden curriculum? It's right under their noses but the teachers ignore it. The most powerful and important things I learn in school I get from the other kids. Call it peer teaching—and I don't mean help on math and reading. It's peer help on the really basic skills! Like communication through clothes and language. Like how to make it with the opposite sex. Like who shoots dope and how it's done. Like how to get by without flunking out, or if you're getting good grades, how to talk about it so it doesn't mess you up with your friends.

Teacher: I know quite a lot about the hidden curriculum apart from what the kids teach each other. I see a hidden aspect in what is not taught in the real curriculum . . . what is not thought of or not allowed. There are sins of omission that speak loud and clear. For example, ignoring the contributions of women and minorities in the textbooks makes a statement although it's unspoken. We can't teach everything, but the ideas and topics omitted stand as ghosts in the background, denied, ignored, but nonetheless a heavy presence.

Parent: Speaking of minorities and women, we seem to be unable to eradicate even the most blatant sexism in the classroom. My daughter wanted to take five solids in high school next year. She is bright, ambitious, and eager to learn all she can. Her counselor said, "You can't take that many heavy subjects. Why don't you take typing?" "I've had typing," my daughter replied. "Well, that's fine, then you should be excellent in stenography; why don't you take shorthand?" When I spoke to the counselor about this, she was surprised that I was offended. She said, "I think shorthand would be very good for her if she's going to college. Think how it would help her take notes in class." I said, "And how many of your bright boys are you putting in the shorthand class?" The fact is, there were none! It's just one example of the continued sabotage of girls' expectations . . . one of the strongest facts of the hidden curriculum!

Student: The hidden curriculum is the obvious and real one, it's the official one that is actually hidden, from me at least. I never know exactly what it is I'm supposed to know or to learn about a subject, but I have learned that the real subject for study is the teacher. You have to figure out what it is she wants . . . what does she believe . . . what turns her on in a paper. I know a couple of kids who learn just to be learning and seem to love it, but they don't make good grades. If you want the grades you have to study the teacher. The problem is, you may not learn what you need to know for the class that follows. That happened to me in Spanish. I got along just great with my beginning Spanish teacher. Everybody told me which jokes to laugh at and which to keep a straight face over. I knew which parts of the material would be emphasized on the test, so I did fine. But, in second year Spanish I had a different teacher. The first year's A's didn't help.

Parent: Jokes! Yes, that's part of the hidden curriculum! I like a teacher with a sense of humor, but how can it be that my child goes to school where teachers use the classroom for talking about themselves, their lives, problems, interests, and rarely are accountable for the time they waste in my child's life? Sure, teachers are people, but learning and teaching are the job of the school. The classroom shouldn't be a soapbox for the teacher's personal views. It also should not be a place where kids sit, clocking seat time, until a bell rings.

Teacher: Does the hidden curriculum always have to be negative? I know we all teach values in one form or another, indirectly, through the curriculum. Sometimes that is bad, sometimes good. Perhaps anything so subtle it seems hidden should be revealed and examined—maybe some of it is legitimate. For example, some so-called middle-class values like responsibility, cleanliness, respect for property, appreciation of the arts, are not all to be discarded.

 **AFTERWORD**

"I've often thought there ought to be a manual to hand to little kids, telling them what kind of planet they're on, why they don't fall off it, how much time they've probably got here, how to avoid poison ivy, and so on. I tried to write one once. It was called Welcome to Earth. But I got stuck on explaining why we don't fall off the planet. Gravity is just a word. It doesn't explain anything. If I could get past gravity, I'd tell them how we reproduce, how long we've been here, apparently, and a little bit about evolution. And one thing I would really like to tell them about is cultural relativity. I didn't learn until I was in college about all the other cultures, and I should have learned that in the first grade. A first grader should understand that his or her culture isn't a rational invention; that there are thousands of other cultures and they all work pretty well; that all cultures function on faith rather than truth; that there are lots of alternatives to our own society. Cultural relativity is defensible and attractive. It's also a source of hope. It means we don't have to continue this way if we don't like it."[19]

A Query

What has been described as urgent realities and what has been explored in the goals section are not new. They echo the refrains of diversity characteristic of modern society. The kaleidoscope of opinion, research findings, personal anecdotes, and reflections at best provides only impressionistic insights into our human conditions in this time and space. If we know these things, even if but dimly, why do we not act to move beyond our condition? What prevents our breaking through to a fuller realization of our dreams and goals for human fulfillment?

Spanish with Joy

"We are determined to move ahead, even if there is great resistance from the power structure. No longer will Chicanos in New Mexico grow up feeling like second-class citizens. No longer will they feel misunderstood or scorned. In the old days they received the worst kind of schooling. They were made to feel . . . they have nothing worthwhile to say or contribute. The Anglo teachers, the Anglo-run school system looked down on Chicanos. We were given no credit for our own values, for our culture

[19] Kurt Vonnegut, Jr. "Afterword." In: *Free To Be . . . You and Me*. Conceived by Marlo Thomas, developed and edited by Carole Haut, *et al*. New York: McGraw Hill, 1974. p. 139.

and traditions. And the contempt showed on the people; they felt ashamed, inferior. They never learned to speak English the way the teachers did. They never learned to express themselves in school and they dropped out soon, usually well before high school was over. We hope to change that. We can't do anything about what has already happened. The old people are the way they are—it is too late for them to change. But it will be different for the young. They will have pride in themselves, and they will not only think well of themselves, but speak well. They won't have memories of Anglo teachers laughing at their Spanish, or punishing them for using it. They will speak Spanish with joy."[20]

Paulo

Six years ago I was hired by this university to develop a multicultural program. The university indicated that I needed to publish, do research, and become involved with the community to be promoted. But, when the university promotion and tenure committee reviewed my case for promotion, I was informed that I had become too involved with the Latino community at the expense of scholarly productivity. There is no way that I could have done the job that they wanted me to do without becoming deeply involved with the Latino community. Any Latino could tell you that. But there are no Latinos on the university review committee. The university makes impossible demands on us Latinos. On the surface, it looks as if they are giving us a bona fide professional opportunity. In reality it's all a fraud.

Counterpoint

Universities are faced with a twin dilemma. On the one hand they are attempting to meet the moral and legislative demands for affirmative action by hiring more minorities and women. On the other hand, they face budgeting restrictions that force cutbacks in faculty and inhibit the awarding of tenure and promotion. Minority candidates especially feel the pressure. Because of their limited numbers and high visibility they are faced with demands for their services beyond normal faculty requirements. While the community service is needed and appreciated, it does not adequately serve to define an outstanding faculty member. In this day and age, outstanding faculty members are the only kind universities can promote.

[20] Robert Coles. *The Old Ones of New Mexico*. Albuquerque: University of New Mexico Press, 1973. pp. 4.

Investment in Learning

According to a study carried out by Howard R. Bowen, a college education will yield a return on one's investment at least three times the original cost. Beyond specific cost benefits, Dr. Bowen found that a college education has a positive influence on the quality of family life. College-educated families tend to have fewer children, their child-rearing practices are more elaborate, and their offspring are generally higher than average achievers who stay in school longer. It was also found that the traditional differences between the sexes with regard to interests, attitudes, and behavior patterns are narrowed considerably by increased education.

In addition, Bowen found that a college education seems to improve consumer practices with college graduates getting higher returns from their incomes than do other people. They are more likely to read and less likely to watch television. They are also more likely to attend adult education courses and cultural events. As a group, college graduates are more active in community affairs and display greater propensity to vote. As Bowen notes, "The non-monetary benefits—personal development and life enrichment, the advancement of knowledge and the arts and satisfaction—are far greater than the monetary effects."[21]

"A Volkswagen is not a cheaper, lighter Cadillac; it is a different car designed for different purposes. Similarly, college for the masses is not a low-standard version of college for the elite; it is a different kind of education with high standards true to its own purpose."[22]

Musings of a High School Teacher

"Why don't they say it like it is? Unemployment among the young is sky-high. Unemployment has reached 40 percent among black urban youth and that is an official Labor Department statistic! And who is the first to be blamed for all this? Teachers and schools are always accused of not preparing the young for the real world. And now we are told that vocational education is our job; as if we could create jobs that are non-existent.

[21] Based on a report by Patricia McCormack, UPI. In: *Los Angeles Times.* January 11, 1978. Part 10A. p. 6.
[22] Patricia Cross. "New Forms for New Functions." In: Dyckman W. Vermilye, editor. *Lifelong Learners—A New Clientele for Higher Education.* San Francisco: Jossey-Boss Inc., Publishers, 1974. pp. 87-88.

"Of course, there are unskilled jobs that sometimes remain unfilled. But the politicians are surely not asking us to improve vocational preparation so that high school graduates can take unskilled jobs. They know that more education means higher vocational expectations. Why should a kid with a high school diploma take a job sweeping floors? No matter how well we may prepare the young, we can not produce one extra job, unless it's the job of being a vocational education teacher. What bothers me is this: When the public realizes that career education programs have not resulted in more jobs for the young, will we be blamed even more?"

Committee Reflections on Pluralism

A key concern of contemporary social observers is how American educational institutions can encourage ethnic and racial plurality while maintaining a unifying national ethos. This urgent dilemma, the clash between assimilation and pluralism, intensified by the rapidly changing ethnic patterns in American schools, can be confronted through a commitment to a fluid conception of culture that is responsive to social, economic, political, and cultural contexts.

When looking beyond their own culture, educators tend to view culture as something of a straight jacket, an all-encompassing yet vague "force" that "causes" particular types of behavior in particular groups. The redefinition of culture proposed here is one of an adjustable framework, very responsive to social and economic conditions, out of which aspects of behavior develop. In this sense, human interaction can be perceived as continual and active construction and reconstruction of patterns. This means that each individual in everyday life is recreating, modifying, or interpreting his or her own cultural background. The important feature of this approach is its recognition of the dynamic and **multidimensional** life patterns within any cultural group.

How does this perspective of culture as dynamic, creative and responsive help resolve the issue of unity versus diversity? It suggests that cultural diversity does not necessarily result in complete divergence of interests. Maintenance of any ethnic identity within the U.S. is not a result of adherence to rigid cultural laws and territorial boundaries but occurs within the context of social, economic, and cultural conditions at the national level. Therefore, the institutionalization of pluralism will not produce static boundaries between separate sets of monolithic cultural forces. Rather, we may see a socio-ecological balance of groups with varying ethnic identities but similar behavior-developing processes—each group being interested in the survival of the whole.[23]

[23] Based on an article by Carlos J. Ovando. "School Implications of the Peaceful Latino Invasion." *Phi Delta Kappan* 59 (10) :230-34; December 1977.

All Over the World...

"All over the developed world, children left their homes this morning and went to school. All over the undeveloped world, parents were wishing their children could do so.

"All over the developed world, millions of children are accepting school as an unavoidable bore, or actively hating it. Some weep, some play truant, some produce psychosomatic symptoms to avoid going to school.

Most just put up with it and long for the holidays. Some lucky ones enjoy school, at least until the age when the shadow of public examinations falls over their lives. Yet all over the undeveloped world, angry or wistful teenagers see schooling as the means to a good life—a means withheld from most of them."[24]

Teenager: Nuts! Is this another guilt trip? I *like* school in general, but am I supposed to be completely devoted to school and never criticize anything? Most of the kids I know feel toward school the way their parents feel about work—good days, bad days, some teachers better or worse than others. It's not all good, but it's not all bad, either. Am I supposed to feel guilty because school is available to me, but not to kids in some other parts of the world?

A Commentary on Curriculum Voids and Institutional Violence

"All over the World" is an indictment against the institutionalization of learning as it exists in both the developed and underdeveloped worlds. As such, the issues of what kind of education and for whom emerge as pressing realities to be confronted by a people aspiring toward the realization of an improved quality of life. In today's industrialized world, institutionalized education no longer seems able to assist individuals in developing an improved quality of life. Instead, the curriculum has remained unchanged and in light of rapid social change becomes progressively irrelevant. As a result, the violence education does to people is primarily a violence of omission.

What is not learned in school (though it is the place where it could be learned) has left a frightening void in the skills necessary to deal effectively in a complex technological society. Indeed, the skills omitted have exacerbated people's helplessness in even the most basic activities of survival—activities that were once commonplace.

What is more, the industrialized world's curriculum has been em-

[24] Rosemary Haughton. "Deschooling and Education." *Commonweal* 26:367; January 1973.

braced by developing countries irrespective of its irrelevance to their needs. One result of burdening the young of these countries with the study of the curricula of the affluent societies is the production of an over-abundance of technocrats ready to build an industrial state while the country's ability to feed and clothe its population remains primitive. This is institutional violence in its most insidious form. In order to feel a part of the affluent world, the people themselves demand the very curricula that continues their oppression.

Compounding the paradox of the unequal distribution and irrational institutionalization of learning opportunities are the political, social, and economic imbalances which characterize this poverty-saturated world. A *sine qua non* to the fulfillment of humankind's learning needs is an environment devoid of "structural violence"—i.e., a learning nucleus that provides for the needs as well as the aspirations of all members of society through equal access to relevant opportunities and materials.

Schools are for getting . . .
for getting grades,
for getting by . . .
for getting jobs . . .
for getting in . . .
for getting out of . . .
forgetting . . . kids.

Rico: Justice

The halls of Public School 119 were alive with sounds of young voices telegraphing the message of a drug bust. A bank of lockers on the second floor of the west wing appeared to be the target this time. Rico caught the word from Benny just as he came out of math class. The call for all students to stand by lockers 2W20-2W60 crackled over the intercom as Benny turned the corner and headed upstairs to watch. Rico took his time. He wasn't threatened. He wanted to catch sight of Barb and signal her to come and watch. He was clean and it would provide a chance to score a few points at the expense of the fuzz.

Barb joined him as he waited at the foot of the stairs. "Want to see a good show?" he said as she hooked her hand in his arm. "The 'Prince' is going through lockers again. I can really give him a hard time. Remember last time when Mike Levin pretended not to want him to look in a bag in his locker and all he had in it was a moldy peanut butter sandwich? Well, this time I've been saving a plastic bag of maple leaves I collected for biology class. He'll think he's found a real killing."

The "Prince" and the fuzz were already standing impatiently by number 2W20. "Open it up," Mr. Reynolds said. He didn't exactly command, but there was no missing his intent. Angelo complied, smiling broadly to his assembled public arranged in clusters at either end of the line of lockers.

Rico watched one after another as they came nearer to 2W49. The ritual had to be played out at each opening. He knew the rules. Locks locked until you were "requested" to open them. Once unlocked, step back and permit the patrolman to check your things. He didn't think it was fair. He had never been into drugs. He didn't have anything to hide, but his locker was the only place at school or home where he could stash his own things.

He twirled the dial left, right, back again. The "Prince" stepped forward to fulfill his role in the continuing charade. Forcefully opening the door of the locker, he exposed a clutter and disorder of typical teenage miscellany. "What's this, Martinez?" he asked, picking up the plastic bag.

"Just some leaves, Sir," "Leaves?" Mr. Reynolds asked incredulously.

"Only some maple leaves," Rico said, trying to add a hint of fear to his voice.

"Only maple leaves? We'll see." With that he opened the bag and took a deep sniff.

Rico's moment had arrived. "Look, they've replaced the police dogs," he laughed just loud enough for those assembled to hear.

Mr. Reynolds began to pick through Rico's other treasures more carefully. His hand came up with a pearl-handled knife. It was the only thing Rico had ever won . . . recognition for being the best camper at the YMCA summer camp five years ago. "Don't you know it's illegal to have weapons on school property?" Reynolds barked. "Report to the office at once!"

"I can't even make a joke and do it right," Rico sighed, ears reddening at the sound of snickers from the group standing at the end of the hall.

Bakke Case Turmoil

After failing to win a satisfactory decision on his application for admission to 13 medical schools, Allan Bakke won a favorable decision from the Supreme Court of California. The legal merits of the case were accepted as the basis for appeal by the United States Supreme Court. At issue was a feature identified as "reverse discrimination"—favoritism of minorities at the expense of the white majority. Whether justice has been done to Bakke or to minorities is a point in question.

A host of arguments and issues have been raised.

1. Is the Court's substituted judgment fairer than the admission committee's?

2. Is the Court to determine fairness or justice?

3. Does the admission of an additional white to medical school at Davis benefit society more than an additional minority?

4. Do the scores used to establish an academic rating have any reliability in terms of probable success in practice?

5. What is the relationship of state residency to selection standards?

6. Will Bakke at age 38 contribute to society as much as a minority candidate of 23?

7. Are the ratings and decisions of a single university to be judged deficient when similar results were achieved at 12 other institutions, several with very few minority students—one (South Dakota) with none?

The arguments can and will go on. They were not resolved by the Court's decision.

What has been the immediate outcome? Officials of the Black American Law Students Association point out that educational opportunities are already decreasing for minority students in the face of institutional uncertainty. "The University of California already has cancelled one scholarship program for minorities," according to Tallea Gooden, vice president of ALSA. Alfred Fitt, Washington, D.C. lawyer has noted that "for judges to order his (Bakke's) admission now would not mean the righting of a wrong; rather it would be no more than to declare him the winner of a retroactive lottery conducted for his private benefit."[25]

Grandma Goes to School

Granted, she was in her 70's and looked every bit her age. Her white hair was rolled up into a tight scroll around the back of her head. Her hands were coarse and wrinkled and had obviously known hard labor. But she walked straight and her eyes were as clear a blue as if she were 17. Altogether, she looked like a determined old lady, which was what she was when she entered the school's main office wanting to enroll in a night course on human biology. She hungered—I am not exaggerating—to know the world around her, about herself; and now that schools were beginning to offer more and more night classes for adults, she saw her chance.

I was with her, but she sent me to sit on a bench at the front of the office. As she walked over to what was obviously the reception desk, the lady behind the desk seemed to steel herself for what was apparently going to be an ordeal for her. I wondered if my grandmother had gotten

[25] Alfred B. Fitt. "In Search of a Just Outcome." *Change* 9: 22-25; October 1977.

the same impression and if the lady had many people like my grandma coming to her desk. Whatever my grandma said, the lady responded crisply with a long application and a question about high school attendance. No, grandma had never attended high school. Yes, she could read and write some, but wouldn't there be a teacher to talk to the class? In any case, some sort of placement exam would have to be taken before she could take the class for credit. Yes, the placement exam would be necessary even if she did not want the credit. She could take it right away. Just walk next door.

My grandmother came over to the bench, her head shaking slightly as if she had come to realize that enrolling was going to be a problem all by itself. Still, she was determined and we sat for a long time trying to fill out the application. She was not sure of the exact date of her birth, but she took the day she received her citizenship and a year that approximated her apparent age. She had no plans and could not put down a purpose other than that she wanted to know. Would lack of specific purpose keep her out of the class?

With the application completed, we went to the next room where I sat on another bench along another front wall. I cannot describe my feelings well for I was both proud and ashamed of grandma—proud that she had the will to persist and ashamed that she obviously did not fit in. As she sat in the hard wooden seat with its little desk surface, she looked even more the European peasant than she ordinarily did. All through the exam, she just went on shaking her head. Finally, she stood up, folded the exam carefully in half so that it would fit into her purse and walked over to me as straight as I ever remember her walking, her head held very high and said, "Come." We never discussed the exam. She never took an evening course.

A Commentary on Education: Two Levels of Crisis

Education is in crisis. Little can be said today any more prosaic than this. It is important to recognize, however, that the very prosaicism of a statement may interfere with our fully understanding the nature of the situation to which the statement makes reference. We have a kaleidoscope of societal crises before us. In one sense, public education is simply another among many crises afflicting our times. The students are alienated, their parents are dissatisfied, administrators feel futile for all their efforts seem to do little to alleviate the multiplying complaints. What the reasonable interaction of people with people should be is up for grabs. This is part of the internal crisis. Schooling is a functioning institution caught in problems not too different from those that can be observed throughout society.

There is, however, a kind of crisis that is unique to public education. Public education cannot ignore all the other crises affecting society. It must take cognizance of the surrounding social ferment and somehow become a broker of "insights" for its students.

But how can the schools be brokers when the very questions for consideration create a constant flow of crises? Should out-of-wedlock relationships be explored as part of the social studies program? Should the value questions involved in abortion and birth control be examined? Regardless of what the schools do, they will be perceived as not doing what they ought to do. Some will say they are usurping others' prerogatives, while others will respond that they are ignoring learnings central to our personal and societal aims.

To avoid the problems and only deal with skills that might be relevant in confronting all our other problems will not extricate the schools from their "crisis of brokerage." If the skills are too specific, too vocationally oriented, obsolescence will be the spectre of crisis; if, instead, more generic processes are opted for, such as the development of critical thinking, then the detachment of schooling from daily reality becomes the core of crisis. The very need to deal with a society in crises is a crisis.

Education cannot ignore its times. It must confront a broad spectrum of concerns. But what does this mean? How shall it be done? What shall the nature of brokerage be? What are we willing to allow? What are we demanding? What do we want from our schools? What is possible?

Alternative Schools Multiply and Go Public

Alternative schools have little in common with each other except that they hope to offer youngsters something different from the traditional public school program. Their numbers have increased so rapidly that the public schools can no longer ignore them. Indeed, public school systems have begun to develop alternative schools of their own. Some systems, such as Indianapolis, have adopted some aspects of the alternative concept as the premise for an optional program for all schools.

Among alternatives being offered by public institutions is the academy which harks back to studies thought vital by Benjamin Franklin. Grading is very strict and the academy is really considered suitable for college-bound students. Another alternative has youngsters taking pass-fail courses in such subjects as guitar, golf, and creative expression. Leaders of the alternative schools movement have expressed concern that the movement is being misused by the public sector as a means for keeping potential dropouts in school while sorting out those who would go on in higher education and placing them in "elitist" type programs.

Eldon, Missouri Bans Dictionary

The American Heritage Dictionary of English has been banned from use in the schools of Eldon, Missouri. The school board voted 6-0 against the dictionary because it contains obscene words. The school board acted on a complaint filed by a parent.

U.S. Commissioner of Education Urges "More Variety" in High Schools

The U.S. Commissioner of Education was recently quoted as saying, "There is an urgent need for more variety in our approaches to the upper grades. The school is the only institution in America where we take the entire population and assume that everyone will perform in the same way for an extended period of time." He went on to suggest that "a network of basic skills centers around the country that would bring together school and college people to look specifically at approaches that work" would be of great benefit to public education. He expects federal funds to be shifted toward increased support for equipping teachers who are already in the field to deal with new educational situations.[26]

Campuses Quiet Again, Gift Giving Increases

Gift giving to American universities and colleges is again on the rise. The total sums received by these institutions is actually down since the federal government has decreased its contributions for higher education. Nevertheless, private contributors are giving in record numbers, and the general feeling seems to be nationwide relief that the riots of the 60's and early 70's have significantly abated.

A Query

What are the problems of the traditional schools? What can we do about them? Is it legitimate to expect the schools, or any institution, to handle the immense array of personal and social expectations and problems that we see all around us? How do we break through?

Eunice and Camille

Some educators see alternative public schools as just one more way to track students along racial, ethnic, and class lines. According to their views alternatives perpetuate the socioeconomic inequities already present

[26] *The New York Times.* June 20, 1977.

in our society. Others see alternatives as socially and ethnically democ-
ratizing institutions which allow parents and students to choose volun-
tarily an integrated school with a curricular emphasis suitable to their
beliefs or needs. In truth the picture is a confused one. The purposes
and motivations of alternative school sponsors and of the individuals
that attend them represent a complex and broad range of possibilities.
The experiences of the following two students in alternative school settings provide examples of the diversity.

Eunice, a 15-year-old Latina sophomore at a magnet high school in
Chicago, was admitted to the alternative public school on the basis
of her high achievement scores on standardized tests. Despite a difficult
one-hour trip to school by public transportation, Eunice feels good about
the opportunity to attend this academically oriented school comprising
40 percent white, 40 percent black and 20 percent Latino, Asian-Ameri-
can, and Native American students. Asked how she feels about the rigor
of the school's curriculum, she notes that because students are selected
on the basis of academic ability, learning essentially is seen as something
one does without too much trouble. Moreover, if a student needs academic assistance, tutors from nearby universities are readily available.

Though the recently constructed school enrolls approximately 1,500
students, she claims that such problems as graffiti, broken windows, gangs,
riots and absenteeism do not exist. She is quick to credit the supposedly
high level of intelligence of the student body for the absence of such
deviant behavior. "We are basically all the same," she explains. While
the student body reflects a diversified ethnic/racial mix, the students get
along well, by Eunice's account. She attributes this harmony to her belief
that intelligent and well-informed people are more likely to get along
with other races and ethnic groups.

One gets from Eunice the feeling that everybody in the school is a
winner. Because counselors, administrators, and teachers want the students to go to college, there is constant testing to determine academic
weaknesses and strengths in order to match the instructional process to
the individuals. According to Eunice, the staff is always telling the students that because of the availability of grants and scholarships, financial
problems should not keep able students from going to college. Eunice is
less certain about her plans than the counselors seem to be. "Right now
I'm not thinking too much about college. After I graduate I know I
don't want to work in a factory or anything like that. I'll probably try
to get a job in an office. You know, some people are saying college doesn't
really help you that much anymore because you can't find a job afterward
anyway."

Like Eunice, Camille is 15 years old and enrolled in a public alternative school, but there most similarities stop. Camille is from an American missionary family and spent most of her childhood in Southeast Asia. She is now living in a midwestern university town where her parents are studying folklore and linguistics. After a few weeks at the conventional high school, Camille asked to be transferred to the community's alternative high school because she felt very out of place in the student culture of the conventional school. She felt it would take her too long to meet traditional graduation requirements. After a few months at the alternative school, these are her observations: "If you think this place looks bad, you should have seen the building we were in at the beginning of the year. It was an old abandoned school out in the country with everything falling apart. They say the building we're in now has been condemned, but at least we're in town and there are separate rooms for classes.

"The kids who come here—when they *do* come—are all kinds. Mostly they couldn't get along at the regular high school. They got expelled or something, so they wound up here. I think the kids are O.K., but some are pretty rough, too. At least they know what's going on in the world. One girl I know ran away from home when she was 13 and was on her own in Phoenix for four months before they sent her back. When she came back she couldn't get along with the teachers at the regular high school, so they sent her here.

"The teachers are really nice here, easygoing. And it's nice to have such small classes, too. In a way it's like a big family.

"Most of the kids, either they're too young to drop out, or their parents won't let them drop out, so that's why they're here. Me, I just want to hurry up and finish the requirements for graduation so I can start college. I want to study religion, and I can get a scholarship from a Bible college in Texas where my uncle teaches. I'm the only one in the school who wants to go to college."

Institutional Credibility

Americans still believe in schools. Multinational corporations, agribusiness, the church, the Pentagon, legislative bodies, the CIA, universities—all have been under siege by a public that in this decade has felt betrayed first by the Vietnam war and then by Watergate. During this time, schools have by no means escaped criticism. Across the country there are mumblings and rumblings about the school's inability to educate children adequately. The 1977 Gallup Poll indicates Americans still believe in the ability of the educational system to transmit the necessary skills for a complex technological nation as well as to imbue children with the appropriate values for a democratic society.[27]

[27] *The Gallup Opinion Index.* Report Number 140. March 1977. p. 24.

A Query

How can we talk of institutional credibility when everywhere the failures of schools are being sold to the public by educational muckrakers who seem able to tell us only what's wrong, not what we can do. How can Americans still believe in us?

Taxpayer Revolt

Schools throughout the U.S. are faced with a taxpayer's revolt. Numerous times in the past five years voters in Ohio have turned down tax increases for support of schools. Schools have been closed for weeks at a time. Cleveland has joined Youngstown and Toledo as centers of fiscal and educational crisis. Bills go unpaid and multi-million-dollar payrolls are not met as local banks refuse to extend additional credit to the beleaguered boards. Had the Cleveland bond issue passed, the total tax on a $25,000 home in Cleveland in 1978 would have been about $400, not a large expense for a child's education if one thinks in terms of purchasing services for six hours a day for 36 weeks a year.

The Ohio superintendent of public instruction indicated that Cleveland is only one of 130 school systems in the state that can expect financial trouble.

News reporter: The taxpayers are revolting!
Educator: I couldn't agree more.

Taxpayer Revolt Indeed! Freeloaders—that's what we are. We are a nation of freeloaders. We want good roads, good schools, good services, but we don't want to pay for them.

Thoughts of an Inner City School Principal

This lunch program is getting to be quite a headache. It's a complicated process just to get everybody fed when it rains; I think it's rained every day this week. My noon staff is about ready to go crazy. Then a mother came in yesterday demanding to know why 80 percent of the children here get free lunches while she has to pay for her daughter's. According to her, most of those with free lunches have parents who are in a position to pay for the meals the same as she does. All I could tell her was that finding out the specific earnings of a family is not my job. My task is simply to administer the program on the basis of the information I receive on the applications.

And then there are the children who are supposed to pay who, when lunchtime arrives, claim they've lost their money. We feel that we have to give them *something* to eat so they won't go hungry. Yet after school these are the same children who can't wait to get to Mrs. Gonzales' candy store across the street. What am I supposed to do? Currently there's a rumor that one of the high schools in our district is paying the students 45¢ a day just to show up. I'll have to check that one out. . . .

Years ago, when I first became interested in leaving the classroom and moving into administration, I had no idea how much the structure of our schools would change. Everyone's said it a million times before, but the paperwork is absolutely unbelievable, thanks to our government. I can honestly say I believe things were much simpler before—decisions were more "cut and dried" then. Oh, I'm proud of all the new things I've brought in for this school—the federal dollars, the state programs, the bilingual component, the artist-in-residence concept—but all these things have brought more difficulties for me as well. There are so many strings attached to Title I, Title VII, Early Childhood and all the others! Right now my entire staff is in a tizzy getting ready for the Title IV-C evaluation. And then, there are the "democratic governance" guidelines, the requirements that the parents be involved in budgetary and curricular decisions. The idea is a beautiful one. I'm not denying that. But in reality, there are a few parents on the Advisory Council at this school who kind of "manipulate" things. They don't really represent the community as a whole; instead they form an elite group to push their own special preferences.

Added to that we've got a problem now with our bilingual program. My professional staff as a whole is committed to the concept of pluralistic education; we've worked hard to achieve what we consider to be a good language maintenance program. Now we've got a strong group of parents who are telling us English/Spanish bilingual programs are O.K. through the third grade, but they want the school to concentrate on English from then on—they'll take care of Spanish maintenance at home. They think that if schools maintain Spanish instruction the children won't learn English well enough to compete with Anglos. Well, what can we do? I can't tell the parents they're wrong, but then on the other hand my staff isn't about to give up a program they really believe in either.

Another issue right now is back-to-basics or a well-rounded curriculum. I believe inner city children have as much right to the finer things of life as any other child, and that's why I've worked so hard to develop a strong arts program in this school. The children love it; I've got sixth graders now who don't want to miss a single day of school so they can keep working on the film their class is making. Yet principals at neighboring schools have criticized me for stressing the arts because they think the parents around here don't really care about these things. Well, it's true that some of my parents have said they want our school to concentrate on the basics so that their children can get ahead in the tire factory. But as an educator I don't feel that I can let such feelings destroy a valid program. To me, self-expression is the most basic need, but I suppose pretty soon someone will come along and tell me that I'm "oppressing" these children by giving them creative experiences instead of giving them the "meat and potatoes" curriculum which some say they need to catch up with their white, middle-class counterparts.

We used to think of educators as "detached professionals," but today I have to think more in terms of being a community politician. It's a very, very difficult role to play.

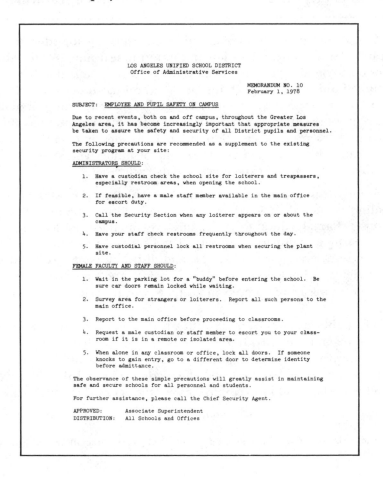

LOS ANGELES UNIFIED SCHOOL DISTRICT
Office of Administrative Services

MEMORANDUM NO. 10
February 1, 1978

SUBJECT: EMPLOYEE AND PUPIL SAFETY ON CAMPUS

Due to recent events, both on and off campus, throughout the Greater Los Angeles area, it has become increasingly important that appropriate measures be taken to assure the safety and security of all District pupils and personnel.

The following precautions are recommended as a supplement to the existing security program at your site:

ADMINISTRATORS SHOULD:

1. Have a custodian check the school site for loiterers and trespassers, especially restroom areas, when opening the school.

2. If feasible, have a male staff member available in the main office for escort duty.

3. Call the Security Section when any loiterer appears on or about the campus.

4. Have your staff check restrooms frequently throughout the day.

5. Have custodial personnel lock all restrooms when securing the plant site.

FEMALE FACULTY AND STAFF SHOULD:

1. Wait in the parking lot for a "buddy" before entering the school. Be sure car doors remain locked while waiting.

2. Survey area for strangers or loiterers. Report all such persons to the main office.

3. Report to the main office before proceeding to classrooms.

4. Request a male custodian or staff member to escort you to your classroom if it is in a remote or isolated area.

5. When alone in any classroom or office, lock all doors. If someone knocks to gain entry, go to a different door to determine identity before admittance.

The observance of these simple precautions will greatly assist in maintaining safe and secure schools for all personnel and students.

For further assistance, please call the Chief Security Agent.

APPROVED: Associate Superintendent
DISTRIBUTION: All Schools and Offices

Committee Reflections on Rules

Public education is beleaguered by its own rules. Rules for safety, for dress, for being on time, for grades, for absences, and so on till the mind tunes out. The very number of rules renders us nearly unable to judge the quality and importance of the rules. The significant and the trivial receive like treatment. A teacher spends many hours weekly on the lunch money accounts and a similar amount of time updating the grade sheet. The bell rings every 50 minutes, and five "hard" subjects make a full load. Johnny receives a three day suspension for smoking in the toilet and five days for fighting in the schoolyard. The Civil War must be studied, but if the Vietnam War is bypassed, that is all right. On and on till there is hardly any sense to be made of an institution designed, above all, to help us make sense.

A Commentary on Learning: Formal, Nonformal, Informal

In our society, we have often mistaken schooling for education and education for learning. Education, in contrast to learning, is "an elaborate extension to do and presumably enhance what he [humankind] once did for himself quite naturally."[28] Just as the wheel has become an extension of our legs, education has become an extension of learning. Extensions operate as intervention agents. Education intervenes and seeks to enhance the natural learning process. Education is neither inherently good nor bad. It can either assist and boost learning or hinder and stifle it. Fundamentally, education and experience feed on each other.[29]

Schooling is an extension of education, perhaps the most obvious one. schooling is the educational network's most formal branch. Schooling and most formal education programs are intended to legitimize and certify learning in American society. Teachers and professors are seen as the processors, evaluators, packagers, and distributors of a certified product, students; schools and formal education are expected to serve as promoters of a learning process in keeping with the national materialistic ethos.

The public equates learning with a tangible payoff, often in the form of socioeconomic mobility. In the process, the notion that there is intrinsic merit in learning has been pushed aside. The bureaucracy of institutionalized education has, perhaps reluctantly, embraced this materialistic view of education and incorporated it with the very structure of schooling.

[28] Edward T. Hall. *Beyond Culture*. New York: Anchor Press/Doubleday, 1976. p. 31.

[29] John Dewey. *Experience and Education*. New York: Macmillan Publishing Co., Inc., 1948. *passim*.

Even those within the bureaucracy who would wish to operate from other perceptions of learning are stymied by this rigid view.

As practiced, schooling is a poor facilitator of learning. Its persistent view of learning as product interferes with significant learnings connected to such complex processes as inquiry and appreciation. What often passes for education is noise that interrupts the natural flow of learning. Schooling too often fragments learning into subject areas, substitutes control for the natural desire to learn, co-opts naturally active children for hours in assembly line classroom structures, and ignores both individual and cultural differences. Students are segregated according to age and mental ability. There is no *gestalt*.

The formal educational system often destroys opportunities for learning from elders, from each other, and from the new generation. Unfortunately, elders past 65 are regarded as historical monuments with no significance for the present; peer learning is tacitly discouraged in formal learning situations; and credentials are often mistaken for valid skills.

Schooling in the United States tends to fragment one's life and to disassociate persons from their actions and reflections. Much is known about the learning process but little has been applied to education. "American education assumes a brain that compartmentalizes and localizes knowledge as an S-R organ in which a single stimulus leads to a uniform response."[30] The American education system is not making use of brain research findings, findings which shatter the S-R learning myth. Pribram, for example, maintains that the brain is a holographic rather than cataloguing organ which seeks to integrate rather than compartmentalize information.[31] Clearly, an individual's needs, abilities, and experiences are involved in reacting to a stimulus. Necessarily, this means that individuals, institutions, cultures, and groups will vary in the type of intensity of response to a given stimulus.

Fortunately, not all learning environments create this kind of sterility. Many nonformal learning opportunities are not connected to certification or the drive for tangible outcomes. There are nonformal education networks which support fresh perspectives of the learning process. The very informality found in settings of some day-care centers, street academies, and open universities offers ways of getting around the obstacles that have arisen in the public schools. In some instances, nonformal education has generated new goals, processes, concepts, and strategies which subsequently have been incorporated into formal education curricula.

In addition to nonformal learning there are informal learning opportunities frequently overlooked in our society and by our schools. This type of learning occurs as a natural part of our lives. People walking, watching T.V., listening to the radio, reading billboards, observing people, dialoguing with family and friends provide opportunities to learn

[30] Hall, *op. cit.*, p. 174.
[31] *Ibid.*, p. 179.

informally and often subconsciously. The power of the informal learning process lies in the fact that unlike the formal learning network, it does not use anxiety, fear of failure, or the necessity to conform in achieving its goals. In informal learning, the selection of activities lies with the learner.

On the other hand, in the formal schooling process most students must undergo regulated and packaged experiences at specific times and places; there is an articulated effort to homogenize learning experiences. The nonformal learning environments are in a sense in an intermediate position between the formal and informal and often exhibit the advantages of both while minimizing the disadvantages, especially of the formal system. The question is how to get those advantages into the bureaucratic structure of the American schools.

NEWS BULLETIN

We interrupt this program for the following bulletin: Jake Jarrow, 11-year-old son of Mr. and Mrs. Lawrence Jarrow has been missing since shortly after 3 p.m. today. Report cards were distributed at school and friends of Jake say he was very upset by his grades in English and mathematics. They think he may have run away rather than show his parents the card . . . The Sheriff was notified at 7 p.m. this evening and a district-wide hunt has been undertaken. If you see a 5'1" blond, blue-eyed 11-year-old boy wearing a red shirt with the words WATCH OUT across the front, blue jeans, and dirty white sneakers, please notify this station or the Sheriff's office. His parents want him to know they do not care what his grades are. "Just come home, Jake," they said.

 Sign over entrance of P.S. 119: THROUGH THESE PORTALS PASS OUR NATION'S MOST PRECIOUS RE-SOURCES.

Committee Reflections on Insecurity

Inner fears and lack of self-esteem have been part of the human experience since the beginning of human life. What is new is the staggering rate of change, and the concomitant overwhelming awareness of personal impotence. There seems to be a general aura of fear emanating from the core of human life throughout the world. In America these fears are based on both specific life-threatening conditions as well as more subtle generalized anxieties stemming from psychological uncertainty and loss of confidence in the self and in society. The physical threats of crime in the streets and in the schools, the continuous threat of economic disaster in the face of inflation, the fear of physical debilitation through accident or as a result of aging: all present quite real situations which intensify an individual's sense of aloneness and vulnerability.

Less apparent are the forces which cause psychological disability, such as the fear of "not making it," the fear of rejection and loss of status, the disintegration of inner belief in oneself. Rather than helping individuals overcome these fears through strengthening their skills in problem solving, reflective thought, and ability to relate to others, the school has often contributed to the further deepening of fears. Threat of failure has been consistently increased. In terms of school practices, it is not inaccurate to state that competition is a pervasive element which is encouraged to such an extent that interpersonal skills are diminished and individual self-esteem is damaged.

Competition is institutionalized in schooling with divisive effects. Under many guises, it is promoted throughout the entire process of schooling. Admittedly, not all competition is destructive; however, its usual manifestation in classrooms too often results in isolation of individuals from one another and sets them against each other as adversaries. Narrow self-interest and the desire to be "first" is apparent in schools from negotiations at the state and district level to the classroom level where students and teachers engage in myriad forms of competition.

Survival in the system depends upon the ability of one individual to obtain distinction above others, often at the expense of others and the loss of personal integrity. Competition permeates the whole fabric of society, but in schools it remains the chief motivating mechanism. Grades and tests are invested with a power and authority disproportionate to their limited function as stimulus to learning.

We are fooling ourselves if we think only schools create competition or foster it through grades and contests. Competition is what makes America go round. It is the energy that makes America great.

"Money makes the world go round, go round, go
round, go rounnn . . ."
"No! Oil makes the world go round."
"International competition is nations fueling around."

The Wizard of Menlo Park, 1847-1931

His was a fertile mind, a creative mind, a troublesome mind. Thomas Alva Edison challenged the established ways of behaving and doing things. His life was epitomized by a sense of urgency and purpose. He seemed to always function from a search for ways to improve the condition of humankind and meet the needs of society. He grew up in the period of exploding industrial and technological revolution, adding his own genius to the push for expansion and technological answers to human dilemmas.

From his childhood efforts to hatch goose eggs with the warmth of his body and his attempts to make his playmates lighter than air by feeding them Seidlitz powders, to his work in his 80's on the distribution of electricity and the storage battery, he exemplified the concept of intentionality in learning. His was a near perfect wedding of societal and personal goals. He responded to the urgencies of his day and in the process contributed to their acceleration.

Wizardry is not without its detractors, however; one person's intentionality may very well be another's impediment. Edison never seemed to doubt himself nor did he shrink from learning even though formal schooling was not to be his avenue. He was a voracious reader in all areas of human endeavor. He early learned the ways of self-education when he left school at age 12 and refused to return because his teacher called him "addled." In later years he recalled, "I remember I used never to be able to get along at school. I was always at the foot of the class. I used to feel that the teachers did not sympathize with me and that my father thought I was stupid."[32]

There can be little doubt that there was cause for Edison's difficulties with schooling and with his family relationships. He burned down his father's barn at age six to see how it would burn; he accidentally destroyed a train in his teens when he dropped phosphorous on the wooden floor of the chemistry laboratory he had established there; he was responsible for at least one train wreck caused by his sleeping while he turned his watchman duties over to one of his telegraphic inventions. Through it all he pursued his own dreams, sorted his priorities, and learned. Few of his em-

[32] *New York Herald Tribune.* "Edison Obituary." October 19, 1931.

ployers during his childhood and youthful years as "tramp" telegrapher appreciated his inventing, drawing, mapping, and audacious personal decision making pursued on their time. His wide experiences in many locations on many jobs were frequently the result of having been fired.

But throughout his life he was sure of where he was going and what he wanted to do. He may not have always got his priorities right, made judicious decisions, or foreseen the consequences of his acts, but he had a will to learn, a strength to be his own man, and the ability to gain over 1,400 patents that have benefited society. He learned early and continued to learn that all manner of situation, material, and ideas may be helpful tools in one's education if intentions are clear and are pursued systematically.

 A six year old's view of school: "School is a waste of fun."

Musings from a Master Teacher

A few years ago, I had my first student teacher. She was really a sweet kid and all fired up about how her students were going to become inquirers, seeking answers to questions that they cared about but that were still of some social importance. Who could disagree? But I had all kinds of misgivings. I mean, how was she going to do all she planned and still reach the Civil War by Christmas vacation, as had been established in our district's curriculum guide? And besides, she looked younger than most of the students she was going to teach. And so soft spoken! I wondered if the kids would even listen to her let alone follow her in all of those teacher-college ideals she was going to lay on them. Those university people!

I decided not to discourage my little student teacher right at the outset. I would be around to help her in case a crisis developed. As far as teaching ideas went, she had quite a bag full. Frankly, the first week went pretty well. She used a game of war that had the students trying to decide what they would do if they found themselves caught in the same strategic situations the generals of the American Revolution had to face. Then, after the kids made their decisions, the whole class read the textbook to see what was actually done. I haven't seen kids that interested in years. But the time it took! How she would get through that textbook in a term going at the rate she was going was beyond me.

Anyway, I said nothing. She was so thrilled with her success. The next week, she assigned the kids reports to do and gave them class time for research in the school library. I really shouldn't say "assigned." She told them to look into an area of the American Revolutionary period that might interest them. That brought an uproar from the kids. Couldn't she give them a few examples? How many pages did the report have to be? What if they weren't interested in anything? Things were almost out of hand when she finally stated that everyone would get an "A." She wasn't trying to threaten them with grades. She just wanted them to deal with a topic that was important for them while they were doing library research. I don't mind saying, she went into the best lesson on library research I've ever heard.

Well, to get to my point, things fell apart pretty quickly for my student teacher after that. The reports she received were a great disappointment to her. They were sloppy for the most part. Some weren't even half a page long. One was obviously copied directly from an encyclopedia.

She had a heart to heart talk with the students which went very badly. First of all, they resented her throwing all that responsibility on their shoulders and then being told their reports weren't any good. It was her job to select what was important for them to study. She didn't even say how many references she wanted! Then, when she told them to do the assignment over, a whole bunch of the kids just kind of looked bored and groaned. She then tried to reteach the research lesson of the week before. The kids began talking to each other, almost ignoring her. And no wonder. She just continued talking to them in that soft tone of hers as though nothing had happened. Once in a while, she would stop and call the name of some kid who was really being offensive. But you could barely hear her. Finally, I stepped out of the adjacent office, raised my voice and told the students that they were to follow her instructions *exactly* and if they didn't, their grades would show the difference. After that, things shaped up.

Later, my student teacher and I talked the situation over. I tried to explain to her that she couldn't walk in and expect kids who had been used to one way of working in school for several years to just suddenly adopt a new way. Besides, grades gave them something to work toward. And if she raised her voice once in a while, that was a way of saying to the kids that she cared. It also gave them a certain sense of security to know exactly what was expected of them. I mean, didn't she like to know when she was a student exactly what was expected of her?

Things did get better and my student teacher pulled through with flying colors. As a matter of fact, she has a job in my school. The other day, I just happened to be passing her room, and the scene I saw really gave me a laugh. There was that little sweet girl with her arms on her hips just tongue-lashing the heck out a half dozen 6 feet tall teenagers who all seemed to cower before her. Deep down I think they know she's right and they appreciate that she cares. And they know she'll give a "D" and even an "E" if she has to.

A Commentary on Built-in Roadblocks to Change

Two phenomena seem to be preventing any real change from occurring in the public schools. On the one hand, youngsters begin their attendance in school at the age of four or five and they absorb, much as they absorb their native tongue, the proper ways of learning and behaving. They are not yet capable of judging these ways, they simply learn them as being good. These ways become a part of their innermost expectations about what ought to go on in formal education. They come to expect grades even as adults—indeed, they have probably come to depend on them although their powers of reasoning will doubtless tell them that such a dependency is silly, that it is what they personally gain from education which really counts. These deeply held expectations of students often work to lead the innovative teacher back into the traditional fold.

On the other hand, teachers do not usually take very long in returning to the fold. High school teachers, especially, return quickly for they see their students' academic performances improve when grades are brandished and a bit of tough talk is used. Furthermore, they must, to keep their jobs, abide by established bureaucratic rules that require them to cover given materials by certain preset dates as well as to use one or another traditional grading system. Regardless of their attitudes before they find teaching positions, several years of behaving in ways that are not consonant with what they believe will change what they believe so that it conforms with the ways they are behaving. In psychological terms, this is Festinger's Theory of Cognitive Dissonance,[33] which, more or less, means that the thinking individual cannot long behave in ways contrary to his beliefs without trying to achieve congruity between his beliefs and his behavior.

Unless ways can be found to mitigate the expectations of students, built into them at such an early age, and to give teachers new modes of behavior which free them from grades and the like, there is little chance that education—even if couched in a new terminology such as lifelong learning—can be significantly redirected. Curricular ideas lacking congruent instructional support and a student body willing to modify its expectations of what is appropriate scholastic behavior cannot achieve the educational difference that has been so valiantly sought throughout the last half century.

If there are ways of behaving we learn because we are members of an ethnic group, and ways of behaving we learn because we attend public school from the age of four or five,

[33] Leon Festinger. *A Theory of Cognitive Dissonance*. Stanford, California: Stanford University Press, 1965.

what happens if these ways are very different or even incompatible with each other? Does the school adjust for such cases? Should it adjust?

Scenes from a Staff Development Meeting at a 95 Percent Latino Elementary School

The chairperson, Ardra, a black teacher from a non-bilingual second grade class, stood up to make an announcement just as everyone was getting ready to go to lunch: "We've made the final arrangements to start a reading lab next semester for second graders who need extra help. Pat says she wants ten children for the lab. So each teacher's quota would be about one child."

As the teachers got up to leave there were mumblings and grumblings among them to the effect that "A lot more of my kids than *that* need help!" The unspoken meaning seemed to be, "Boy, I sure have some dumb ones."

In the midst of this noise, Sofia Oropeza pointedly asked Ardra: "Is this lab for English reading or Spanish reading or both?" Ardra replied, "English," with the "of course" unsaid but clearly communicated. This brief exchange generated a number of arguments involving two or three teachers each, but Sofia's voice rose clearly distinguishable above it all. Her point: At the second grade level a good two thirds of the children are in Spanish reading and only one third or less are in English reading. Therefore, the program would serve only a minority of the children. She asked Margaret, the ECE coordinator, why there was a designated lab for English given these small numbers. Margaret, seemingly surprised that the announcement would have caused such a controversy, replied in her perpetually calm voice, "Sofia, the Los Angeles School District doesn't care what our Spanish scores look like. All they are going to look at are the English scores. It doesn't matter how bad the Spanish reading is."

Of the 12 or so teachers and coordinators no one came to Sofia's defense. The comments were essentially pro-English lab only. "It's about time the English-speaking children got some help around here. The Spanish-speaking ones are always getting special stuff." "After all, it's harder to learn to read in English than in Spanish."

Margaret managed to get everyone's attention. "O.K., Sofia, let's just look at the numbers. Everybody send us the names of the English and Spanish readers who need help. We'll see where we go from there. But remember, we've got nine classrooms with second graders but only about ten slots; so you can only send us one or two names."

Walking down to the lunch room an Anglo-bilingual teacher is heard to comment to another, "Now I suppose we are going to have to listen to Sofia at lunch telling us how we discriminate against the Spanish."

Postscript: The following day Ardra came into the lunchroom with another announcement for her colleagues who were in the middle of sandwiches and a discussion of the horrors of serving yard duty. She didn't sit down. "I've just talked with the principal, and all she has to say is that this school does not operate a *Spanish* remedial reading program." Sofia looked up and shrugged her shoulders. "O.K., but it's not fair to most of the kids."

 Did you know that in the 1930's the median educational attainment for the nation was around eighth grade? Today, it is nearly 12 years of education. High school graduation has become the standard for the nation.

And yet, for the whole population of Spanish origin in the United States the average school attainment (as of 1977) had barely reached the tenth grade level.[34]

Committee Reflections on Change

It is hard to acknowledge, now, as we look back, how little real change took place in the 60's. Those of use who lived through that decade of hope and idealism, of inquiry and humanism cannot help but be stunned by the pall of apathetic conformism that has settled around education. Those of us who worked for a conception of education that would lead the young to deal broadly and humanely, flexibly and rationally with the quality of their lives both as individuals and as members of society cannot but feel a tremendous sadness before the ever increasing popularity of performance objectives and their administrative translation, accountability. Grades, standardized tests, and national norms hang about our collective neck like the Ancient Mariner's albatross.

It hurts to admit it, but we who fostered that surge for renewal are largely to blame for its inauspicious passing. While we preached the tenets of a new education, while we fumbled with process-oriented curricula and the intriguing methods of sensitivity training, while we tried to make education the solution of all our economic and social problems, the long-standing bureaucratic traditions of public education became even more firmly entrenched. We paid too little heed.

As we tried to figure out what we were all about, long lists of specific performance objectives were being incorporated into the curricula. Most of the factually oriented, subject-centered curricula offered by the public schools easily accommodated such lists. We failed to recognize the intellectual and political attractiveness of a performance-based curricular design, which at one fell swoop outlined the specific content to be learned, included evaluative feedback that was easily translated into report card

[34] U.S. Bureau of the Census. "Current Population Reports." *Educational Attainment in the United States: March, 1977 and 1976.* Series P-20, No. 314, December 1977. p. 33.

language, and led the teacher, step by step, through the teaching process. Aware that what we were about could not be quantified via the existing measurements of scholastic progress, we did little to devise more adequate systems of evaluation.

We were intellectually and politically weak. We were still working out what we meant scholastically by process and inquiry, love, and taking the child "where she's at." The complexity of what we meant and the flood of indiscriminate federal funding worked against us. Eventually, the federal government and the school's bureaucrats clamored for "proof" that the public's funds had been spent well. With the usual lack of discrimination, they adopted I.Q. tests and achievement tests that have dominated the American school system as the basis for their evaluation. We went along with them only vaguely whimpering that the nature of our goals were different—that the tests were not measuring the kinds of skills and attitudes we felt to be central, that standardized criteria did not take into account our efforts to meet the special needs of individuals as well as of diverse ethnic groups. We went along with them and we were slaughtered. The Ohio-Westinghouse study typifies the slaughter. Head Start made little difference in future scholastic performances as measured by standardized tests. These tests were based on traditional goals of education and not on the goals established for Head Start Programs.[35] Jensen came forth with his well-publicized analysis of the efforts of various compensatory programs and grandiosely concluded that they did little good. It was all in the genes; it was better to leave education to the biologist instead of the psychologist.[36]. All of Jensen's conclusions were based on the outcomes of standardized achievement and I.Q. tests, which, time and again, have been demonstrated to be closely related to reading skills and long-standing goals of traditional education.

On top of this crisis in evaluation, the very nature of the goals we sought—creativity, open enededness, discovery, coping with one's own identity, etc.—prevented us from devising "teacher proof" materials. We could make suggestions but we could not give a recipe for how to achieve "discovery." We were asking teachers to do what they had never themselves experienced in school. We were probably asking more of them than most could give, however willing.

We needed time and the freedom to work out our ideas in tentative ways. The job crunch of the late 60's and early 70's stopped us and we remained stuck with our early failures. Public clamor for skills training and career education elevated specific performance objectives to even greater bureaucratic favor. The government bureaucracy took its money away from those of us who would not or could not develop programs

[35] Marshall S. Smith and Joan S. Bissell. "The Impact of Head Start: The Westinghouse-Ohio Head Start Evaluation." *Harvard Educational Review* 40: 51-104; February 1970.

[36] Arthur Jensen. "How Much Can We Boost I.Q. and Scholastic Achievement?" *Harvard Educational Review* 39: 7; 1969.

based on lists of performance objectives and suited to the measurement of student performance and ACCOUNTABILITY.

In our present state of disillusionment and resignation, we are still to blame. Scientists work through decades of adversity and failure to establish a new conception or a vaccine for polio, or a cure for cancer. Yet, we, who are working with the most complex matter known—the human mind—seem to have given up after relatively few failures.

Musings of a Teacher

I used to think college professors were being unrealistic. I even wondered what was wrong with the way things were being done in schools. But I don't wonder any more. The kids seem hell bent on tearing the school apart. It's almost as if they were daring us to teach them, and most of us just don't have the courage to take them up on the dare.

I think the professors go wrong because they keep on thinking everyone is ready to change—wants to change. Maybe I am ready, but most of the complaints I hear are not about change. People are not complaining about what we do in school, but that what we do is not done well enough. What do you think all the hoopla over basics is about? Same old reading, writing, and 'rithmetic—just teach it better. People don't want inquirers for children, and most of them don't even worry about their kids being apathetic; they could care less about the development of core values or the appreciation of art. They want good "solid" basics that will get their kids into the factories with pay and benefits beginning somewhere around $10 an hour.

The more we try new ways, the more we hear demands to strengthen the old ways. Even the kids want us to get down to basics. Next thing I'll have to dust off my McGuffey reader.

What Schools Need Now is Time to Teach

New Federal and State Programs, Though Well Intentioned, Could Cripple District

"Too many people are demanding too much, too fast, from the Los Angeles Unified School District. This great educational institution is about to collapse from the sheer volume of administrative work demanded of it in recent years, albeit with the best intentions, by state and federal legislation and the orders of various courts. And as a result, the quality of the district's educational program has been seriously impaired.

"Among the administrative burdens placed on the city schools in the past three years are the following:

—Student integration as mandated by the state Supreme Court in the Crawford Case.

—Teacher integration, ordered by the office for civil rights, of the Department of Health, Education and Welfare.

—The Early Childhood Education program, required and administered by the state.

—Programs for students speaking little or no English, required by the U.S. Supreme Court's Lau decision as well as by state legislation.

—Collective bargaining for school employees, as mandated by the state's Rodda Act.

—Participation by girls in team sports and similar changes in curricula required by Title IX of the 1972 education amendments act.

—Special assistance for the handicapped, as ordered by recent federal legislation.

—Surveys and research work in connection with AB 65, the school finance reform bill passed last year by the state legislature.

"Each of these programs has a noble purpose behind it, nor do I have any argument with the goals of the legislation and the court orders involved. These reforms are needed. My sole concern is with the overburdening of the school officials who must administer such reforms. They face deadlines that would be difficult even if the programs had been added to the educational system one at a time. But the changes are all relatively new, and most are extraordinarily complex.

"These mandated programs bring with them thousands of rules, each requiring school employees—at all levels—to plan, organize, implement and then report results back to the originating agency. They all take the time of our teachers and administrators, drawing them away from their primary responsibility— the classroom education of our children. . . .

"Classroom teachers and school administrators need time to plan, organize, use and most important, follow through with their efforts— both in teaching and in responding to the requirements of outside public agencies. Yet the totality of these requirements now threatens to severely cripple the district's ability to maintain or improve the quality of public education in Los Angelis. . . .

"We ask a great deal of our district employees, from the superintendent to the teacher in the classroom to the secretary of the neighborhood school. Their dedication and plain guts may well be why the system, engulfed as it has become, has not yet actually collapsed.

"Is it unreasonable to ask legislators, judges and others who have lately issued orders to the school district to call a halt to their demands for a while, to give us a little breathing room in which to carry on our task of education while we absorb the disruptions of their demands? After all, we are dealing with our most precious asset—our children."[37]

---

[37] Phillip G. Bardos, Los Angeles Board of Education member. "What Schools Need Now is Time to Teach." *Los Angeles Times*. February 19, 1978. Part VII. p. 5.

A Commentary on a Break in the Walls of Time and Space

The walls of the school as a stereotypic building, and the walls of the classroom as an independent unit, must be breached in order to let people and learning flow in and out. Of course, classrooms have been opening up both literally and figuratively in recent years. Open classroom organizational models, with teachers working as teams and parents involved in the daily work of the school, have contributed to removing the isolated egg-crate character of separate classrooms.

However, research on open space schools and open classrooms has been discouraging. Findings do not indicate that such arrangements promote any real differences in learning. Mere architectural change does not seem to affect educational outcomes; sometimes they mask abuses such as overcrowding. What is needed in order to truly open schools is greater openness in the mind-set of educators. The architecture of open space is not a sufficiently pervasive modification to overcome the years spent by both teachers and students in the restricted structures of traditional schooling. Intentional concentration on overcoming the mind-sets fostered by these traditions is essential to any significant change. In other words, teachers and students must plan together how they will behave differently in innovative structures.

Innovative structures, furthermore, need to be seen as more than architectural changes. Spaces beyond the classroom and the school have potential for learning. Many interesting and creative approaches have already been launched in this direction, using business offices, bank space, factories, museums, zoos, libraries, and stores as places where groups of students can meet for specific purposes under the aegis of the school.

The use of the school facility itself as a community center provides a type of reciprocity with the community which is mutually beneficial. For example, using schools for community education or activities during the summer, at night, and even during the school day reflects a raised consciousness about the role of the school in the ongoing education and life of the community. Some schools, where enrollment has declined leaving empty classrooms, have experimented with shared arrangements whereby a community group (such as a well-baby clinic, a vocational school, or a business) can use space formerly in use as classrooms. When such space is wisely shared it provides another opportunity to link school and community in independent, but advantageous, association.

Time as a barrier must be looked at with fresh imagination. Time in school is often used wastefully and is controlled arbitrarily by those in authority. A sense of morality with regard to the spending of time, both the teacher's and the learner's, must be built into a new perception of schooling. The use of invariable time schedules for the school year, the school week, and the school day often inhibits learning. Classes with rigid time periods, courses of specific duration, curriculum sequences and prerequisites arbitrarily followed, students grouped by chronological age regardless of background, interests, or abilities all create barriers to learning and are formidable obstacles to reform in education.

Equally disturbing is the lack of respect for the individual's time when students are forced to sit idly waiting in non-productive class situations—waiting until the teacher gives the signal to begin. Educators must act on the belief that wasting time is wasting life, that using time is spending life. Wasting another human being's time is a violation of human life and human rights.

"Students (vandals?) have shown so much ingenuity at getting into school during holidays, we are asking all teachers to check ventilation screens to be sure they are securely fastened in their homerooms. Don't be the one to let kids in!"

—from a note sent to teachers in a Midwestern high school

THURSDAY EVENING NEWS

Lifelong Learning Council Formed

MONEY APPROPRIATED FOR POST-SECONDARY EDUCATION

The California legislature has appropriated money to develop the idea of post-secondary education as lifelong learning. The reasons given for this movement toward lifelong learning were (a) the potential for the reduction of such social ills as functional illiteracy, welfare dependency and social instability, and (b) the enhancement of the state's cultural, political, and economic life as well as the . . . quality of life.[38]

Adult Education Publication Changes Name to "Lifelong Learning"

UNIVERSITY INAUGURATES NONTRADITIONAL PROGRAM

American Educators Look to European Models

For many years, Sweden has had a well-established variety of channels for open access to lifelong education. Education has been designed

---

[38] Richard E. Peterson and J. B. Lon Hefferlin. "Post-Secondary Alternatives to Meet the Educational Needs of California's Adults." Final Report of a Feasibility Study Prepared for the California Legislature, September 1975.

for both individual and societal needs.

Concepts such as the opportunity for each individual to live a full and meaningful life are a basic part of the ideology of the government. Such statements as "school should keep one step ahead of the times" and "self-actualization through socially oriented pursuits" are basic tenets of the educational structure.[39]

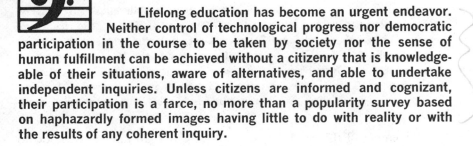 **Lifelong education has become an urgent endeavor. Neither control of technological progress nor democratic participation in the course to be taken by society nor the sense of human fulfillment can be achieved without a citizenry that is knowledgeable of their situations, aware of alternatives, and able to undertake independent inquiries. Unless citizens are informed and cognizant, their participation is a farce, no more than a popularity survey based on haphazardly formed images having little to do with reality or with the results of any coherent inquiry.**

Who Needs Schools?

A Brazilian chief recently surprised the Brazilian legislature by showing up armed with a tape recorder, not only to deliver a full report of his lobbying efforts to his Amazonian tribe, but also as a means of illustrating, to any who would listen, the difference between a politician's words and actions. Given the fact that this middle-aged chief had not come in contact with whites until the age of 17, his effective use of such a technological device as the tape recorder is an interesting case of one kind of lifelong learning. Without enrolling in any night school, this individual had also developed strategies that enabled him to deal cogently with a totally new political and economic environment.[40]

Sage Advice

Eddie English at age 73 flew a biplane he built himself. From a childhood memory of working around the local airfields, and the exhilaration of standing in the wash of the old prop planes while holding them down, came a dream of someday flying his own plane. The dream did not die—but it was deferred for a few years until he could have enough money for lessons. He soloed at age 71.

Eddie's advice to those facing retirement is: "Don't sit down—get something else to do."

[39] Zaher Wahab. "Ideology and Adult Education in Sweden: Lesson for the U.S." Paper presented at the Nation's Bicentennial Adult Continuing Education Congress, New York, November 18-23, 1976.

[40] Based on an article in: *The Los Angeles Times*. May 4, 1977.

A Commentary on Lifelong Learning: For whom? By whom?

It is a fact that most Americans who develop plans for lifelong learning are members of an elite group—a group comprising more or less the upper 10 percent of the population in terms of education, income, and occupational freedom. Members of this group are most likely to identify themselves as middle class, or possibly "upper middle" class. But as Novak points out,

Sometimes we wrongly let ourselves think that "middle class" covers everyone from about $10,000 per year to $20,000 per year—as though "the rich" were the top hundred thousand families. If we leave aside the 20 percent or so of Americans who live in or near the state of poverty, and the 10 percent who earn more than $20,000, 70 percent live in a world far more accurately described as "working class." They are diverse, complex, invisible, and unknown in America. Our ignorance about them is as astonishing as if they lived on another continent.[41]

A member of this working class more likely than not has little or no college education, punches a time clock, engages in rote manual labor, and unlike Eddie, has never been on an airplane. Our talk about a knowledge-based society and enriched jobs, about such things as egalitarianism and social change, is just that, *our* talk. Members of the working and the lower classes have ideas about changes they want to see, but exactly what is the nature of their aspirations? It is the upper ten percent who are the leaders, the opinion makers, the image makers; "the public image of the nation is vastly out of tune with the public reality."[42] If we are to seriously entertain the idea of developing a learning society with all segments of society involved in learning lifelong, we must come to a clear understanding of reality for the vast middle class.

Is it possible for lifelong learning, designed "from the top," to be good in terms of human fulfillment for the rest of society? Might it not be more beneficial if the aspirations and the content for lifelong learning were of grass-roots origin?

Universities and the Lifelong Learning Market

The day the university could sit back and pursue research interests and teaching with the expectation that students would continue to clamor for admission is past. Not only has the birthrate dropped, but youth are reevaluating the worth of a college education. In addition, businesses such as IBM, AT&T and G.E. now confer bachelor's degrees, and the MBA in management has been authorized by the state of

---

[41] Michael Novak. "The Beleaguered Middle Class." *Los Angeles Times*. Sept. 14, 1975. p. 5.

[42] *Ibid*.

Massachusetts for the Arthur D. Little Company. Universities must compete. Included in the competition are over ten thousand proprietary schools enrolling over three million students each year. Eighty-five percent of the profitmaking schools are owned by major corporations such as IT&T, Control Data, Bell & Howell, and Minneapolis Honeywell.[43]

As a result of the competition, lifelong learning has taken on new significance for the nation's colleges and universities. One outcome is a reconsideration of alternative modes of meeting university standards and criteria; another includes an expansion of existing administrative patterns, such as continuing education, into new marketing areas. In addition, the development of new programs has taken on an air of desperate intensity.

The University Extension, University of California, San Diego, has moved beyond the old pattern of television courses to courses by newspapers. The lessons are carried without charge in over 250 newspapers. Those seeking credit register with the university. Anyone is free to purchase text materials and pursue learning on his/her own.[44] Other institutions are developing cooperative programs, sending senior professors to branch locations, giving credit for experience, and accepting transfer of extension work that formerly was not considered acceptable.

Some of the debate that has been coursing through academia is captured in the report of the study sponsored by the W. K. Kellogg Foundation called *Patterns for Lifelong Learning*.[45] Academics are by no means unanimous in their support of efforts to modify the traditional role and function of the university. But it is clear that "the lifelong university"[46] is here to stay, if not in a unique administrative guise, at least in a renewed awareness of the changing educational scene and new life-styles that bring a more adverse public to universities and a more diverse university fare to the public.

Committee Reflections on Universities as Business

Why should universities compete? Was Robert Hutchins right when he wryly pointed out, "Education is almost as profitable a business as poverty."[47] Education is big business. But are its goals comparable to the

[43] Wellford W. Wilms. "Profile of Proprietary Students." In: Dyckman W. Vermilye, editor. *Lifelong Learning—A New Clientele for Higher Education*. Washington, D.C.: Jossey-Bass Inc., Publishers, 1974. pp. 34-35.

[44] Caleb A. Lewis. "Courses by Newspaper." In: Dyckman W. Vermilye, editor. *Lifelong Learners—A New Clientele for Higher Education*. Washington, D.C.: Jossey-Bass Inc., Publishers, 1974. p. 67.

[45] Theodore M. Hesburgh, Paul A. Milter, and Clifton R. Whorton, Jr. *Patterns for Lifelong Learning*. Washington, D.C.: Jossey-Bass Inc., Publishers, 1973.

[46] A term copyrighted in 1973 by the Board of Trustees, Michigan State University, East Lansing.

[47] Interview on CBS, *The Remarkable Schoolhouse*, 1967.

goals for industrial production? Taking a cynical view, one may be led to the conclusion that the burgeoning interest in lifelong learning or life-long education is being spurred on by the promise of new and expanded educational markets in the face of too many buildings, a decreasing population pool interested in traditional school and college offerings, and increases in leisure time. There have always been a large number of informal educational enterprises and institutions engaged in various forms of educational endeavor outside the bounds of the governmental educational system. Major businesses and industries have had a variety of educational and training programs. But is the delivery of training programs the main business of universities? Should universities scurry to increase the production of credit hours regardless of their real worth just to show increased productivity?

It appears that the education industry may be a part of the problem that universities face today. Universities are caught in the economic competition of our society and have lost the space and disposition to reflect on the outcome of society's actions. We are caught in a vicious circle of marketing products in terms of societal demands rather than providing intellectual leadership that will call in question the direction we are going.

A Commentary on Lifelong Learning: Conflicts of Purpose

There is little debate about the growing interest in problems and issues related to lifelong learning. As recently as 1974 the ERIC information retrieval system had no descriptor for lifelong learning or for most of the other terms associated with it. But by 1975, a descriptor had been added and a probe revealed 519 articles related to the topic. This suggests a more recent genesis for the concept than is the case. It is only in the United States that the concept has been slow to emerge. Concern for lifelong learning has been a longtime concern for many nations of the world, but in large measure it has been submerged in the field of adult education.

The Scandinavian countries have been the historic leaders in the development of lifelong learning. Denmark, Norway, Sweden, and Finland have each contributed uniquely to the models of free schools and folk schools that serve to extend educational opportunity beyond the limits of the typical public or governmentally controlled school system. In Sweden, for example, the folk high schools are largely independent of state control and have been "the bastion of individual liberty and personal development."[48] Their expressed goal is "to improve the student's power of independent thinking and critical judgment and further his maturity and his interest in learning."[49]

[48] Gene G. Gage. "The Nordic Example." *Saturday Review* 2:20; September 15, 1975.

[49] *Ibid.*

One becomes aware of reasons for the slow emergence of interest in lifelong learning in the United States when one compares the variety of programs and the purposes attached to them in other nations. Part of the lack of interest in lifelong learning as a special area in the United States may be traced to the existence of a strong and fairly effective public school system that, for all its shortcomings, has provided an avenue for learning that seemed adequate to meet the needs of the first 200 years of American development. On the other hand, Third World or developing countries have been vitally interested in aspects of lifelong learning for several years. Their interests grow out of a desire to increase general literacy, a desire to improve training for economic growth, and a concern for improvement of individual life conditions. The leadership provided by Mahatma Ghandi in India is a significant example of one variety of program, as is the work of Pedro Orata in the Philippines and Paulo Freire in Brazil and Chile. In these cases, the types of programs are unique efforts to achieve greater indigenous involvement in formal education and to help members of society move from marginal existence into participation in the economic and cultural mainstream.

From its inception, lifelong learning was tied most directly to adult education and continuing education. The 1919 Report of the Adult Education Committee of the Ministry of Reconstruction in Great Britain recognized that adult education was "a permanent national necessity, an inseparable aspect of citizenship [which] should be both unusual and *lifelong.*"[50] From such beginnings it is not unexpected that the emphasis on adult education has continued to predominate consideration of lifelong learning even though a more comprehensive view was projected by the publication of *Learning to Be* by UNESCO in 1972.[51]

Irrespective of the differences in parameters of educational concerns within the area of lifelong learning there is common acceptance of the need to develop an attitude toward learning throughout one's lifetime as a normal and necessary condition for human fulfillment. In large measure the competing perspectives within the field have arisen from the different historical, social, political, and economic needs being served. While each focus or emphasis in lifelong learning in the United States has elements in common with programs and ideas found in other countries, there are a number of critical distinctions and contributions present in the practices and intent of various programs. At least three distinct purposes may be identified.

As suggested earlier, basic literacy education is a primary concern of developing countries. Governments generally accept the caveat that an

[50] F. W. Jessup. "The Idea of Lifelong Learning." In: R. H. Dave and N. Stiemerling. *Lifelong Education and the School.* Hamburg: UNESCO Institute for Education, 1973. p. 19.

[51] Edgar Faure. *Learning to Be: The World of Education, Today and Tomorrow.* Paris: UNESCO, 1972.

educated populace is needed if a stable government is to be achieved with a growing economic base. A developing society needs trained workers for its labor force capable of moving the society from a preindustrial state to a modern industrial state with maximum efficiency; but at another level, a nation psychologically needs the world recognition that accompanies the achievement of a literate populace. At the same time, for individuals education is an important local commodity that leads to improved economic and social standing in nearly all societies. However, emphasis on basic education is not an effective equalizer of social classes. Efforts to increase educational opportunities have succeeded only in increasing "enrollment from every social class with continuing class disparities," [52] whether the country is India, Gabon, Norway, or the United States. Efforts to solve major social, economic, or political problems by changing aspects of the educational system will be doomed to failure because of cultural disparities between individuals and segments of the society.

Besides national economic improvement and improvement of national standing in the worldwide community, emphasis on lifelong learning has served to foster a strong nationalistic identity. Especially in Scandinavia, but to some extent in most developing countries as well, there has been a conservative cultural feature to lifelong learning that focuses on personal involvement in and contribution to the culture and subcultures of the nation. The appeal of such an approach is in the sense of identification the learners develop with the broader community. Often the participants have been cut off from the more traditional, formal paths of post-secondary education which have been reserved for an elite.

A third purpose for lifelong learning has emerged more recently, even though it has been present in the background for many years. It is a general concern for improvement of the quality of life. While arising from a desire for more effective use of leisure time, it has encompassed an expanded arena including environmental awareness, consumer advocacy, and more effective political involvement. This purpose often leads to challenges of existing political, social, and economic systems instead of the aggrandizement of an idealized cultural and national identity. Persons involved in development of lifelong learning models and in fostering lifelong learning programs need to be clear about their purposes and aware of the implications of their efforts.

A Teacher's Reactions

Lifelong learning sounds like a lifetime "custodianship" for the schools. Whenever there isn't a job for someone, they send them back to school! The young, the old, the sick, the unemployed, all back to school.

[52] Joffre Dumazedier. "Continuing Education and the Education System in France." *The School and Continuing Education: Four Studies.* Paris, UNESCO, 1972. p. 43.

And to do what? Basket weave? Belly dance? Fix motors? Some human fulfillment!

Besides, where is the money coming from? As it is, they keep on trying to increase taxes. Millage after millage has gone down to defeat. How are we going to extend educational opportunity—support new ways of learning—when we can barely support teaching calculus and German?

If anything is going to come out of lifelong learning, the schools cannot just be shoved into taking it over. Lifelong learning has got to be thought about in a different context from schooling. Not that I think we should give up schooling—but just that some kind of reasonable relationships between teaching immature youngsters and continuing education for a lifetime has to be worked out. There is no way that my school could contribute to lifelong learning under the present setup.

The Committee's Coda

We are caught in a crossfire of demands from diverse publics urging basic education, career education, ethnic education, and other kinds of specialized training. Society acts as if a particular content appropriately planned, organized, and presented would be sufficient to resolve all the problems it faces. Like the Sorcerer's Apprentice, we have begot a monster laboring to unload buckets of knowledge. The more we learn by way of facts, the more there is to learn. The more learners, the more knowledge produced, the more knowledge, the more, the more, the more . . . and still the common model of the learner remains that of the collector of knowledge, trying to stuff pennies in a little bank when the needs call for millions as a starting investment. Individuals end up chasing someone else's plan. The course is set. There is no room for dreamers.

Segments of the leadership within the educational community have noted the problem and have tried to change the model. To date, the incidences of success have been so infrequent as to be remarkable. But in most cases the efforts have been directed to the organization and packaging of knowledge rather than to addressing directly the problem of determining whether the substance of schooling ought to be knowledge or process or valuing or socializing, or some combination of these aims. Why are we wanting a learning society? What is the role of educators and educational institutions? One of the most urgent realities for us professional educators is to ask ourselves what we are about. Are we protecting turf? Shouting into the wind? Or merely jousting with windmills?

PART III

Coming to Terms

"... it was the spring of hope, it was the winter of despair, ..."
Charles Dickens, *A Tale of Two Cities*

Introduction

We have struggled with the identification of goals, as individuals and as members of society. We have considered some of the urgent realities that confront us directly and as members of diverse communities. At the same time we have sought to identify particular obstacles that impede our efforts to achieve the potential "good life" we desire. And ultimately, we must face the existential now. We must decide what we'll do on Monday.

We resolve to face it hopefully. We are by nature hope-filled creatures able to anticipate and look forward, able to set goals, draft plans for the achievement of the goals, and anticipate the consequences of our plans. If we are to rise above the level of doomsayers and idle dreamers we must bring to bear on our condition the best thinking and strongest commitment of all segments of our society. A feature of great civilizations has been their ability to look forward, to strive for new goals, to dream new dreams, and to marshal the energy and will to meet the challenges. America and American education stand at a critical junction. Will we rise to the challenges or retire, convinced that the obstacles are unsurmountable? The whole world seems to teeter with us, even when antagonistic to our interpretation of the human dreams, as we decide to act or not to act, to affirm or not affirm, to lead the new revolution or to dig in our heels and try to stem the onrush of change.[1]

Historic commitments, practices, and traditions are challenged from without and within. The challenges provide opportunities for leadership and excellence. Individually, we have opportunities to come to terms with those aspects of our reality that are within our spheres of influence. As citizens we have an opportunity to be a part of the larger commitment to a just social order, open to diversity, sharing society's beneficence with all, continuing the struggle for expanded human rights and fulfillment. As individuals we have a responsibility to ourselves to realize our greatest potential while simultaneously bending our will to the broader goal of human fulfillment.

This part of the yearbook reflects the individual efforts of the authors to come to terms with those aspects of reality that are especially critical from their perspectives. Readers may wish to challenge the judgments and interpretations or add to the suggestions that are made. That is part of coming to terms.

"We are human to the extent that we are able and willing to make the choices that enable us to transcend genetic and environmental determinism, and thus to participate in the continuous process of self-creation which seems to be the task and the reward of humankind."[2]

How will you come to terms?

Open Education — A Coming to Terms with Uncertainty

Wilma S. Longstreet

There can be little doubt. Public education is on the verge of total irrelevancy. As we struggle through intragenerational disjunctions, as we increasingly recognize the inability of our senses to comprehend the realities of technology, as the fear within us grows that technology has already escaped the kinds of control available to a democratic society, statehouses are legislating lists of performance objectives designed to hold teachers and students alike accountable for competencies that are, and were even in the past, trivial; textbook companies add to the trivia as they continue

---

[1] Cf.: Jean-François Revel. *Without Marx or Jesus*. Garden City, New York: Doubleday and Company, Inc., 1970. passim.

[2] René Dubos. *Beast or Angel?: Choices That Make Us Human*. New York: Scribner's, 1974.

to push for a return to the basics, meaning, of course, reading, writing, and arithmetic packaged between a pair of hard covers; and school administrators continue to accept the models of business and industry to guide school operations as though schools were part of a free enterprise system having discrete products as outcomes. The world is staggering through a maze of unknowns—uncertainty is an integral part of our daily lives. Yet, what we do in schools is being progressively pushed toward the clearly discernible and the easily described.

Sadly enough, such precisely defined studies are irrelevant to the basic cognitive needs of our present circumstances. The multiplication of computers and microprocessor chips, of communication devices of all kinds are revolutionizing how and what we know. All this, while our children memorize the dates of the Civil War at least three different times during their school careers and repeat meaningless grammar and arithmetic exercises without understanding. They are being made complacent about the stability of human knowledge in the midst of a major upheaval.

The Impoverishment of Human Fulfillment

The incongruency, however, goes beyond the obvious incompatibility between how we must live and how we are taught. It goes to the very way human fulfillment is conceived and related to formal education. The claims on the schools are many, ranging from those who would make the personal, affective development of individual youngsters the core of the curriculum to those who insist that the disciplines and the academic skills ought to be central to all children's studies to those who see vocational preparation as the major purpose of schooling. Fulfillment, of course, is variously conceived; some would say it is the affective, inner contentment of individuals with themselves; for others, it is the cognitive reaching out to different ages of human history so that the cumulative greatness of humanity may become the possession of each individual; for still others, it is the successful participation of individuals in the social, economic and political aspects of society.

If these conceptions have anything in common, it is that each, taken alone, is an impoverishment of the nature of human fulfillment which comprises all of the conceptions mentioned in ways neither discrete, nor clearly understood, nor predictable. What is more, there can be no human fulfillment without both self-fulfillment and societal fulfillment. Both defy empirical precision; both bear the instability that is the hallmark of human beings exercising their will to be and to act differently as individuals and as members of society.

It must further be understood that human fulfillment involves not simply the balanced interaction of self-fulfillment and societal fulfillment, but the tension between these as well, that is, the conflicts of individual and societal purpose and need that defy resolution and remain as con-

tradictions even in the most benign of historical periods. Human fulfillment always develops in the midst of uncertainty and imprecision.

Technology and the dominance of business industrial complexes have
led us to expect to deal primarily with the clearly delineated and the
precisely defined, and to lend little credence to whatever it is that escapes
such precision. In this vein, if the "quality of life" is studied, the effort is
usually to achieve empirical descriptions of what that means and some
form of precise, quantitative measure. Implicitly, we seem to have rejected the nonquantitative and whatever defies empirical observation.

When we in the schools discuss "human fulfillment," the effort, all
too frequently, is to reduce the concept to ideas and forms that can be
modeled into measurable performance. Human fulfillment, in official
quarters, is often translated into lists of specific performance objectives
and/or competencies. So-called "soft" topics such as justice become the
object of fill-in questions, and discussions of love and goodness are rele-
gated to being curricular afterthoughts for they do not fit measurable
formats. In a time when the exploration of a universe—the dimensions of
which boggle human imagination—has been undertaken and the very
essence of life is being probed, the inadequacy of such an approach must
surely be obvious. When viewed in the light of our ever increasing uncertainty about what ought to be the criteria of worthwhile human life, the
approach goes beyond simple trivia to the dangerous.

The long lists of performance objectives that legislators[1] have imposed, or are thinking of imposing on the schools, are dangerous because
they ignore the major realities of the human condition while heralding
their practicality. We need *ongoing tentativeness* if we are to be capable
of action in what promises to be a persistent state of uncertainty and
imprecision. We need an in-depth understanding of technologies that
have developed in ways only peripherally related to reading and writing.
We need to become involved in creating new sets of values applicable not
only to ourselves as individuals or to society as a whole but to the tensions
which loom enormously between these, to a whole range of new experiences for which we have no criteria. We need to talk of love and goodness.
Such needs cannot be met with lists of performance objectives, even if they
are legislated. We simply do not know enough.

Openness as Part of the Curriculum

In order to confront the uncertainties, the schools must incorporate
openness into the very texture of their curricular designs. Often, when
the concept of openness in schooling is discussed, it is viewed as something "unstructured," while what is actually going on in the schools is
thought to be "structured." Without reentering the debate regarding the
effectiveness of traditional curricular structures, it is important to point

[1] As of this writing some 35 state legislatures are considering some form of com-
petency or performance objective requirements.

out that the concept of "openness" by its very nature implies structure. A door can be closed in its structure or it can be open; it can be neither without the structure. Furthermore, a door can take many different forms whether it is closed or open.

Making a metaphorical leap to curricular design, it is possible to develop many different kinds of studies which allow for the direct input and decision making activities of students just as it is possible to develop numerous kinds of curricula that tell the student what to do every step of the way. A closed door describes the space it outlines completely; an open door describes the breadth and form of its outline, even the measures of its openness (a tiny crack to wide open), but to the extent that it offers open space, whatever passes through will influence the qualities that the space will take on. This is the inherent imprecision and uncertainty of openness even though organization and structure are present: it is the quality which makes the open curriculum suited to the needs of our young and the uncertain times they will live through.

This is not to say that a closed structure is *never* desirable. The teaching of a specific set of mathematical procedures might be best done through a closed curricular design. Rather, it is the dominant use of the closed structure leading to the exclusion of uncertainties from school studies that undermines the validity and relevancy of the curriculum. For instance, the nature of science remains, even today, a vigorously debated topic full of imprecisions and uncertainties. It cannot be validly discussed without openness, however, discussion of the meaning and validity of science is rarely held in today's public school even though several years of science study are included in most curricula.

The Qualities or Parameters of an Open Curriculum

Regardless of the specific contents selected, there are qualities or parameters that ought to be included in the framework of an open curriculum given our present historical circumstances. To begin with, the importance of controlling the production, uses and diffusion of information must be scholastically recognized. If we are to continue to participate significantly in a democratic form of governance and in the power that governance holds over human fulfillment, the understanding of new kinds of information devices must be widely diffused among the public at large. Without such general understanding, democratic participation can be likened to a group of blind people voting on the colors they want for a flag; there is no relevant data basis for the vote and it becomes a haphazard selection based on factors extraneous to the question. Indeed, extraneous voting of this type is a phenomenon that has already been observed with some frequency in our society.

The schools are the logical vehicles for helping the public at large to become capable of working with and comprehending both the limitations and advantages of the data generated by new information devices, though

most schools at present seem satisfied to stop with reading and writing.
Most schools have ignored, for instance, the microprocessor revolution,
which is bringing computer technology out of the specialized data processing lab into an array of everyday uses. The schools seem barely aware
of what is happening. Microprocessor chips can already be found by the
millions in our automobiles, dishwashers, cameras, microwave ovens, sewing machines, etc. The infiltration is vast while the diffusion of knowledge
about how such chips are created and controlled is limited to a relative
handful of technicians. The potential for the development of an elite of
technicians able to direct if not totally control the nature of human fulfillment looms all the more dangerously, for the danger is not yet recognized by either the schools or the public at large.

What is more, the schools continue to ignore the no longer new
modes of information development and diffusion, that is, television and
radio. While they sometimes use these forms to assist their teaching of the
young (even boring them to tears with too many movies), the young remain passive absorbers of what these devices offer, ready to take a fill-in
quiz over the information that has been delivered and utterly incapable
of actively creating or rationally evaluating the quality of information
thus memorized. The schools do seem to have understood that the active
participation of students in the skills of writing is useful to them in learning how to control the graphemic form of communication for it helps to
show the limits as well as the power of that medium. Nevertheless, they
have ignored the importance of active student involvement with either
radio or television encoding, relegating most of our populace to the position of entertained audience unable to estimate what the information thus
received can do to them. Sadly, we seem to be on the verge of allowing
this to occur again as computer technology advances into every aspect of
our society. A major parameter for the open curriculum must involve not
only the inclusion of an increased array of information-bearing devices,
but the pursuit of creative and evaluative skills related to the active control of such devices.   *understanding*

Another necessary quality of the open curriculum needs to involve
the intention of dealing with uncertainty, that is, of making uncertainty
part of the basic content to be studied. Uncertainties are of many kinds
and a reasonable range of study could be established including, say, the
welfare of big business and society as a whole, the influence of various
technologies on our personal lives, and the tensions between individual
and societal fulfillment caused by big business.

As young children we become certain of what life is and how we
ought to live it; this is probably necessary if we are to have any sense of
stability through childhood. But herein lie the seeds of conflict that have
already led most of us into crises of intragenerational identity, the likes of
which preceding generations have not experienced. To the extent that
rational analyses and control of information devices can help in confront-

ing the uncertainty of our adult lives, the schools ought to take the responsibility of helping us learn how to deal with uncertainties. Instead, for the most part, they continue to fill the heads of youngsters with illusions of certainty based on factual memorization.

Dealing with uncertainties implies still another parameter, that of value development understood not as the indoctrination of values passed on from preceding generations, but as the active involvement of students in the creation of their own values. This means confronting such questions as whether there is a basic human need for values (why should we have values at all?), the desirable interaction between fundamental and relative values (are some values more fundamental than others?), the resolution of major conflicts between individual and societal fulfillment (shall individual values take precedence over societal values?), and so forth. This also means involving students in an ongoing effort to develop societal values with which their own values would need to interact.

The process of value formation, it should be noted, is not an arbitrary one. It requires a continual reappraisal of new conditions and potentials. For example, the increased human potential for more wealth requires the reassessment of the values pertaining to welfare. To sustain the traditional values about welfare in the light of so many greater resources could be immoral.

Two other qualities need to be incorporated into the structure of an open curriculum if present circumstances are to be met effectively. One involves the skills of scientific inquiry, which have made modern technology and the development of new information devices possible. The other is perhaps the most nebulous of the qualities discussed here, that is, decision-making skills such as these are related to the exercise of democratic citizenship and to the ability to reach decisions and take action while surrounded by uncertainty. If the skills of democratic decision making could be equated to the skills of scientific inquiry, the inclusion of decision-making skills in the open curriculum might not be so uncomfortably nebulous. But such an equation is not possible.

In scientific inquiry, the scientist may stipulate his definitions and ignore those usages that do not comply; in democratic decision making, the citizen is beseiged by any number of inconsistent usages which cannot be ignored, for to do so would mean to neglect circumstances important to the understanding of how our human society works. For example, the fact that "free enterprise" is used differently and even inconsistently, not only by different people but by the same person at different times, yields insights regarding what is believed about "free enterprise" and under what diverse circumstances it is employed. To ignore such information could easily lead to the taking of action that is irrelevant to the real problems society may be having with the enactment of the "free enterprise" concept. To simply stipulate a definition would not change how the term is perceived and used by people at large and would probably add to the confusion. The citizen must be a student and observer of society in all of its diversities.

The scientist may choose the concerns to be dealt with to fit his or her best circumstances; the citizen must meet problems under circumstances frequently not of his or her choosing. The scientist may refrain from reaching conclusions until there is sufficient data; the citizen must often decide even when the data is conflicting and inconclusive. The citizen must decide and take action even while doubting the decision. The citizen must operate with ongoing tentativeness as opposed to the scientist's sporadic questioning of conclusions in the light of new data.

Both scientific inquiry skills and decision-making skills are important if effective democratic participation is to persist in an increasingly technical society. While there is already considerable understanding of the nature of scientific inquiry, the skills of democratic decision making remain vague and imprecise.[2] They are no less important for this. All that can be hoped is that the very intent to concentrate scholastic efforts on improving our understanding and implementation of them will help us to do exactly that. We do know that flexibility, a willingness to reconsider decisions, an avidness for seeking out new ways for doing things, an ability to suspend judgment without the individual allowing such inconclusiveness to lead to apathy are traits related to citizen decision making and can serve as starting points in an open curricular plan. Admittedly, we cannot describe these traits in terms of specific performance. We cannot assure a legislature when these will or will not have been accomplished. Nevertheless, they need to become a part of the public's education if ever present and increasing uncertainty is not to mean the demise of democracy.

Implementing an Open Curriculum Design

Although specific content has not been discussed, the following qualities or parameters have been offered as basic to an open curricular structure in our present circumstances:

1. *Information Device*—The development of skills necessary for the action control and evaluation of various information devices with a concomitant knowledge of the ways in which the structures of the devices influence the quality of knowledge.

2. *Uncertainties*—The treatment of a range of uncertainties including the tensions between individual and societal fulfillment.

3. *Value Development*—The active analysis, evaluation, and development of value systems.

4. *Scientific Inquiry*—The development of scientific inquiry skills.

[2] A more complete discussion of the differences between scientific inquiry and democratic decision making may be found in: Wilma S. Longstreet, "Decision Making: The New Social Studies." *Decision-Making: The Heart of Social Studies Instruction, Revisited.* Occasional Paper Number 1, Social Studies Development Center, Indiana University, 1978. pp. 19-32.

5. *Decision Making*—The development of citizen-oriented decision making skills, including the concept of ongoing tentativeness in the light of continuing uncertainty.

If the preceding parameters are to be valid aspects of the curriculum, the metaphorical door cannot be open just slightly. The openness itself must be sufficient so that each individual will be a significant influence on the final version of the curriculum. It is not reasonable to expect to encourage ongoing tentativeness or the willingness to deal with uncertainties while excluding the background and capacities of the students who are the objects of such encouragement. Their input must be an important determinant of the curriculum.

A specific example might help to clarify the development of an open curricular design comprising the preceding parameters. Say that the topics of "Family Life," "Success in Business and Industry," and "Lifelong Achievement" have been selected as the material needing to be dealt with. Each of the five parameters, when paired with the topics creates a format within which students may undertake a series of studies determined by their own background and, to some extent, by the skills they possess or are most interested in. Student "A" in dealing with the intersection of Family Life and Information Devices might explore the ways in which microprocessor chips are being used in the home and the kind of influence these may have over family life. "A" may relate this intersection with the ones on Uncertainities and Value Development by deciding to proceed with a study of the influence of microprocessor chips on the possible future of family life and the sets of values that may be needed to maintain an acceptable quality of family life.

Student "B", on the other hand, may have a father who works for the Internal Revenue Service and therefore is more interested in investigating the kinds of control the IRS has acquired over families because of the diffusion of information devices. Scientific inquiry might lead "B" through an objective investigation of the existing state of affairs. Uncertainties could be developed as areas that have not lent themselves well to objective inquiry and Decision Making could involve "B" in hypothetical cases about taxes to be levied and how these ought to be collected. The problems and uncertainties involved in these governance decisions could be emphasized.

Instead of topics, a discipline such as mathematics could be used as the source of content. In such a case, the implementation of openness still remains viable even though more directed guidance at certain preliminary stages of each new mathematical procedure may be necessary. What is important to understand is that the proportion of directed learnings is held to a minimum rather than, as is now the case, being the dominant *modus operandus*.

For the sake of discussion, let us say that elementary algebraic equations are being studied and that the concept of such equations has been the topic of a lecture by the teacher. Now, each student would develop his or her curriculum based on the intersections of the five parameters with what has been taught. Student "A" explores the employment of algebraic equations in calculators designed for use with family budgets, while student "B" decides to study how the qualities of American family life can be analyzed via computer devices employing simple algebraic equations. Uncertainties for Student "A" may involve the typical conundrums of a family budget and the inadequacies of the equations for the real-world situations. For student "B", it might be an effort to seek an estimate of the error to be expected when trying to describe a particular quality of American family life via a given education. Value Development for "A" could mean trying to find an algebraic equation that would represent the major priorities of the family within the family's budget. For "B", Value Development could mean studying the influence of the algebraic equation on the description of family life and determining, via Scientific Inquiry and Decision Making, to what extent such influence is acceptable.

A diagrammatic outline of the way an open curricular design comprising the five basic parameters would function is shown in Figure 1.

Figure 1. DISCIPLINE/TOPIC/PROBLEM

Basic Parameters	(Determined in Curriculum Development Phase)		Student Input
1. Information Devices	Possible Areas of Directed Teaching	Not Specifiable in Advance ◄------------------	
2. Uncertainties	Possible Areas of Directed Teaching	Not Specifiable in Advance ◄------------------	
3. Value Development	Possible Areas of Directed Teaching	Not Specifiable in Advance ◄------------------	
4. Scientific Inquiry	Possible Areas of Directed Teaching	Not Specifiable in Advance ◄------------------	
5. Decision Making	Possible Areas of Directed Teaching	Not Specifiable in Advance ◄------------------	

[handwritten margin note: meaning → purpose fulfillment]

School Practices for an Open Curriculum

The development of an open curricular design, regardless of the content we may adopt, leaves us a long way from achieving, in the public schools, open education. Even assuming that there would be a willingness to modify the closed structure of today's public school curriculum, it must be recognized that curricular design is only one of several types of structures operating within the present school system. Both the bureaucratic/organizational structure, which involves such administrative activities as scheduling, building design, class function, record keeping, etc., and the teaching structure, which arises from the decisions that teachers make within their own classrooms, have far-reaching effects upon the final nature of the curriculum. If administrators insist on lists of specific objectives, standardized norms, the purchasing of textbooks to be utilized for a minimum five year period, etc., the results of schooling are not likely to reflect an open curricular design; and if teachers insist on students knowing the right answers or awaiting directions before any investigative study is undertaken, the curriculum may appear different but the results are likely to be as usual. In the sixties, numerous curricular revisions, based on concepts and inquiry, were developed. Nevertheless, as Goodlad's survey revealed, teaching structure remained unchanged, being "predominantly telling and questioning . . . with children responding one-by-one or occasionally in chorus."[3] For the most part, the curricular revisions, under such conditions, had almost no impact on the outcomes of schooling.

The different types of structures operating within the public educational system are in constant interaction with each other. This may seem an obvious, perhaps unnecessary statement, and yet, the interaction of education's diverse structures has often been ignored in the past. New techniques such as modular scheduling or new architectural forms such as the open space classroom have been adopted and then exaggeratedly used to indicate that open education had become a reality. All too frequently, the open space classroom has meant sonorous bedlam for the numerous self-contained classes that have found themselves thus unfortunately relocated; and modular scheduling has often supported (perhaps beneficially) the discipline-oriented, closed curricular design. In sum, open education must involve the opening up of the various types of structures operating within the educational system. There needs to be a coordination of "openness" so that there is a consistency among the various school structures in their operations and purposes.

Within the context of the parameters of openness proposed in this paper, the bureaucratic/organizational structure, for example, could profitably modify its record keeping so that the unique studies of individual students could be stored and retrieved by teachers whenever guidance about the scope and depth of youngster's studies were necessary. Inputs into this kind of retrieval system would need to be made by teachers *after the fact,* that is, after students had determined the exact nature of their curricula. Such record keeping would allow other teachers to know about specific experiences youngsters had already had and would enable them to help broaden the experiential base of their students as well as achieve increased continuity of study.

The bureaucratic/organizational structure could also profitably modify its way of evaluating the success of curriculum and instruction. It would refrain, for instance, from adopting nationwide standardized tests on reading and try, instead, to estimate students' abilities to manipulate and communicate a variety of subjects of their own choosing via two or more information devices. A "think tank" group similar to the one sup-

[3] John I. Goodlad. "Schooling and Education." Unpublished paper, 1969. pp. 52-53.

ported by the Rand Corporation could be established annually to assist in the development of this kind of evaluation.

There are numerous teaching modifications which would also support an open curricular design. Among these is the reconception of teaching from an activity which takes a clearly delineated content and manages it in such a way that the content is well learned by students to an activity which involves helping youngsters to develop the final versions of their curricula. In other words, teaching would need to become the act of supporting certain kinds of undertakings, the inputs for which would be largely in the hands of students. Developing and communicating the structures of openness as well as supporting a better quality of student input would need to be major teaching functions.

In terms of specific instructional methodologies, teaching would need to embrace more degrees of freedom than is now ordinarily the case in the public schools. Four major teaching styles—the lecture, the Socratic approach, the discovery mode, and the open-ended approach—may be used to represent the gamut of instructional openness available to teachers. The lecture represents the closed end of the gamut because it limits the student's freedom of response and activity to whatever may occur within his own mind. If the lecture is presented as a set of conclusions which students must memorize for the test, it is at the extreme of limiting degrees of freedom; on the other hand, if it presents a series of problems with which the teacher is struggling, it does offer more degrees of freedom to students even though still within the limits of the lecture format.

The Socratic approach requires the students' active input and yields increased freedom by leading them through ways of thinking that at certain points require their judgment. The students usually end up where the teacher thinks they ought to be, but the degrees of freedom have increased so that some other outcomes are a distinct possibility. The discovery mode increases even further the degrees of freedom available to students in their responses and activities. Via some set of materials, events, etc., students are encouraged to develop their own ideas and/or conclusion. Given the nature of the materials provided, the overall types of responses a student might make, though greatly increased over the Socratic approach, are generally forseeable. Nevertheless, students have considerable control over what is happening. They can be far more creative than in the preceding methods.

The open-ended approach represents the maximum degrees of freedom available instructionally. It can only be achieved if the teacher does not truly know the answers sought and is thus on a par with his/her students. If the teacher does know some of the answers while really believing that other answers, unknown to him/her, are possible the approach decreases in its degree of freedom, but remains primarily open-ended.

The preceding description of four major teaching styles representing a continuum of instructional openness makes quite clear the underlying consistency that the discovery mode and the limited open-ended approach have with the qualities of an open curricular design proposed in this paper. In this regard, it is important to note that the open curriculum does not mean that any activity undertaken by students will do. Activities need to conform to the constraints that have been built into the design. The discovery mode is especially consistent with the structured openness of the design. It should also be kept in mind that while the discovery/ open-ended portion of the continuum would need to dominate for the survival of openness in the curriculum, some limited employment of methods at the closed end of the continuum is necessary if students are not to ignore the power of already acquired knowledge.

It stands to reason that a teacher who is dealing with some estab-lished, widely accepted knowledge, whether it is a simple listing of facts or the presentation of a set of procedures, will, at that point, use a method involving fewer degrees of freedom for student performance than would be necessary if he or she were involved in helping students reach decisions about how they will develop the intersections of their study. This is not merely an eclectic view of teaching, but rather a recognition that the Socratic approach, and especially the lecture, can serve as powerful ways of helping students understand the instruments, concepts, theories, etc. that they are to use when undertaking studies of their own design. It is really a question of retaining a proportional mix of instructional ap-proaches such that the nature of the curriculum is validly represented in the actual learning experiences students have in the classroom.

The consistent interaction of administrative effort, instructional methodology and curricular design is a prerequisite to any significant change in school study. It is all the more necessary for an open curricular design that in its very nature avows *uncertainty*. Such openness can be effectively undone if either administrators or teachers follow the tradi-tional modes of operating which posit and often require *certainty*.

Coming to Terms with Curriculum as a Human Agenda

Virginia M. Macagnoni

To be on the cutting edge is to see the curriculum as a human agenda. Such a curriculum calls for the continuous release and development of the person as a holistic being. The person is in the process of becoming. He is not a finished creature. His potentials are physical, emotional, social, intellectual, aesthetic and spiritual.[1] The order can be viewed as hierarchical to an extent, moving from survival potentials to the more transcendent ones. However, the hierarchy breaks down, because the potentials are not mutually exclusive. They always interact. Experience evoking any one response calls up all of the others.

The purpose of schooling is to enable the person to perceive and to integrate his six potentials as he encounters the problems of his existence that are real to him at the moment. An assumption underlying this chapter is that formal schooling just gets people started in systematic learning. The person has to continue his growth independently, though he may return to some type of formal schooling at crucial points in his life. The curriculum as a human agenda anticipates lifelong education.

It is the proper activity of the curriculum leader in the home setting to influence the communication, conceptualization, clarification, and acceptance of humane perspectives as purpose of education. Those who design curriculum must insist upon purposes that have been understood and agreed upon by all who are involved. In addition, those who design curriculum have an obligation to insist that they be given an opportunity to participate in the formulation of purposes. Once there is consensus and commitment, the designers can clarify and translate purposes into alternative curriculum designs. It is the responsibility of the curriculum leader to see that designs result in purposive activity in educational settings.

What we must not overlook is that design as a process is a basic human act within which there is concern for qualities such as form, balance, continuity, and movement in relation to human purpose and function. The design process, then, results in the life-enhancing aesthetic product. To design a curriculum as a human agenda is to use the design process to create varieties of settings within which learners can attain form as "that radiance from within, to which a shape attains when in a given situation it realizes itself complete."[2] The learner becomes his own aesthetic product, continuously producing something new in the process of becoming. The curriculum as interface between the person and his potentials is catalyst for creativity.

There can be no one design for the curriculum as a human agenda. As educators, if we believe in schools where persons in a pluralistic society can further their becoming, we have to reject all attempts that coerce us into accepting a single modality for viewing curriculum. Even though there is little consensus on meanings of curriculum, established views seem to be variations of the one basic design dwelling on predetermined objectives and systematic and unidimensional movement from objectives

---

[1] For another description of six aspects of humanness, see: Arthur W. Foshay. "Toward a Humane Curriculum." In: *Essays on Curriculum*. New York: Teachers College Press, 1975. pp. 151-71.

[2] Bernard Berensen. *Aesthetics and History*. New York: Doubleday, 1948. p. 72.

to selection and organization of content and activities to evaluation. Specification of behavioral objectives in separate subject matter areas with little consideration for value orientation or the part in relationship to the organic whole is often viewed as curriculum in its entirety. Emphasis is on external variables, empirical verification, and middle class values.

It is not that this basic paradigm has not served us in the past, but like all paradigms it has its unique weaknesses, which are especially evident in today's world of rapidly changing cultural realities. The world of curriculum making dealing with today's cultural realities in practical school situations is a complex human enterprise, requiring a variety of modalities. The undergirding cultural reality is that education is deeply affected by rapid change and by the predominant presence of discontent. Many see the school as a potential agent for generating restorative powers in their lives, and when this does not happen, they become further alienated from themselves and from the educational process. The educational effort is inseparable from the societal effort.[3] What society is not providing, we have come to expect schools to offer. Problems of society become the problems of the school. Yet schooling alone cannot compensate for the lack of humanization in the social order. However, humanizing the social order does indeed involve humanizing the curriculum, and vice versa. Rugg[4] said in 1927 that not once in the history of the United States had the school curriculum caught up with the dynamic content of life. We believe that much of this lag still persists.

In our over-dependence upon a single view of curriculum we are not only excluding other viewpoints, but we are also discouraging fresh perspectives. Viewpoints that depart from the pre-established parameters of the past need to be solicited and criticized to the benefit of all.

There certainly is a need for sustained investigation of newer forms of curriculum more reflective of the present cultural realities which do indeed "surround us and hound us with their urgency—hunger, strife, fear, ignorance, injustice." Witness the lives of the Does, Ruth the Zoomer, Dave, Bruce, Rico, Juan, Mrs. Spencer, Grandma, Helen Keller. No single societal plan or curriculum design will ensure the ideal fulfillment of human potential. We can only try to create the curriculum as a human agenda from a heuristic perspective which will permit the generation of many forms. Even while we do this, we must assure ourselves that the forms we create inspire even more dynamic forms for the future. Intentionality, fluidity, multidimensionality and creativity are required. The way is not easy. The remainder of this chapter presents an initial view of the curriculum as a human agenda. Six potentials of the person

[3] Virginia M. Macagnoni. "Democratization and Curriculum Renewal: An Exploratory Interdisciplinary Framework for Cooperative Educational Planning." Eugene: University of Oregon, ERIC Clearinghouse on Educational Management, 1973.

[4] Harold Rugg. "The School Curriculum, 1825-1890." *Curriculum Making: Past and Present.* Part I, Twenty-sixth Yearbook, National Society for the Study of Education. Bloomington, Illinois: Public School Publishing Company, 1927.

as a holistic being in the process of becoming are sketched tentatively. Integration of these potentials is a function of personal intentionality, a concept which must be emphasized. Seven propositions relate intentionality to the potentials with reference to schooling. The concepts of perfectibility and temporality are discussed briefly. Perfectibility is related to the curriculum in two ways, concern for goals and for purposive activity.

The Six Potentials of the Person

The Physical. The physical potential is the person's overall awareness of the self as a physical being. The body is the physical form that contains the human energy from which the action of the moment emanates and evolves into further becoming. Leonard presents a dramatic portrayal of body as "ultimate athlete" within reach of everyone.

. . . body is spirit, that its every cell re-enacts the dance of love and death, that in the relationships of these cells we may trace the anatomy of all relationship. There is no single ultimate athlete; there are millions waiting to be born. Running, falling, flying, diving—each of us may get in shape or even set new records. But the body of the Ultimate Athlete—fat or thin, short or tall—summons us beyond these things toward the birth of the self, and, in time, the unfolding of a new world.[5]

Schooling which involves growth in physical potential is concerned with awarenesses such as the following:

1. The person as body.

2. What constitutes the body, its systems, functions, and interconnections.

3. The possibility for optimal health.

4. The possibility for optimal physiological efficiency.

5. The possibility for optimal movement.

In an overall model for viewing physical education, Jewett uses movement as a central focus. Some 22 concepts delineate man as master of himself, man in space, and man in a social world. Fitness, performance, and transcendence characterize each cluster of concepts.[6]

The Emotional. The emotional potential is the person's overall awareness that he has emotions which can be experienced and enjoyed. To be human is to experience feeling from immobilizing fear to liberating hope to ecstasy. To be human is to experience both joy and tragedy and to acknowledge that it takes both to deepen the meaning of life. Schooling which involves growth in emotional potential is concerned with:

1. The person as a sentient being, a sum of "the felt responses of our sense organs to the environment, of our proprioceptive mechanisms to

[5] George Leonard. *The Ultimate Athlete.* New York: Avon Books, 1975.

[6] Ann E. Jewett and Marie R. Mullen. *Curriculum Design Purposes and Processes in Physical Education Teaching and Learning.* Washington, D.C.: American Association of Health, Physical Education and Recreation, 1977.

internal changes, and of the organism as a whole."[7] Langer establishes feeling in the broad sense as the generic base of all mental experience.[8]

2. The person as an emoting being, expressing what is internalized.

3. The person's repertoire of emotions—the love-hate, hope-fear, joy-grief, proximity-distance continuums.

4. The person's special awareness of playfulness as humor, manifest joy, and spontaneity.[9]

5. The person's awareness of his reality orientation, that is, his contextual relation to the environment.

6. The person's exercised use of value orientation, the relationships among her beliefs, feelings, and behaviors.

The Social. The social potential is the person's overall awareness of the self as a social being,[10] that one's very personhood is developed in interaction with others. Caring community is essential for one's optimal development. Contributing to this potential is our awareness that new patterns of human association are possible in today's world, indeed that they may be necessary to maintain life as we know it. Our institutions can facilitate the opportunity for these new patterns to emerge. We have a moral obligation to change those schooling contexts which inhibit the development of awarenesses such as the following:

1. Gregariousness as the person's basic inclination to be with others.

2. Empathy as the person's capacity for participating in another's feelings.

3. Altruism as the person's capacity for uncalculated consideration of the needs of others.

4. Collaboration as the person's capacity for willing cooperation with an instrumentality with which he is not immediately connected in a societal or group effort.

5. Personal heritage as access to the products of cultural evolution.

The Intellectual. The intellectual potential is the person's awareness of the nature of her own mind. It is awareness that through the use of the mind one can integrate the six potentials in one's human environment. Even though the way the mind works remains a mystery, we do know enough to say that the mind contains discrete. abilities. Schooling which is concerned with intellectual growth views the following abilities as potentials to be developed:

[7] Susanne K. Langer. *Philosophical Sketches.* Baltimore: Johns Hopkins Press, 1962. p. 18.

[8] Susanne K. Langer. *Mind: An Essay on Human Feeling.* Baltimore: Johns Hopkins Press, 1972.

[9] Nina Lieberman. *Playfulness.* New Jersey: Academic Press, 1977.

[10] See: Virginia Macagnoni. *Social Dimension of the Self as an Open System: A Curriculum Design.* Research Bulletin of the Florida Research and Development Council, 5 (2); Summer 1969. Gainesville, Florida. The University of Florida.

1. Sensors (eyes, ears, thermoceptors, proprioceptors) which report the effects of the environment.

2. Information as symbolic representation of events.

3. Memory as a storage process determined by the nature of events.

4. Logic as an internal consistency check.

5. Imagination as a process of self-generating events independent of sensors.

6. Effectors as body (muscles, bone, connective tissue) generation of events.

7. Will as determination by choice of imagination and effector generation of consistent and complete subsets of events.

8. Connectors as propagating information between the sensors, memory, imagination, logic and will.[11]

The Aesthetic. The aesthetic quality of the human condition is described by Broudy as four kinds of responses.[12] Schooling which involves growth in aesthetic potential is concerned with these responses:

1. The response to form as the recognition of the purely formal qualities (or properties) of the aesthetic object. This object has properties recognizable to the extent that the object can be classified. The object may be an animate or an inanimate entity, a process or a product. Hence, the object may be: (1) a person; (2) a living thing, e.g., a tree, an animal; (3) an inanimate thing, e.g., a rock, a film, a lesson plan; (4) a process, e.g., a dance, a teaching episode, a political conflict; (5) a product, e.g., a poem, a plan, anything that is the result of a process; and (6) varying combinations of the preceding.

2. The technical response as that response which involves the recognition of the technique(s) used in producing the aesthetic object. Here the person becomes interested, for example, in what the artist used to produce his product; how he used composition, brushwork and color; how he organized for his task.

3. The sensuous responses which acknowledge and seek the appeal of the aesthetic object to the senses. Here the person becomes aware of her own perceptual processes. She notices color, texture, movement. It is through the perceptual processes that the person literally "takes in" the aesthetic form. She develops images in her mind.

4. The expressive response which is a summary of the other three aesthetic responses. In the expressive response, the person assesses the meaning of his encounter with the form. He interprets and evaluates what his senses report to him, incorporating the form as his own experience.

The application of Broudy's four aesthetic responses is especially use-

[11] John David Garcia. *The Moral Society.* New York: Julian Press, 1971. pp. 50-51.
[12] Harry S. Broudy. In: Arthur W. Foshay, *op. cit.,* pp. 163-64.

ful in enabling the person to perceive self as aesthetic form. Perceiving self in this way requires experiencing the complex interrelationships among the six potentials. The person builds upon them. She organizes and develops techniques to produce a product. She relates technique and environmental force. She responds to herself as product. She interprets and evaluates what her senses report, always incorporating new perceptions into her awareness and redirecting her experience. She gains the control of the artist in relation to her potentials.

The Spiritual. The spiritual potential assumes the other five potentials, but rises above the level of the senses so that even physical movement may be transformed into a quality of abstract beauty. It is the person's overall awareness of the self as holistic form in the continuous process of becoming. It is awe at the realization of one's interconnectedness with all that is in the process of becoming, nature and human nature, and one's responsibility therein. It is awe at the power of mind or intentionality when brought into collaboration with nature and with creation. Not only are the potentials perceived as aesthetic form, energized and energizing, but intentionality is extended to pursuit of truth and participation in the quest for perfectibility to the extent that it is possible for temporal beings in the finite state. Schooling which involves growth in spiritual potential is concerned with awareness such as:

1. The incomprehensible as ultimate questions of life, birth, death.

2. Organism or unity as the coming together of separates to form a complete entity, the person seeing the self in its continuous connections or nexus.[13]

3. Individuation as the uniqueness of the person's process of becoming. Though persons are in relation to each other, no two human beings are precisely alike. Each person has a special quality which is needed in the human community.

4. Cosmogenesis as the person's becoming in relation to the becoming of the universe. Realization of potentials as a unique person capable of higher level moral judgments may be essential to the continuous becoming of the universe.

5. Creativity as becoming which is advance into novelty.[14] It is participation in the evoking of the new. Creativity is the universal of universals in prototypic development.[15]

6. Reverence for life as an honoring of all that is in the state of becoming.

[13] A concept developed by: Alfred N. Whitehead. *Process and Reality.* New York: Free Press Paperback Edition, 1969. p. 32.

[14] *Ibid.,* pp. 25-26.

[15] E. Paul Torrance. "Creatively Gifted and Disadvantaged Gifted Students." Julian Stanley, William George and Cecilia Solano, editors. *The Gifted and the Creative: A Fifty-Year Perspective.* Baltimore: Johns Hopkins University Press, 1977. pp. 173-96.

7. Celebration as an honoring of life as exalted expression, characterized by physical, emotional, social, intellectual and aesthetic unity. Celebration cannot be forced and is most often preceded by aesthetic experience. Heightened awareness becomes available to persons experiencing celebration in community with others.

8. Forgiveness as realization that we are imperfect creatures seeking higher levels of awareness, "perfection in a world of imperfection."[16]

In summary, we have attempted to sketch the six potentials in a way that would enable the reader to develop personal meanings for them. Next we give our attention to the concept of intentionality which is the integrating force for developing the potentials.

Intentionality

Basic to the construct of the six potentials is the idea that schooling can facilitate the person's perceiving these in their interconnectedness and incorporating them into consciousness. Intentionality as the human capacity to perceive the six potentials is "the structure which gives meaning to experience."[17] Intentionality is the person's capacity to have intentions, to use the imagination in seeing emerging possibilities for each potential. Intentionality is at the heart of awareness. It is all of the components of the mind working together through an act of will to produce higher levels of awareness. Intentionality involves wish and will. Because we as humans have this uniquely human capacity we can form, mold and change ourselves in relation to each other. Husserl, in defining intentionality, describes learning as follows:

Learning is not the accumulation of scraps of knowledge. It is a growth where every act of knowledge develops the learner, thus making him capable of even more complex objectives—and the object growth in complexity parallels the subjective growth in capacity.[18]

Learning is gaining control over one's creative becoming. Rather than an accumulation of knowledge, it is the multidimensional selection of content to serve the learner in more adequately perceiving and integrating the six potentials. Learning for Ruth the Zoomer is a growth where every act of knowledge, every encounter with the curriculum, develops her as a person, thus making her capable of even more complex objectives and advances into novelty.

Propositions and Strategies

Interpretation of intentionality as a concept in relation to the six

[16] Ruth Nielsen. "The Imperfect Child in a World of Perfection." Keynote Address at the 1965 International Conference on Science and the Arts in Education. The Danish Section of the New Education Fellowship, Vejen, Denmark.

[17] Rollo May. *Love and Will.* New York: Norton, 1969. p. 223.

[18] J. Quentin Lauer, S. J. *The Triumph of Subjectivity.* New York: Fordham University Press, 1972. p. 105. (Translation of Husserl.)

potentials is presented in the form of propositions and strategies as a way of approaching the curriculum as a human agenda.

Propositions	Strategies
1. The six potentials of the self can be translated into intentions as a part of a curriculum design. However, the learner, as the human structure which gives meaning to experience, has to be reached. He has to develop the will to have these intentions.	1. Teacher endeavors (a) to create learner awareness of the six potentials, (b) to encourage exploration of possibilities, (c) to reach the learner with the intention of persuading him to formulate a specific intention. (The teacher views the curriculum as an aesthetic form and continues to engage in design as a human act as he creates the environment for learning.)
2. The learner can develop the awareness of the six potentials, indeed, she must develop the awareness if she is to make any decision to direct her energy toward experiential involvement with problems. Schooling can provide the context within which this can occur.	2. Teacher and learner (a) respond to learner needs, using criteria from the six potentials, once learner awareness of the potentials has been established and (b) focus on a specific aspect of a potential, toward which the learner can direct her energy—toward which she can become involved experientially.
3. In experiential involvement, the learner can deliberately extend his capacity to the six potentials. He can shape increasingly higher levels of these. He can wish or will as a means of generating the energy to get started.	3. Teacher and learner focus on (a) one of the six potentials relating it to the other five and (b) development of the "will" to shape increasingly higher levels of the selected potentials.
4. Schooling can provide the opportunity for the learner to incorporate into consciousness the six potentials of the self as unified personal meaning.	4. Teacher motivates the learner to use consciousness in ways suggested by the four aesthetic responses. These are (a) sensing the properties or the formal qualities of the potential as "form"—e.g., sensing how strength appears as form, (b) sensing techniques which produce strength as form, as well as those which attenuate it, (c) becoming aware of sensory responses to strength as form,—what it looks like, feels like, (d) evaluating sensory responses to the form and incorporating these into one's consciousness.
5. The learner can assume charge of her own becoming, within limits of course. The decision can be made to use one's own imagination to see emerging possibilities, indeed, that the	5. Teacher motivates the learner (a) to assume charge of her own becoming —e.g., her independent powers, (b) to use her own imagination to see emerging possibilities, and (c) to "make con-

Propositions	Strategies

coming day in school can be used to create some aspect of one's own becoming. The curriculum can offer possibilities toward which one can reach.

nections" as she moves through the schooling.

6. Schooling can provide the context within which the learner justifies his choices and verifies and validates his meanings.

6. Teacher questions the learner with regard to his choices and challenges him toward the process of verifying and validating his meanings.

7. The six potentials offer possibilities for foci or organizers which can facilitate the selection and organization of content for curricula from: a) the person's interest, b) the situational context, c) the disciplines of knowledge, and d) the persistent human problems and concerns. The selections can be those which provide rich and satisfying involvement . . . opportunity to develop toward individual potentials. The curriculum can be a human agenda in a very real sense.

7. Teacher responds to the curriculum design as an aesthetic form as she incorporates her responses into an instructional plan which she wishes to implement. Decisions about some of the following are made: (a) foci and organizers, (b) questions, directional objectives, ways to get started, (c) strands of available curricula, (d) media for learner involvement far beyond the ordinary printed and audiovisual materials, extended to all human, natural and technical resources, (e) climate for learning, (f) various models of her own behavior as supporter, motivator, co-learner, (g) modes of inquiry based on the nature of the mind and the subject matter, (h) particular benchmarks by which evaluation of the six zones of potential can be conducted.

The decisions that the teacher does make energize her thought processes as she thinks through her design for purposive activity. The plan remains open-ended.

Perfectibility

Perfectibility is a qualitative state of the six potentials. The person is a unity of potentials. As an incomplete creature, she naturally strives for higher levels of functioning. Yet it is not likely that she will attain the "perfect" with regard to any of the six potentials. Perfectibility can be viewed as a continuum for each of the six potentials ranging from relative absence through increasingly higher degrees of perfectibility. Humans have come a long way in their evolutionary journey. However, we are not yet all that we would hope to be. None of us is perfect. Empathy and forgiveness are essential human qualities. Perfectibility in the person is related to perfectibility in the human species.

Temporality

Humans are temporal beings. Living as a person implies a destiny in time. History can be viewed as the record of human potential. The person can perceive the past while he lives in the present. The choices that he makes in the present become his future. It is in the present that the person strives to integrate his six potentials. He strives for increasingly higher levels of perfection.

Perfectibility and the Curriculum in Schools

Perfectibility can be a way of viewing aspects of the curriculum.

Goals. For example, we could look for the presence or absence of goals dealing with each of the six potentials. The school either does or does not accept this challenge. The "more perfect" school would deal with all of the potentials in a qualitative way. This would be true for all of the subject areas in the curriculum. The "less perfect" school would leave out some of the potentials. Leaving out any one of the potentials would suggest a less qualitative experience for those being educated.

Purposive Activity. We could also look for the presence or absence of purposive activities related to the six potentials in schools. The activity is the context within which the person experiences purpose and goals.

A defined problem is helpful to focus activity. Hunger was the problem selected for the 1976-77 Global Issues Project Program sponsored by the National Association for Foreign Student Affairs[19] in the United States under a contract with the Agency for International Development. Because educational materials are available on this topic in the U.S.A., I will use hunger as an example to examine the process of planning for purposive activity related to the six potentials in schools.

Try to imagine yourself as a teacher or as a curriculum designer engaged in such planning. You realize that you must have sharp focus in order to treat a problem as broad as hunger.

At some point, with your students in mind, you think through questions such as the following as you relate hunger to the six potentials with the intention of motivating students to raise similar questions.

1. *The Physical*—How does hunger make me feel, physically? Does the kind of activity in which I am involved make a difference? How does hunger affect my strength? My movement?

2. *The Emotional*—Does hunger limit the emotions I can feel? The way I handle my emotions? Does hunger affect my playfulness? My ability to maintain a reality orientation? My ability to act on what I believe?

<hr />

[19] *Global Issue: Hunger, Is It Ingenuity or Wisdom Which Has Failed.* Packet distributed by Barbara Dirks, NAFSA Representative on Global Issues, University of Georgia Campus, Athens, Georgia, May 4, 1977.

3. *The Social*—Can I be gregarious when I am hungry? Extend empathy to others? Collaborate with others in an important effort?

4. *The Intellectual*—Does hunger affect my mind? Is it true that a lack of nutrition can cause brain damage? Can I trust my own sensing when I am hungry? My own logic? My own imagination? Can my mind serve its integrating function when I am hungry?

5. *The Aesthetic*—Does hunger affect my capacity to perceive the form and the formal properties of objects in my environment? Does it affect my capacity to translate form into personal meaning?

6. *The Spiritual*—Does hunger affect how I raise and answer the ultimate questions of life, birth, death? Can anyone behave as a whole person if hunger is great? What effect does hunger have on creativity? Can anyone celebrate when he is hungry?

These questions, of course, can be extended to how others feel—people who live in the present, those who lived in the past, and those who will live in the future. Literature, the visual arts, the theater, history, the sciences, health and physical education, are all subjects which assist the student in answering such questions. The media—newspapers, the radio, television—and interpersonal contact with a variety of people also assist the student in answering such questions. Focus of the questions can be extended not only through time—past, present, and future as frame of reference—but also from the local community to the world community, socially and geographically.

Conclusion

It was my choice in this chapter to move from theoretical rationale to the shaping of purposive activity in schools. I believe that we do not have to wait on a full curriculum design to implement the ideas presented. We are obligated to provide purposive experience in schools in each of the arenas suggested by the six human potentials—the physical, the emotional, the social, the intellectual, the aesthetic and the spiritual. Each arena is a valid one for purposive experience. Each discipline contributes to the person's understanding and developing of each potential. In school experience the person should be able to use his or her consciousness and intentionality to assist in developing the potential under consideration, separately, and in relation to the other potentials.

I have attempted to communicate a conception and rationale for a humane education as lifelong process. This is the curriculum as a human agenda, as the interface of the person and the external forces that influence his or her becoming. We cannot afford to exclude each other in this awesome responsibility. The long term result is human intentionality moving beyond awareness to lifelong learning within which past, present, and future merge.

Coming to Terms with the Individual as Culture Maker: A Pluralistic Perspective

Carlos J. Ovando

The present system of education is mirrored in most efforts to develop lifelong learning. Programs and models that have emerged as a result of policy deliberations tend to suggest a "business as usual" attitude. Rather than perceiving lifelong learning as a socially revitalizing concept with potential for moving all humanity toward fulfillment, programmatic emphasis to date continues to be on a regressive incrementalism that preserves the inequities of the status quo while promising significant changes. In taking such a direction we may be binding the mass of society, but especially the rich resources of minority groups, to learning structures and assumptions of the nineteenth century.

The "business as usual" approach to lifelong learning tends to emphasize basic skill development, training for occupations and career changes, use of leisure time, preparation for social and religious volunteerism, as well as institutional aims to keep educational facilities filled and productive.

New players (both adults and young children) have been added to the educational game, but most of the rules regarding certification and resource availability remain the same. Adult learners may be attending night school to become legal secretaries, to get an associate of arts degree in data processing, to become a mechanic, to get a beautician's license, and so on. These are valid endeavors which may meet particular needs, but in and of themselves they do not constitute an adequate foundation for the creation of a learning society with equal access for all. They merely demonstrate the extent to which the dominant social values have co-opted and institutionalized the concept of learning. The position of the learner within the process remains that of an object to be manipulated and filled instead of as a subject with responsibility for creating one's own history. As Eric Fromm has noted, freedom must be more than the absence of restrictions. Fulfillment means:

> . . . freedom to create and to construct, to wonder and to venture. Such freedom requires that the individual be active and responsible, not a slave or a well-fed cog in the machine. . . . It is not enough that men are not slaves; if social conditions further the existence of automatons, the result will not be love of life, but love of death.[1]

[1] Eric Fromm. *The Heart of Man.* New York: Harper & Row, Publishers, 1964. pp. 52-53.

Realization of the potential of lifelong learning demands a recognition that *the primary function of education is the creation of responsible culture makers*. For curricula to be in tune with a changing world, learning content, process and style need to be articulated with the individual's potential role as a culture maker and a participant in social history in mind. As such, knowledge must be linked to well-articulated values before creative and responsible decisions can be made. The currently predominant emphasis on short-range, personal goals designed to make people fit into existing slots and frameworks are dysfunctional to most efforts to develop a society of responsible culture makers. When learning is viewed in terms of existing schooling models, we find the results to be the development of skills for survival, certification for jobs and professions, and socialization to the institution itself. Learners are consequently disadvantaged by schooling in the sense that they are not encouraged to see themselves on the cutting edge of knowledge and culture creation. It is not that they are without value to the social conscience and have nothing to contribute, it is that they and the total society are prevented from being more.

While the failure of schools to foster learning as a tool for culture building and history making is restrictive for the whole society and for the individuals within it, the failure poses a special problem for minorities. Insofar as culture and history are perpetuated and changed incrementally, the majority culture is the one fostered. It is possible for citizens of the majority to see themselves involved in the making of the culture, at least vicariously. But for members of minority groups even the vicarious attachment is strained. The situation makes the avowed aim of recognizing and achieving a level of pluralism within our culture which will incorporate the contributions of all a hollow ideal, casting wispy shadows on cave walls.

Social worth via certification. In most societies what persons might become is determined not only by their knowledge and skills but by accompanying certificates or diplomas. For some, these credentials provide the necessary status, money, and decision-making powers for affiliation with the dominant class. For others, certificates merely keep them out of poverty. Still others, including disproportionate numbers of Blacks, Chicanos, Puerto Ricans, and Native Americans, are marginal members of society who lack some or all of the necessary resources to obtain formal instruction. Consequently, the right credentials for successful upward mobility are not available to them.

When marginal persons do get certificates, the vast majority tend to be limited to low status certification slots. Typical programs designed to meet the needs of depressed minorities stress basic survival skills and social conformity rather than total human development. Any suggestion that minority cultural patterns or minority individuals can contribute to the modification of culture is missing. Policy makers often see minorities as socioeconomic pariahs who need to be psychologically, socially, and culturally modified in order to fit into the normal social stream. The Lifelong Learning Report to Congress reflects this view.

Disadvantaged urban youth who have left the school system, and who have unsatisfactory memories of their experiences there, are among the least likely groups to continue their learning. The consequence may be trouble for themselves and for society; low skills and poor paying jobs, lack of self-understanding and problems within the family, an insufficient grasp of the responsibilities of citizenship, and difficulties with the law and regulatory agencies of society.[2]

While the chicken-egg nature of self-fulfillment vs. social harmony can be argued, the importance of individuals seeing themselves as culture makers is an ideologically important concept that can not be escaped. Within a democratic system the opportunity for each individual to develop and contribute must be nurtured. Part of self-acceptance is bound to one's cultural identification and the recognition given that heritage. While as a society we have given lip service to the idea of contributions from all segments of our diverse heritage to the resultant American culture, the reality suggests more acceptance of some heritages and the ignoring or outright rejection of others. This is pedagogically and socially damaging, and indefensible. If we are to become a nation of culture makers, the so-called "culturally disadvantaged" as well as non-disadvantaged learners need to reflect on and to interfere critically and responsibly with the existing social order.

Currently, the payoff of successful formal learning in our society is not necessarily better human beings and an improving social system, but a certificate of occupational and sociocultural worth marketable within the advantaged segment of society. Formal education in the United States is an extension of the consumer ethos as applied to learning. This is the same world view that has helped to create a racially, culturally and economically inequitable society in the first place.

Social worth beyond certification: minority learning movements. The ability of traditional formal schooling to provide meaningful learning opportunities for our pluralistic society has been strongly challenged from a variety of minority positions. Each challenge is based in a powerful sociopolitical stance regarding the larger social structure. Paulston and LeRoy note that it is collective social class and ethnic movements using nonformal education programs that contribute to structural change:

Ethnic movements offer equally fertile settings for the creation of "liberating" nonformal education programs. Ethnic groups resisting acculturation and/or seeking cultural revitalization and attempting to redefine "who they are," as well as "proper" relations with the dominant society, often initially attempt to make formal schools more responsive to their new goals and awareness. But as formal schools in equilibrium-state societies are highly "functionalist" and acculturative,

---
[2] Penny Richardson. *Lifelong Learning and Public Policy.* Unpublished report. U.S. Department of Health, Education, and Welfare, 1978. p. iv.

members of ethnic revival movements often become resigned to the need for full control of the content and style of their children's schooling.[3]

Within the context of the American civil rights movement, certain minority elements have internalized the belief that it is impossible for them to maintain their identity and also become an integral aspect of the "in" majority. Movements such as ASPIRA, Brown Berets, Movimiento Estudiantil Chicano de Aztlán (MECHA), Black Panthers, and the American Indian Movement (AIM) illustrate the acting out of such a philosophy. These groups have opted to legitimize their marginal position by declaring that they can develop individual and collective self-worth through the creation of symbols and through a commitment to the understanding of their existential reality. These groups have generated types of learning that are directly linked to their perceptions of social, political and economic realities. The realization that all education is value-laden and stems from a particular view of humankind has provided rationale for the creation of ethnically controlled and operated learning contexts. For example, Fields documents how Chicano students who were totally alienated from formal schooling became enthusiastic and effective learners once their lives were linked to the sociopolitical realities of their ethnic group via association with the Brown Berets. In fact, these young people learned to deal with middle-class society quite effectively through the manipulation of the media and social help organizations.[4] Unquestionably, movements such as AIM, MECHA, the Black Panthers, and the Brown Berets can serve as types of catalysts for social transformation. They call attention to and act upon the absence of harmony between humanistic values and technical/material progress. Their antiestablishment function is important to a society in need of messengers reminding us of the less than perfect nature of the educational system.

The bilingual-multicultural education movement is also based in minority self-assertion, but it does not constitute a total rejection of the social structure at large. Rather, the intent is to force the system to live up to its own ideals. It diverges from a central tenet of traditional formal schooling in its belief that heterogeneity rather than homogeneity should be a goal of schooling and that the curricula should reflect the learners' reality and not only the power holders' reality. Therefore, bilingual-multicultural education has much to commend it as a critical part of a diverse learning environment. The acknowledgement of the legitimacy of diverse linguistic and cultural traditions produces added dignity for diverse cultural groups, and it suggests the possibility of building future society and culture from a positive base—that of acceptance of one's own

[3] Rolland G. Paulston and Gregory LeRoy. "Strategies for Nonformal Education." *Teacher College Record* 76 (4): 593; May 1975.

[4] Rona M. Fields. *The Brown Berets: A Participant Observation Study of Social Action in the Schools of Los Angeles.* University of Southern California, 1970. Unpublished Ph.D. dissertation. *passim.*

sociocultural background. In addition, bilingual-multicultural education provides a context of creative tension that has the potential to affect the structure of schools and society. In its attempt to bring egalitarian principles into behavior-forming institutions such as schools, it requires a confrontation of basic democratic concepts:

> Equality of treatment, or equality of opportunity? The rights of groups, or the rights of individuals? Unity in order to maintain freedom or freedom to maintain diversity?[5]

While more radical groups such as AIM and Black Panthers may have tended toward a "separate but equal" philosophy, and while the bilingual-multicultural movement is generally characterized by a belief in civil rights and social harmony through mutual respect and understanding, the Reverend Jesse Jackson's Operation PUSH illustrates another challenge to traditional modes of learning. In this case, however, the focus of the challenge is much more clearly aimed at the individual than at the institution. The objective might well be described as achievement through assertive but well-mannered infiltration of the system.[6]

Operation PUSH is open to the possibility of change and improvement of the learning structures, but its primary focus is on the total psychological involvement of the community and on the development of a spiritual reaffirmation of commitment to learning. It is imperative that the individual be motivated toward self-improvement through successful learning *regardless* of the level of quality of the learning institutions. The structure of the PUSH program itself is based in mind sets—the creation of a "love triangle" between the home, the church, and the school. It is an affirmation of self as culture maker from the perspective of one celebrating and accepting the strength of the black subculture that has been incorporated as part of the national history. The movement demonstrates not only a need to, but also a way to link productively the individual and society at the local level. Marginal groups can easily drift into the belief that they can have only that which the power elite wants to give them. However, Operation PUSH is an attempt to force individuals to take clear responsibility for their personal history. Structuring programs in such a way that they are widely accessible is crucial to the development of pluralistic learning programs. Jackson's philosophy, however, calls attention to the fact that no learning system can be perfect, and therefore that the development of a learning mind set is as important as the development of programs or policies which look good on paper.

Configurations for Becoming Culture Makers

All three types of minority movements discussed above remind us

---

[5] Carlos J. Ovando. "School Implications of the Peaceful Latino Invasion." *Phi Delta Kappan*. December 1977. p. 231.

[6] Eugene Eubanks and Daniel V. Levine. "The PUSH Program for Excellence in Big-City Schools." *Phi Delta Kappan*. January 1978, pp. 383-87.

that much of what normally occurs in school is incongruous with the sociocultural rhythm of life experienced outside its walls. Educational experiences often miseducate rather than strengthen the natural perceptions which the learner has about home, community and school. As noted in *Learning to Be:*

> Education suffers basically from the gap between its content and the living experiences of its pupils, between the systems of values that it preaches and the goals set up by society, between its ancient curriculum and the modernity of science. Link education to life, associate it with concrete goals, establish a close relationship between society and economy, invent or rediscover an education system that fits its surroundings—surely this is where the solution must be sought.[7]

The American education system has undoubtedly failed to address itself with sufficient energy and conviction to the crucial socioeconomic and political issues which arise out of the multiethnic history of the nation. Cultural homogenization has been the stated or unstated goal, while at the same time people are highly segregated according to age, ethnicity, occupation, and social class. This attempted overlay of conformity among relatively isolated groups is counterproductive to lifelong learning. Instead of regarding individual, cultural or group differences as obstacles, a pluralistic learning society should have as its basic goal the ideal of unity through diversity, with all members viewed as contributors to its history and culture.

Of paramount importance in developing lifelong learning experiences within the framework of American society is a redefinition and redistribution of human resources. Unfortunately, our educational system has failed in utilizing many of the potential resources for interactive learning. In the traditional method of instruction, the teacher has been perceived as the principal valid learning source and the students, consciously or otherwise, become passive consumers of the learning process.[8] In formal learning situations, the teacher controls the learning environment in an effort to transmit the "right" values, attitudes, skills, perceptions and behaviors. Although much learning can and does occur through the interaction between such societal actors as the individual, the group, and the culture, the formal education system makes little attempt to acknowledge or to understand these configurations. Certainly, to evaluate the quality of the relationship between the individual and society, one needs to grasp the essence of their respective power bases. Yet the isolation of schools and other institutions which provide educational environments prevents them from coming to terms with life in the communities around them. If educational environments remain as static clots within the community mainstream, lifelong education cannot become pluralistic. There-

---

[7] Edgar Fauré, *et al. Learning To Be: The World of Education Today and Tomorrow.* Paris UNESCO, 1972. p. 69.

[8] Paulo Freire. *Pedagogy of the Oppressed.* New York: The Seabury Press, 1973. *passim.*

fore, coming to terms with the learning needs of all members of society requires a curriculum that incorporates a variety of human potential configurations: individual to individual, individuals and institutions, and individuals and groups or cultures.[9]

Individual to individual. The individual-to-individual interaction is undoubtedly one of the most powerful linkages for bringing about long-lasting learning experiences. In an attempt to maximize the opportunities in our society for people of all races, ethnic and class backgrounds to interact with each other, peer matching, as suggested by Illich[10] and others, is a strong concept. This would involve obtaining the names, addresses, and telephone numbers of persons in the community who have diversified interests, knowledge, skills, and resources. Illich, for instance, suggests creating a computerized master file of interests to link people to each other. The locus of activity would emerge from the interests and needs that exist, not from absolute credentials, age, ethnicity, race, ideology or any other label which keeps people apart. Even though the mechanics of such a web may seem to be on the impersonal side, if handled in a creative and humane fashion this approach could lead to more pluralistic and interwoven types of relationships. The nationwide emergence of free universities illustrates this. In a given city interested persons may enroll by calling telephone numbers listed in a Free University catalogue and by arranging to meet with a person who offers his/her skills. Typically, the free courses cover a wide variety of topics.

Within more formal learning situations we need to encourage the ethics of knowledge sharing. Individuals can be helped to realize that what they have come to know is an important resource that should be shared on a nonhierarchical basis. This will require that students be encouraged whenever possible to work together in projects, and that the teacher-student hierarchy be broken down. The practice of such an ethos creates reciprocity in learning in addition to facilitating human interdependency and appreciation.[11]

Individuals and institutions. Most Americans have come to experience their lives in affiliation to an institution, be that a church, school, factory, university, government, military or whatever. Such institutions have tremendous power to define lives. More and more they have become bureaucracies that blame the victims rather than the structures for whatever failures occur. According to Hall,[12] "Bureaucracies have no soul,

---

[9] Harbans S. Bhola. *Diffusion of Educational Innovation.* Morristown, New Jersey: General Learning Press, 1977. The linkages discussed in this section are adapted from Bhola's CLER Model for educational change, pp. 13-16.

[10] Ivan Illich. *Deschooling Society.* New York: Harrow Books, 1972. *passim.*

[11] David W. Johnson and Roger T. Johnson. *Learning Together and Alone: Co-operation, Competition and Individualization.* Englewood Cliffs, New Jersey: Prentice-Hall, Inc. 1975.

[12] Edward T. Hall. *Beyond Culture.* New York: Anchor/Doubleday, 1976. p. 181.

no memory, and no conscience." On this same point, Illich notes that humankind's ability to survive may very well depend on its ability to extricate the truth from the mythologized reality created by institutions. Because institutions perceive their integrity to be more important than that of the individual, the individual must be highly creative and strong to keep himself from becoming so enmeshed that he loses his sense of personal vision and personal integrity. Given their traditional socioeconomic marginality, minority persons are particularly vulnerable to institutional co-optation.

It has been suggested that institutions should employ individuals whose sole mission is to serve as gadflies. Their task would be to serve as independent evaluators of institutional processes, goals, and means within the context of how they affect human lives. Institutions could also develop a contractual educational system that provides linkage with the needs, interests, and abilities of individuals in learning settings that are free from the prescriptive nature of credential programs. For example, universities contain or have access to a host of human and material resources which need to be made more freely available to the surrounding community at large in the manner of free universities mentioned previously. Multiple possibilities exist whereby the environments of home, work, school, and leisure can be woven into powerful, available learning milieus that use institutional strengths outside the usual restrictions of institutional time and space for all segments of society.

Individuals and groups or cultures. It is a sociological and anthropological principle that sanctions and behaviors established by the group serve as the guideposts for the individual member of society. Through the formulation of individual behavior within the context of group norms a sense of personal identity is achieved. People arrive at this sense of sociocultural equilibrium principally through primary associations. Therefore, although technological and communicative advances have tended to provide a homogenized overlay for large segments of the American experience, primary group associations are still functioning strongly as reference points for individuals.

Because lifelong learning has the potential to become a search for the lost community, the asymmetrical power relationships between the group or culture and the individual should be addressed within the learning environment. The individual needs frequent opportunities to become cognizant of and to re-evaluate his/her place within and outside the group. In turn, group organizations need to reflect on the extent of their power to co-opt the individual to their norms. The marginal individual can in fact serve a valuable function for the group's clarity of social vision.

Though there are approximately 160 specific definitions of culture, social scientists generally agree on three characteristics; it is shared and in effect defines the boundaries of different groups; the various facets of culture are interrelated—you touch a culture in one place and everything else can be affected in some way; it is not innate, but learned.[13] This implies that people can change their world if they do not like the direction in which it is moving. Collectively shared world views and behavior patterns do much to provide a design for living a free or an oppressive existence. But if individuals are to be able to free themselves from any potentially damaging aspects of their lives they need to become conscious of their own and other cultural patterns. To be aware that specific cultural characteristics are not absolutes but rather human-produced guidelines for living becomes a powerful concept for freeing individuals from certain sociocultural constraints. A possible approach to operationalize this concept in formal and nonformal learning contexts would be to utilize Freire's *conscientização*[14] by having individuals or groups describe their reality and then begin conceptualizing ways of making their environment non-oppressive. For this model to be viable the teacher-facilitator must not impose his/her solutions. Instead, this approach to possible sociocultural transformation must be generated by the learning community. For example, the existing and the potential roles for women constitute a vital cultural and social issue for many young minority women. In recognition of these issues, problem posing and problem solving processes should pervade the lifelong learning curricula for these individuals.

The learning community could provide one form of cultural reflection and communication through multicultural pavilions where individuals make use of cultural resources from their groups as well as from others. Persons who belong to diverse age, sex, racial, ethnic, and socioeconomic status groups would engage in a process of discovering other perceptions. This type of human recycling could be done in many formal and nonformal learning situations. Again, such interaction would be facilitated by having information in a computer file which is accessible to all members of the learning community.

Groups or cultures interacting with each other. The concept of culture finds its expression through groups, and one of the most exciting learning configurations is that of groups interacting with one another. It is within this learning framework that integrative pluralism can be achieved. Groups have much potential power to develop and change cultural systems, as well as attitudes toward them. In our society this point has been dramatized by the rise of racial and ethnic awareness.

The rise of minority group awareness in recent times has to a large extent been a media phenomenon. In modern society in general, groups tend to perceive each other via nonpersonal modes of communication. The more socially, economically, and culturally separated the groups, the more likely that this is the only acceptable and readily available means of contact. Therefore, the intergroup attitudes formed, upon which *action* is

[13] *Ibid.*

[14] Freire, *op. cit.*, p. 19.

based, carry all the limitations and distortions that the media implies. For a structurally pluralistic learning society to become a reality, opportunities for personal communication between diverse groups is essential.

The coming together of extremely diverse groups for the intentional purpose of social learning is a highly unnatural event. Yet, because of the potential wealth of outcomes, the fostering of such opportunities would be socially and personally worth considerable personal and social risk. For example, divergent groups (e.g., ethnic, age, social class) might periodically converse, in the presence of a moderator, to discuss particular social issues. Such a blending of ethnic, age or social class groups would create a ground for coming to terms with respective allegiances and biases. As one type of model for this configuration, the National Conference of Christians and Jews and the National Council of Churches, as well as other organizations, sponsor group sessions, campus discussions, weekend seminars, etc., which encourage interracial and ecumenical dialogue among groups that are experiencing conflict.

In the multination study *Children's View of Foreign Peoples*[15] it was discovered that the best-informed children were the ones found to be the least racially and culturally prejudiced. If this is true, then each learning community should strive to keep itself open and informed regarding the content and structure of its surrounding society. If lifelong learning is to have any single *raison d'etre,* it may well be to provide universally accessible opportunities for in-depth reflection and action on the total and varied human experience. It is this author's belief that individuals, groups and institutions committed to providing diverse intercultural and interclass learning environments can radically alter the nature of a society by activating the resources of all its members. Lifelong learning can be the vehicle which will thrust marginal populations as well as the dominant majority into more socially and personally satisfying roles as culture makers. This is a goal worth pursuing.

Educational Leadership – Coming to Terms with Responsibility

Edna Mitchell

At this time in history when future directions for education are taking new turns, with public disenchantment focusing on the schools in

[15] Wallace E. Lambert and Otto Klineberg. *Children's View of Foreign Peoples.* New York: Appleton-Century-Crofts, 1967.

general and on teachers in particular, with new sources of decision-making power developing outside the schools, with the emergence of alternative institutions which show signs of replacing the schools as primary institutions for educating human beings, professional educators must respond with fresh vision and vitality or see themselves bypassed as vestigial remnants of a former era.

Urgently needed is educational leadership exercised by educators. Professional leadership should come from those who know the problems of the schools in intimate detail, but who also have the wisdom to analyze those problems in a broad social framework which requires an understanding of the complexities of a changing world. Educators need not work in isolation, but need to initiate partnerships with other interested groups in order to link human resources which can jointly extend educational opportunity and solve continuing educational problems. Educators must be willing to examine critically and forcefully the barriers to fulfillment of educational ideals which lie within the institution of schooling itself, and which, therefore, may be within their power to remedy.

Leadership for Reform

Professional educators can take the initiative in applying both micro and macro analysis in charting the future of education and designing a new role for the educator. We need to take a close look at schools and classrooms, and at the same time take a long-range view of the needs of the society in which schools operate. We must critically examine ourselves as educators, becoming aware of our own motives, special interests, and limitations; and in the process develop an image of educational leadership consonant with a new vision of education. Further, we must examine the structure of schooling, as it now exists, to eliminate rigidities which prevent schools from fulfilling their responsibilities. We must look to the community and society at large for direction in developing educational opportunity and meeting educational needs. Educators should not be hesitant to give leadership to new directions. We can hear and accept public criticism of schools, at the same time we can give criticism reciprocally and constructively about broader problems facing our society. If educators are to be leaders we must not limit our concerns and responses to those issues which impinge directly on education nor should we unquestioningly assent to fulfilling any and all goals set before us. We must develop a new image as active philosophers and responsible activists whose energies are committed to the improvement of the whole of human life, not merely to narrow self-interest in schooling. Educators as a professional group should be identified by their continuous determination to recognize and comprehend the complexities of problems facing humanity locally, nationally, and globally. It should be made clear by the actions of educators that we are philosophically committed to a holistic view of human development. Such a view includes a respect for the wholeness of human life and learning, a recognition of the potential for learning and personal development throughout an entire lifetime, and a view of learning which integrally links the school and society. Such a philosophy requires that educators, who are part of school systems, go beyond the school to utilize all available resources for promoting learning. Efforts to link the school with the community have been extolled in rhetoric for decades; however, in practice this linkage has been limited to merely bringing community resources into the school. These artificial connections give an illusion of real-life contact, but have actually further isolated the school.

For example, in our effort to teach economic responsibility we bring in a local banker to talk to our students and have them manipulate play money on the stock market. We substitute talk and games for real world involvement. Recent efforts to break through the isolation of the school have required almost revolutionary action. Where creative and vital connections have been made between a learner and her/his real life, these have most often been arranged through nonformal channels by groups not associated with schools, such as service clubs, churches, Junior Achievement, art associations, and private music lessons arranged by and paid for by parents.

The successful expansion of nonformal educational groups such as 4-H Clubs, Boy Scouts, church groups, and adult education programs in foreign language and political education has intruded into areas of learning once considered the prerogative of schools. The intrusion may be a guide to future educational patterns. Jesse Jacksons' Operation PUSH, speed reading and remedial reading programs run by volunteer agencies demonstrate the ability of nonformal education to deliver, at least in selected areas. Professional educators should be leaders, not passive reactors, in breaking through the limits of institutionalized schooling to develop opportunities for learning of which formal schooling may be only a part. The professional educator can play a central role in making available, developing, and linking together resources for learning.

Educational leadership should recognize the limits of the learning experiences provided within schools, should accept the validity of nonschool learning, and should act as an organic link to coordinate and unify learning opportunities both within and beyond the school. Without such coordination, learning in the schools will lack relevance, the function of the school will be usurped by others, and schools will become increasingly like museum pieces preserving the practices of an archaic period. We need not defend the schools out of professional self-interest. There are no institutions or programs which can fully provide what society has expected the schools to provide. We must keep schools, but we must exert leadership in changing them.

The emergence of a new perspective on schooling may come slowly and will require painful changes in, and thoughtful study of, areas in which breakthroughs are necessary. Target areas for revision can be categorized in three groups: (1) the need to develop a new sense of responsibility to the learner, including a new perception of who the learners are, and a fresh respect for time and space as personal resources; (2) the need for revision in administrative structures, breaking down old hierarchical administrative patterns which inhibit communication and change within a community of teachers and learners; and (3) the need to counteract unexamined psychological attitudes and rituals which are impediments.

Responsibility to the Learner

Learners are no longer only the young and immature, but increasingly include persons of all ages throughout the life span. The orientation toward youth as students in schools and the view of education as preparation for future life, which has generally characterized American education, is disappearing. Entry points and termination points for schooling are being drastically modified, and chronological age groupings are becoming inappropriate in many situations.

While the specific developmental needs of learners of different ages do vary, some principles apply to all learning situations. Learning cannot take place effectively in environments which violate basic human needs. Rankings and hierarchies of human needs have been identified by Maslow, Raths, Havighurst, Erikson and others, pointing out clearly the necessity of providing for physiological and psychological needs before optimum learning can occur. The learner, whether child or adult, must work in an atmosphere in which there is safety both physically and psychologically, an environment in which a sense of self-esteem, achievement, economic security, and sharing of mutual respect exists. In order to provide an environment with these qualities, the schools must consider many more factors than merely the organization of curriculum and presentation of prescribed content.

Recent trends toward packaging total curricula, sometimes cynically referred to as "teacher-proof materials," illustrate one aspect of the problem. Packaged curricula cannot adequately consider the varied backgrounds of individuals, special abilities, unique personal interests, immediate problems and needs, and the previous experiences of individual learners both young and mature. These considerations call for talented and well-trained teachers who can orchestrate a wide variety of learning resources both in the school and in the community at large.

Often personal human needs take priority over educational needs. Poverty, illness, hunger, psychological depression, and combinations of all interrelated miseries, have been major causes of educational deprivation in our society. Recognizing these priorities, the schools have added social services, welfare services, guidance services, food programs, and other special programs all in response to human needs but also as prerequisites to support and to facilitate the teaching-learning program. Such services are, of course, essential and schools should be even more active in locating and utilizing necessary social services. However, a serious problem arises when schools duplicate or assume responsibility for the maintenance of such programs. Schools can offer leadership in the coordination of the delivery of human services without becoming the agents responsible for providing them. Moreover, important as these services are in creating a favorable climate for learning, the school remains uniquely a place for formal instruction. This role should not be forgotten.

Even when special services are provided within the budget and philosophy of the school, the classroom atmosphere may still be marked by practices which violate human needs. Often, the special services themselves are used as rationalizations for ineffective teaching. Furthermore, acceptance of some special services offered by the school may result in an individual being stigmatized or stereotyped unfavorably. All human beings have special needs and special problems. These needs change with different life circumstances and through lifelong development. Schools must adopt a broader view of the spectrum of human needs which create barriers to learning. Services which empower, actualize, and motivate, without labeling and categorizing learners, should be maintained.

People of all ages, with purposes and needs which may be only incidentally related to their ages, will be clients for the future learning systems. Such a broad profile of learners will require a responsive educational environment which, by recognizing unique personal goals, will also contribute to the realization of broader societal goals. As we revise our perceptions of the learner as client our sense of responsibility to that learner will include a fresh awareness of the need to respect individual time and choice of space for learning.

An optimum learning environment will consider the uses of both time and space to enhance individual learning, to develop individuals who respect their own goals, and to empower individuals with the skills to control and direct their own learning. Schools have too long been the instruments of social control rather than liberators of the human spirit and activators of human potential. A new pedagogy should free educators from the restrictions of a model of teaching limited to narrow time frames and specific institutionally controlled space and allow them to see themselves as facilitators of learning in a lifelong continuum in a global setting.

Breaking Down Hierarchical Structures Inhibiting Communication and Change

The personnel associated with schooling, when considered as a total, constitutes an enormous body of highly trained people devoting their lives to the education of others. Strong educational leadership should emerge from this body. However, if the resource of educators is to be used in transforming education, we must first transform ourselves. We must identify the key factors within the school environment and within our professional and personal structure which prevent us from realizing the utopian ideals of educational philosophy. The problems of transforming the schools are not just problems of making changes on the inside; however, reforms from the inside can strengthen educators and unify them for working on problems which have roots in other institutions.

Frustration and despair created by inequality and impotence permeate every corner of human life. These conditions are magnified by many experiences within the school. For example, relationships within schools are often characterized by inequality and imbalance of power. Hierarchies which structure human relationships, with covert role and behavioral implications affecting the learning environment, extend from the Board of Education to the superintendent's office, the principal's office to the classroom teacher, and finally to the students and their families. Within the classroom, further inequalities exist creating a comparable minihierarchy shaping the relationships of teachers, aides, and pupils. The most important persons in this structure, teachers on the one hand and learners on the other, have the greatest sense of powerlessness. They experience the least opportunity for decision making about issues which directly affect them.

With teachers' organizations and school boards often on a collision course, with teachers and administrators viewing each other as adversaries, and with both groups identifying the public as the enemy, a change in the structure of decision making must be accompanied by a change in the psychological climate in which educators need to support one another, to grant intentions of good will to colleagues, to work to counteract the insidious destruction inherent in the divisive effects of superior-inferior hierarchical relationships. Being human seems to carry with it inescapable problems associated with miscommunication, misunderstanding, justifiable anger, and conflict. Such experiences may be unavoidable, however they need not be accepted as unmanageable or as inevitably destructive. Knowledge of organizational behavior should enable us to devise organizational structures which carry out the principle that those affected by decisions should share responsibility for making them.

Rituals and Psychological Impediments

In addition to the organizational structures that directly and indirectly control personnel, the sheer mechanics of operating schools produce factors inhibiting change and depressing educational achievement. Schools are bound by rules, rituals, procedures, and ceremonies rooted in unexamined tradition. These often unrecognized conventions bind educators rather than free them. The concept of credentialing is one such ritual. The process of credentialing teachers has become, in many places, an issue of political power and vested interest with little connection to the original intent to identify the skills, knowledge, and characteristics needed by teachers. Professional educators are now locked into a view of credentialing which gives pretentious preciousness to various forms of credentials from paper promotions grade level by grade level, to the Carnegie unit requirements of high school diplomas, course credits for college degrees and professional certifications. Traditional dependence upon formal credential rituals has prevented recognition of the validity of forms of education other than schooling. We should link the school with these vital out-of-school forms of education, related to life but unrelated to unit and course credits. We must break out of institutionalized learning, even for ourselves as educators. The fact that we are products of our own experience, and successful consumers of the system, may mean that we have been co-opted into maintaining the status quo. Similarly, institutionalized oppression inflicted on students also affects educators who experience comparable confusion, fear, and loss of power. Educators have both perpetuated the oppression and have been victims of it.

Professional educators must liberate themselves and each other if they are to provide leadership in transforming schools. We must move into a questioning role, questioning the school and the society. We must move away from the role of victim, rationalizing our failures, projecting blame, personalizing criticism, and defending practices which no longer have a rational base. Educators can learn, together and with others, how to interact in a powerful way with an institution which was created by earlier generations for purposes no longer totally relevant. We must ask ourselves if we can belong in the system, be part of the traditional institution of schools, and yet maintain integrity by protesting and reforming those factors which prevent fulfillment of educational purpose. As educational leaders, can we learn to communicate with the community, not just with other educators? Can we vigorously participate as part of the broader community instead of as a group defending a personal investment in the schools? Can we become allies with other agencies in the community which have a legitimate place in the educational process? Have we the professional maturity to provide educational leadership without demanding total control?

In coming to terms with our responsibilities as professionals, as educators, and as participating citizens we can offer leadership in solving educational problems only to the extent that we demonstrate maturity as a profession, overcoming our paranoia and sensitivity to criticism. We can reshape our relationships with each other, strengthening and empowering each person engaged in teaching and learning.

Schools as Linking Agents

Schools in our complex society, providing for many of the educational needs of diverse population groups, should become clearing houses for the multitude of educational opportunities already available, though often unknown, to those who could make use of them. The schools could simplify the present fragmentation and multiplicity of options which are overwhelmingly confusing to the consumer. Many people do not know how to obtain access to services or educational opportunities already existing. Enormous effort and energy are required to seek these out and use them. Schools should be facilitators in identifying the specific resources which would be most useful to an individual at a particular time in life.

Many school systems are developing new programs to link the school and the community. For example, the Regional Learning Service of Central New York is attempting a program of educational brokering in which consultants gather information on programs available in a given field and pass this information along to those over 16 years old who want to further their education or career development. The New Castle County School System in Delaware has developed a comprehensive catalog listing hundreds of persons or organizations willing to visit schools or have students visit them. The San Jose, California, schools have developed a program, reported to be highly successful, to reduce crime by involving students directly in solving school, family, and neighborhood problems.

Programs which open up the school to the community include those reported through the Early Childhood Education Outreach Program of Title III in which there are more than 50 projects using empty classroom space as headquarters for programs helping parents work with their children, some of them beginning with infants.

Linkage within and between school systems are also beginning through efforts to build support mechanisms for professional improvement. In Alaska the State Department of Education has developed a talent bank of teachers in which excellent teachers are identified and periodically released to serve as consultants to other teachers. The League of Cooperating Schools in the Los Angeles area, funded by the Kettering Foundation Institute for the Development of Educational Activities, offers another structural model of mutual support of individual teachers and schools across district lines in their efforts to effect institutional change. The League has offered a clearing house of ideas, consultant services, workshops, and systematic training in educational change. An informal newsletter links the network of schools and teachers. Research on this project provides evidence that educational change can occur, even in unfavorable settings, when a supporting network is available to individual change agents within schools.

These and other efforts mark the beginning of some important changes, even though they are largely isolated projects focusing on a few specific activities which attempt to broaden educational opportunity and improve educational environments. A breakthrough may be occurring as small projects make cracks in the old institutional barriers. Information about innovative experiments should be made available through a resource data bank so they may be used as seminal ideas in the development of local and regional holistic plans. Future educational planning should be designed to make accessible every available educational opportunity to individuals during each changing phase of life by maximizing the use of coordinated resources including agencies, people, places, spaces, and time.

Educational leadership for the future will be in the hands of those who can visualize and actualize mechanisms for linking the school with resources for learning available in the society at large, as well as those who can apply their energies to improving the school as an environment for learning in itself. The creation of networks which put people in touch with opportunities for self development, including the school as one of those opportunities, should become the new mission of schooling. Responsibility for the teaching of skills and knowledge will still rest squarely on professional educators, but the processes for delivering educational opportunities will draw from a wide variety of sources beyond the limits of the school. If professional educators are to be the educational leaders they must be able to coordinate learning opportunities from many sources, while remaining in tune with the individual being served.

Currently the teacher's role is limited to competence in the classroom. While such competence will remain a necessity, the teacher must look beyond the classroom to share in a broader view of learning. Although students' lives are increasingly enriched by out-of-school learning, the teacher seems more than ever locked inside the classroom box. Students often have more access to learning and living than do their teachers. Teachers are often unaware of the importance of using the students' learnings from out of school.

The teacher must be a learner as well as a leader, a consumer of education as well as a coordinator. The practice of lifelong learning is essential for the educational leader as well as for the clients served by the schools. The need for continuous growth as a lifelong learner applies to the development of the educator as well as to others. The educator must not only be a creator and operator of a system coordinating all useful learning resources, but must also be a living participant in the process.

If educators are to come to terms with their responsibility for leadership in education, pathological reactions to criticism of schooling must be converted to aggressive problem solving which includes an objective examination of the obstacles impeding educational progress. There are new opportunities for educational leadership and new roles to be assumed by educators. The school need not be obsolete, but can become much more responsive to the lifelong educational needs of the society.

The role for the future educator may be envisioned as that of one who works within an educational system whose overall aim is to manage and deliver resources for individual learning and development. The focus will be on the individual, but the learning resources will be tapped from local, regional, national, and even global, sources. The concept of education will be widened so that formal schooling, the traditional educational ladder, will be only one component, although still a legitimate one. With the individual as the central focus, educators will recognize the many facets of educational need: intellectual, social, economic, ethical, personal, psychological, physical and vocational.

Schools, and special personnel within schools, can take the initiative in coordinating, organizing, and delivering educational opportunities to persons of all ages. When there is no appropriate resource for meeting a special learning need expressed by the client, the school could take the initiative in spearheading the development of that resource somewhere in the community. Schools need not attempt to be all things to all people, and should not assume responsibility for every learning experience. Learning activities should permeate all of life throughout the total community. Educators could view their responsibility as serving as linking agents providing access to appropriate learning situations.

Many educators, of course, still will focus their expertise on teaching within their own discipline or classroom. However, all educators will be able to utilize, through the coordinated school clearing house, every reasonable available resource in creating opportunities for learning. At the same time they will be better able to demonstrate respect for the need and right of the individual learner to set personal goals, and they will be better able to recognize and provide for personal differences in the types of environments and experiences necessary for learning.

It is educators, themselves, who should provide leadership in breaking out of the constraints which bind schooling to institutionalized space and time, separate from the broader stream of education flowing throughout life. Professional educators are the self-committed persons in our society who, through deliberate choice, have dedicated themselves to work on educational problems. Leadership can emerge from the ranks of classroom teachers as well as from administrators and academicians. Talented articulate spokespersons, with the skill and vision to be transformers in every sphere of education, must be identified and encouraged to speak and act with confidence, affirming our ability and assuming our responsibility as educational leaders in educational reform.

Coming to Terms
with Monday Morning

Norman V. Overly

Monday mornings have a way of arriving after Sunday night whether we intend them to or not. Daily we are faced with the problems and promises not only of noble dreams and a new day, but of a continuation of past experience into the future, of efforts to come to grips with the unknown in terms of goals and realities not totally of our choosing nor totally in keeping with the new day we desire. In the face of conflicting goals and demands on our time and resources, in light of many worthy and equally urgent realities, whether classroom teacher, administrator or parent, it is customary to be concerned about what we shall do on Monday morning. While in the abstract we may appreciate the complexities and paradoxes of modern life and recognize the importance of learning throughout life, in reality we want to know what lifelong learning means and we want to know what we are supposed to do about it.

Each of us has a job to do. The pressures and ambiguity of the moment force us into a search for the clearly definable and doable. But if the world about us is in chaos, at least we hope to maintain our sanity and equilibrium by having a semblance of order and familiarity in our world. Almost by accident we fall into a search for easy answers. Regardless of our role or our relationships to formal education, the searches are characterized by similar motivations.

If we are parents, we seek schools for our children with clearly defined curricula extolling the basics and discipline that will guarantee capabilities in adult life. If we are fifth grade teachers, we seek programmed texts on fractions and the decimal system, American history, ecologically oriented science, and basic grammar. With such help we propose to plug kids into the lifelong learning stream. If our own learning needs attention, we seek an inservice training program or college course for credit. Tell us how many pages are required for each paper and we'll go through the motions of learning. If we are administrators, present us with a list of competencies for being a principal, a curriculum coordinator, a superintendent. These we'll learn if courses are available on Saturday morning, Monday evening, or in the summer during our vacation. If we are in higher education we "retool" to meet the challenge of changing markets for university services; postdoctoral studies and sabbaticals for midcareer changes are encouraged. Those of us in education —alas, the whole of society—have become so obsessed with having clearcut things to do that we seldom take the time to reflect seriously on why we are doing them or the impact of what we do or are told to do upon the achievement of *our* goals. If we take time to reflect we discover we have few goals that we ourselves have generated. But we are more apt to avoid reflection and immerse ourselves in action to meet goals prescribed by others or that are emerging at the moment.

There can be no denying that coming to terms involves action and acting—for ourselves, for others, and with others. As we face the enormity of the task of translating a desire for a lifelong learning society into action, where can we begin? What does it mean to me to be a lifelong learner, beginning where I am today? What does it mean to me as a professional educator to be a facilitator of lifelong learning for others? What does it mean to me as a parent, as a businessman, as a religious leader, as a student, as a laborer?

Coming to terms with the present reality of lifelong learning would be easier if there were a single model. But the concept is too complex to permit a singular response. It is at once adult education and the whole spectrum of learning opportunities available to humanity from conception to death. It is a process involving individual as well as societal choices with regard to content, mode, and setting for learning. It takes place through a variety of experiences and activities, requires different resources and material for differing goals and is evaluated in diverse ways for a variety of reasons. The vision of lifelong learning is not unlike the ideal of Greek culture Werner Jaeger had called *paideia*. Lewis Mumford captured the vitality and distinctions of this ideal succinctly:

> *Paideia* is education looked upon as a life-long transformation of the human personality, in which every aspect of life plays a part. Unlike education in the traditional sense, *paideia* does not limit itself to the conscious learning process, or to introducing the young into the social heritage of the community. *Paideia* is rather the task of giving form to the act of living itself; treating every occasion of life as a means of self-fabrication, and as part of a larger process of converting facts into values, processes into purposes, hopes and plans into consummation and realizations. *Paideia* is not merely learning; it is making and shaping a man himself as the work of art that *paideia* seeks to form.[1]

Some part of Monday morning must be invested in intentional reflection on the ideal of *paideia* and the extent to which that ideal can be made a part of one's personal vision. Lifelong learning is a glorious ideal which educators and leaders the world over have taken as their motto. It remains for each of us as individuals, citizens, professionals, persons of faith and commitment to focus our attention, resources, and skills on lifelong learning so as to raise it above the level of a catch phrase or fad.

Whatever practices we adopt for Monday (and we may make mistakes) need to be grounded in goals which will provide a basis for judging whether what is done is worth repeating. In addition, if practice is not to become sterile repetition of the known and comfortable, the ideals of utopians must be explored as the basis for practice. Thus, the discourse must proceed on several levels at once—dreams, ideals, goals, tradition, even easy answers that provide breathing room for creative reflection.

To make sense of our caring, to bring order to the competing demands on our time and resources, we must identify a level of discourse with which we are comfortable and from which it is possible for us to move into meaningful action. For some, it will be tempting to remain at the level of talk and reflection. For others, there will be an ultimately defeating attraction to rush into action without adequate thought or sharing. If we are to succeed, we must combine the critical elements of

---

[1] Lewis Mumford. *The Transformations of Man.* New York: Harper & Row, Publishers, 1956. pp. 242-43.

reflection and action in a rational commitment to achievement of carefully considered, meaningful goals.

To be sure, we live in a time of high hopes and depressing reality. The mid-American frenzy to ride roller coasters has thousands standing in lines for quick trips on a vicarious mockery of life's vicissitudes. Such frenzy is a contemporary reflection of our condition as much as Dickens' somber description of London and Paris in an earlier era reflected his time. But while the basic paradoxes of life seem to change little, the capacity to control our creation is out of hand. What remains constant is the necessity of individuals to become responsible decision makers, able to create alternatives and direct, if only slightly, the course of the world about them. It remains for us to take responsibility for becoming participants in our own history making.

Harvey Cox, theologian-sociologist, has challenged us to a prophetic-conditional view of history in *On Not Leaving It to the Snake*.[2] His view places humankind at the center of history with responsibility for personal becoming rather than in the apocalyptic position with its controlled determinism of awaiting the end resignedly, or in the chiliastic position of waiting upon a Messiah to deliver us. His view is in keeping with the educational emphasis placed on decision making within the past twenty years. But the gap between recognition of the need to act, or the desirability of personal action, and the ability to decide to act and to act responsibly on Monday morning is wide.

The explosion of knowledge, the emergence of new political alignments, the transient nature of relationships, and the technological developments of science and industry are but some of the forces which challenge our perceptions of reality, threaten cherished traditions, and shake the foundations of our culture and our life space. We are told that linear thinking, which focuses on simple cause and effect relationships, must be replaced by recognition of the more complex, multiple causations and interrelationships of pattern thinking. We are confronted by the disturbing concept of a global village intruding into our consciousness whether we like it or not; and economic, political, and social change bewilder us. At the same time we are caught up in more personal searches for our historic roots—everyone longing for the equivalent of a pilgrim ancestor or Kunta Kinte.

In light of our present and projected condition, how are we to make sense of it? How can we approach the task of improving our quality of life? It does no good to wait for panaceas or grouse about the lack of consensus. Individuals must make their own decisions, pusillanimous and changeable as they may be.

Individual and group efforts to come to terms with Monday morning do not lend themselves to easy characterization. No single format has been

[2] Harvey Cox. *On Not Leaving It to the Snake*. New York: The Macmillan Co., 1967.

used nor does one suggest itself when attempts to come to terms with lifelong learning are reviewed. But irrespective of this lacuna there is a sense of style or "feel" about different approaches that permits one to fit them into two categories, the utopian and the reformation.

The utopian approach is future oriented and aims for ideals; often those functioning from this perspective are oriented toward social change and are impatient with the evolutionary process. Strong leaders with a few dedicated cadres spreading the word and creating new models for the coming age represent the prophetic tradition of the utopian style. Those who look to the future may have little common ground and great diversity, tending to take the ambiguity of the present situation as a basis for projecting alternatives. But even with the diversity, a common disposition exists within the utopian style.

The reformation style of operation is less apt to be alienated from the existing structures and better able to maintain communication with educational institutions and tradition-bound personnel. This is achieved through a willingness to accept the present situation and striving to remove the ambiguity and uncertainty of conditions. While neither style of operation is wholly satisfactory, each has elements which commend it. Deciding on what to do on Monday morning requires practical action as well as goals and a theoretical perspective.

The Utopian Style

Among utopians the emphasis on education is usually secondary to a number of competing primary motivations such as social, economic, or political perfection. Education typically has been viewed as a major socializing tool for strengthening of ties to the utopian community and its fundamental tenets. In most instances, utopias have been conceived as communities[3] either set apart from the world or designed to provide an alternative to the dominant world view. America has always been a fertile setting for utopian thought and action; indeed, we live in a period of renewed interest in utopianism. On the one hand the work of the Futurists such as Fuller, Gabor, Kahn, Soleri, and Platt,[4] to note but a few, hold up for educators visions of alternative futures which challenge us to reconsider our traditional curricular responses to the age old question of "what to teach?" To be sure, each has his own particular perspective. "They do not merely extrapolate current trends or posit a minor shuffling

---

[3] Rosabeth Moss Kanter. *Commitment and Community.* Cambridge, Massachusetts: Harvard Press, 1972. p. 2.

[4] Richard Buckminister Fuller. *Utopia or Oblivion, The Prospects for Humanity.* New York: Bantam Books, 1969; Dennis Gabor. *The Mature Society.* New York: Praeger Publishers, 1972; Herman Kahn and Anthony J. Wiener. *The Year 2000, A Framework for Speculation.* New York: The Macmillan Company, 1967; Paolo Soleri. *Arcology, The City in the Image of Man.* Cambridge, Massachusetts: MIT Press, 1972; John Platt. "How Men Can Shape Their Future." *Futures* 3:32-47, March 1971.

of priorities. They start from a counter-stance to the present and reach out for radically different principles and patterns for human action."[5] While attempting a more measured, scientific approach to development of future planning than the literary or prophetic utopians of the past, this group of dreamers takes the broad view of history and society with a primary emphasis on reflection.

On the other hand, there has been a large group of educational critics and reformers led by such persons as John Holt, Herbert Kohl, James Herndon, Jonathan Kozol, and others in the sixties who have come closer to the activist strain in American Utopianism. For example, the Free School movement that rose on the horizon like a new comet quickly burned itself out,[6] but the resultant interest in alternatives and options to traditional educational patterns are reminders of the continuing search for more effective action on Monday morning. The educational utopians have been at the forefront in stimulating our thinking.

Few Waldens or Summerhills have achieved continued success, any more than did Brook Farm, New Harmony, or the Shaker settlements. But there can be no doubt about the attraction such schemes have for many educators concerned with making learning a relevant, lifelong human endeavor. For whatever reasons, often less than noble as in the case of white flight to escape integration, individuals and groups continue to act out their dreams in educational experiments in widely variant modes.[7] While few of these would be classified as utopias, the urge to experimentation in alternative and optional school patterns is one manifestation of utopianism, the power of which lies in its ability to free humans "from their apathetic or suffering acceptance of the world as-it-is and to give them self-transcending purposes."[8]

There can be little doubt that utopianism by itself is a weak resource for most of us when we attempt to decide what we should do on Monday morning. For some, too little time has been allowed for reflection and the necessary commitment is missing. For others, the golden dream, even in democratically conceived utopias, is found to be grounded in dogmatism

[5] David W. Plath. *Aware of Utopia*. Chicago: University of Illinois Press, 1971. p. x.

[6] Robert D. Barr. "Whatever Happened to the Free School Movement?" *Phi Delta Kappan*, pp. 454-57; March 1973.

[7] Examples of efforts to combine the historical roots of different traditions may be found throughout the U.S. Two in the Bloomington, Indiana area provide differing examples. The Padanarum community of Daniel Wright is a socio-religious group pursuing a communal family life style with its own school system. The Harmony School, a private alternative school, is pursuing a child-centered approach to relevant education within the regular community with parental and community-based support. Students and staff of the Harmony School are now publishing a bimonthly magazine, *Hoosier Harmony*. Leaders of the school are making an effort to fuse reflection and action, theory and practice into a meaningful whole, a step missing in most educational efforts. (See: Daniel Baron. "A Case Study of Praxis." Paper presented to the Curriculum Theory Conference, Rochester Institute of Technology, May 12, 1978.)

[8] W. Warren Wager. *Building the City of Man: Outlines of a World Civilization*. New York: Grossman Publishers, 1971. p. 73.

and ruled by tyranny.[9] And for still others, the seeds of destruction are inherent in the extreme personalism of many contemporary alternative efforts.[10] In addition, we may be moved to reject specific utopian models because they are more dystopian than utopian in their world view, exhibiting lack of hope in human social relations, especially in those situations arising from an effort to escape present realities. This is an outgrowth of a co-figurative or even a post-figurative view of social relationships[11] which fails to grasp the nature of interdependent social relationships of the future which must focus on human fulfillment as a synthesis of individual and societal dreams.

Too frequently the dreams have not been pondered sufficiently, especially in the communal movement within the United States,[12] but also among the utopian educators. There has been a propensity to rush into action without consideration of the costs and consequences. One result is a failure to appreciate the complexity of the human condition and the intricacies of relationships. The dystopian angst has led many to try to go it alone, to withdraw or remain apart from the mainstream of life. But important as personal dreams and times of solitude may be, learning is a social activity dependent upon shared insights and community knowledge. As Bill Flanders has aptly noted, "I was born to be me. But, I've learned in a lifetime I never can make it alone. Far too much of myself needs the giving of others, the parts I can't see till I'm shown."[13] No matter how I long to be totally independent, my humanity demands that I find fulfillment in and with others.

Notwithstanding the drawbacks of the utopian style, it remains a position of value. While one may not go as far as Van Loon in declaring that "it does not matter so much where we are going, as long as we are working consciously for some definite goal,"[14] it is clear that the utopians challenge us to extraordinary visions and dreams. Even though we may be tempted to strive for greater objectivity and control of our tomorrows as we project into the future we need ideals to stretch us and cause us to ponder the consequences of the options before us. Second, the utopian style casts in relief the limitations of a vision created only in terms of what can be done immediately. Probably the most influential of all utopian thinkers were the Old Testament prophets such as Amos who

---

[9] Milovan Djilas. *The Unperfect Society: Beyond the New Class.* New York: Harcourt, Brace and World, 1969. pp. 4-5.

[10] An extreme example of the power and weakness of personalism may be seen in the mass suicide by the members of the Peoples' Temple in Guyana led by the Reverend Jim Jones.

[11] Margaret Mead. *Culture and Commitment.* New York: National History Press/ Doubleday and Co., Inc., 1970.

[12] "Year of the Commune." *Newsweek.* pp. 89-90; August 18, 1969.

[13] William Flanders. "I Was Born To Be Me." Words and music by William Flanders. Copyright © 1968, by William Flanders. In: *Love is a Verb and Other Folk Hymns.*

[14] Hendrick William Van Loon. "Introduction." In: Lewis Mumford. *The Story of Utopias.* London: George G. Harrap and Co., Ltd, 1923. p. xii.

were misfits in their societies, out of step with the drummers of their age. While naive and impractical in their suggestions, they continue to speak to us across the gaps of culture and time.[15]

The utopian perspective highlights the need for personal commitment and decision making. Utopias are not mandated by governments. They are offered by dreamers, open to free acceptance or rejection by all. In that respect they are similar to lifelong learning which can only be made available. The commitment rests ultimately with the individual.

Because of differences in long term goals and style of operation, the utopians have great difficulty in communicating with the reformers and vice versa. Different assumptions, dispositions, and basic aims create barriers. But the contribution each has to make commands attention.

The Reformation Style

The reformation approach arises from leadership within the educational establishment, follows the industrial model, and is grounded in the hope that if we just do better what we are already doing we can extend our present enterprises so as to meet the needs of a learning society. Doing better in large measure means maintaining present opportunities but organizing differently to improve access. The basic assumption underlying the suggestions characterized as the reformation approach is that existing institutions will maintain their present goals but their roles will be expanded with the increased demand for their services or newly emerging nontraditional programs. In the main, while recognizing the need for an expansion of the arena of education and learning opportunities beyond the confines of existing educational institutions the response is centered around existing institutions. As James Cass noted, interest in lifelong learning has presaged a "back-to-school boom." [16]

Educators at all levels have seen in lifelong learning an opportunity to fill empty classrooms, develop new markets, and serve a population of increasingly senior citizens. To date, efforts to develop models have addressed themselves to *aspects* of the problem of lifelong learning, either remaining tied to existing organizational patterns and delivery systems while modifying the content and perception of it or accepting existing content and suggesting modification of the organization. The Life Coping Skills Model of Winthrop Adkins[17] emphasizes development of learning modes through a "fifth curriculum" to parallel present curricula and provide "life problem centered instruction from kindergarten through con-

[15] Chad Walsh. *From Utopia to Nightmare.* New York: Harper and Row, Publishers, 1962. p. 33.

[16] James Cass. "Lifelong Learning: The Back-to-School Boom." Symposium. *Saturday Review,* 2: 14-16+: September 29, 1975.

[17] Winthrop R. Adkins. "Life Coping Skills: A Fifth Curriculum." *Teachers College Record* 75(4):512; May 1974. This suggestion strongly reflects the "persistent life situations" of earlier years. Florence Stratemeyer *et al. Developing A Curriculum For Modern Living.* New York: Teachers College Press, 1957.

tinuing education on predictable developmental tasks, crises, and problems faced by individuals at different stages in their lives." The Life
Involvement Model (LIM) of Kapfer, Kapfer, and Woodruff attempts to
move away from the current "banking concept" of education to a view of
education which makes universal decision-making and decision-executing
behaviors central to curriculum development and implementation. Behavior is conceived as coping with or manipulating objects in real situations with feedback to the learner. "The LIM Model[18] requires subordi-
nating the abstract verbal form to the direct practice or real life abilities."
While dividing behavior into four distinct categories—conditioned responses, verbal processes, motive processes, and conceptual-affective processes—the developers emphasize that the four categories form an organ-
ismic whole with all parts functioning simultaneously. But the model
limits itself to the improvement of education within the existing structure
of schools. Two other weaknesses are its failure to recognize the legitimacy
of alternative learning styles (only a simple to complex, or concrete to
general arrangement of learning activities is suggested) and its exclusion
of preschool and postschool learning activities. Important as the improvement and modification of the existing schools may be, any comprehensive
view of lifelong learning must move beyond tinkering with program in
existing models. If one were to turn to these models for Monday morning
direction, a sense of *deja vu* would be likely to ensue. While each of these
efforts provides a reconceptualization of content and modes of learning,
their unique relevance to lifelong learning is difficult to discern.

The most comprehensive effort to build a model for lifelong learning
has been undertaken by Harold G. Shane.[19] He has endeavored to incorporate the thinking of the utopian futurists within the existing, educational structures. Building on his interviews with some of the world's
leading scientists, logicians and futurists he concludes that the mood of
the decade is reform, not revolution.[20] He then sets forth a model for
changing the infrastructure of public education which he calls the Seamless Curriculum. His model widens the scope of traditional public education, extends the sequence, and adds variability and flexibility to the total
organization. The traditional graded structure would be abandoned "in
favor of a smoothly flowing, seamless curriculum,"[21] consisting of two
major components: (1) a formal educational structure for ages two through
the remainder of life; and (2) a "real world" paracurriculum with special
significance for secondary and postsecondary educational institutions.[22]

[18] Norman V. Overly *et al. Development of a Model for Lifelong Learning.* Report
of the Phi Delta Kappa Commission of Curriculum Models for Lifelong Learning.
Mimeographed, 1977. p. 39.

[19] Harold G. Shane. *The Educational Significance of the Future.* Bloomington, Indiana: Phi Delta Kappa, Inc., 1973.

[20] *Ibid*, p. 60.

[21] *Ibid*, p. 67.

[22] *Ibid*, p. 72.

The paracurriculum is conceived to be any out-of-school experiences that add to or strengthen one's ability to cope intellectually as well as generally in society. In encounters within the paracurriculum one is building on the foundation acquired in the communiversity—the formal educational organization that flows without the artificial boundaries of age-specific learnings and enrollments.

The school acts as both broker for paracurriculum activities and as credentialing agency, providing formal recognition for learnings achieved outside the regular school structure. In part the flexibility would emphasize a reversal of form for educational institutions which foster dropouts and "pushouts" and supplant them with programs for "come-backs" and "drop-ins." For example, following achievement of a societally acceptable majority of 13-15 years of age an individual would be free to enter and exit existing formal education as needed and desired. In fact, the establishment would provide assistance in the personalization of learning opportunities in the communiversity system, in the university system, and in the paracurriculum system. The result would be "ability referenced rather than chronologically referenced groups."[23]

While focusing on the changes needed in organizational framework, Shane is also aware of the need for changes in the content of the learning experiences, in the modes of instruction and learning, and in the role of the instructional staff. But for all the insights there is a sense of new wine in old wineskins and an occasional vineyard not harvested at the appropriate time. One misses a comprehensive rationale for all manner of lifelong learning and all manner of learners. Rather the arena is limited to existing organizational structures and programs. Learning activities are discussed in terms of institutionally selected and directed programs, with little suggestion of learner-initiated and -directed learning. Also, insofar as the postsecondary opportunities are explored, Shane limits himself to adult education, continuing education, university education, and the communiversity. He fails to incorporate the vast array of nonformal and informal learning activities needed by all learners at various points in their lives. The most critical deficiency is the omission of how the young learners will become mature decision makers in reasonable control of the direction their lives will take. How is one to become a maker of culture and history? It is a disposition we must take on if the utopian and reformation styles are to contribute to development of a productive conception of lifelong learning.

Shane's main contributions to the lifelong learning literature are his identification of the paracurriculum, his suggestion that it be recognized as a vital part of each person's learning and that it be intentionally incorporated in one's lifelong learning. Unfortunately, he stops short of the potential of the idea of the paracurriculum which extends beyond those points which have direct relevance to formal learning opportunities. His

[23] *Ibid*, p. 71.

failure on this point is similar to the general insufficiency of efforts to develop nontraditional models. Most efforts end up modifying instructional approaches, time requirements, residency, evaluation procedures, and admission criteria, but continue to aim for publically verifiable authentication in the form of high school certificates or college and university degrees. They are important components of any lifelong learning approach but not sufficient for construction of a comprehensive model.

The Comprehensive Approach

The Comprehensive Approach is presented on the assumptions that both the utopian and reformation styles of addressing lifelong learning are deficient by themselves and that lifelong learning is a complex concept requiring extensive analysis as a prerequisite to development of desirable, relevant syntheses.[24] Further, the approach is built on the assumption that learning is pursued for a variety of purposes which change from time to time and as conditions are modified. If we are to realize the ideal of *paideia* more fully than we have in the past, we must put behind us the attitudes of drudgery and ennui that result from viewing learning as the private preserve of an educational establishment bolstered by societal compulsion and move toward a model that affords greater opportunity for internal control of one's destiny as a learner. This is a very different perspective from the usual models which begin from an assumption of external control of learning by adults, government, certifying and accrediting agencies, parents, and even peer pressures. While all learning is a legitimate part of lifelong learning, the purpose of this comprehensive model is to promote the expansion of the incidental and the common claims made upon existing formal and informal systems that provide opportunities for learning and provide suggestions for moving beyond existing structures.

What is being emphasized here is the need to increase the level of personal and group intentionality or purposing on the part of the learners. A model for lifelong learning for the modern age must value more than mandated minimums and serendipitous occurrences. It must optimize opportunities for purposeful learning and suggest ways to activate purposeful learning. A first step is to recognize the complexity of the learning act. Only then can we identify points at which intervention—personal and societal—will be efficacious. There are four major components of lifelong learning. (See Figure 1.) While all learning requires (1) learners, (2) experiences, (3) resources, and (4) authentication, lifelong learning requires the same components but in extended, more complex relationships than present in a single act of learning. Learners, whether in groups or as individuals use a great variety of resources in even more

---

[24] Material in this section is an extension and modification of work begun in cooperation with the Phi Delta Kappa Commission on Curriculum Models for Lifelong Learning under the leadership of R. Bruce McQuigg, Floyd Coppedge, David Silvernail, and the author. *Development of a Model of Lifelong Learning*. Overly, *op. cit.*

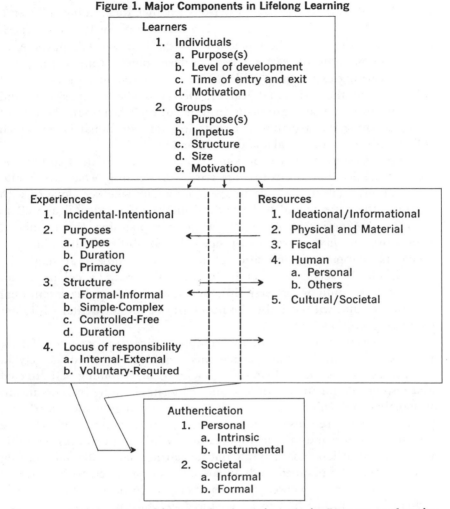

Figure 1. Major Components in Lifelong Learning

Learners
1. Individuals
   a. Purpose(s)
   b. Level of development
   c. Time of entry and exit
   d. Motivation
2. Groups
   a. Purpose(s)
   b. Impetus
   c. Structure
   d. Size
   e. Motivation

Experiences
1. Incidental-Intentional
2. Purposes
   a. Types
   b. Duration
   c. Primacy
3. Structure
   a. Formal-Informal
   b. Simple-Complex
   c. Controlled-Free
   d. Duration
4. Locus of responsibility
   a. Internal-External
   b. Voluntary-Required

Resources
1. Ideational/Informational
2. Physical and Material
3. Fiscal
4. Human
   a. Personal
   b. Others
5. Cultural/Societal

Authentication
1. Personal
   a. Intrinsic
   b. Instrumental
2. Societal
   a. Informal
   b. Formal

diverse experiences to achieve goals of varying merit. In turn authentication is awarded or sought by the learner and others in a never-ending process. It is important to bear in mind that traditional schooling and all existing forms of learning fit within the components suggested. However, no existing system or conceptualization has addressed the problems inherent in attending to the potential for humankind in efforts to broaden opportunities for all levels of society.

The dream is of an enormously rich and varied process that is all embracing, encompassing opportunities and promises of the present as well as of unseen tomorrows. And yet the tools at our disposal are restrictive. If the ideas incorporated within this model are interpreted too statically or without imagination, the result will be a deformed, truncated vision of what the future might have been.

Learners. The first component of the model is learners. (See Figure

1.) Potential learners include all persons whether functioning independently or in groups of varying sizes. They may engage in learning experiences at any time from the moment of birth. The learner's purpose, as well as the impetus for learning, level of development, time of entry and exit in learning experiences, and the level of motivation are all critical influences on the individual learner. Decisions about experiences and resources to be pursued are made in terms of each factor. In the case of group learning the structure of the group is an additional factor which influences learner potential and decision making.

The example of a trip or journey may be helpful in highlighting some of the decision points that are critical in deciding what one should do on Monday morning. If we are going on a trip, whether alone or with a group, there are bound to be both a number of incidental as well as intentional experiences. However, while not planning the incidental experiences, we may strive to keep open the possibility or desirability of incidental happenings and attempt to preclude those that might be undesirable. In such a manner lifelong learning may be enhanced not only by recognition of the serendipitous but also by planning intentional experiences that will optimize the possibility of the incidental while not conflicting with one's goals.

Of special importance in the comprehensive approach to lifelong learning is recognition that participants should be involved actively in the process of realizing their own potential, of becoming self-directed and responsible for their own learning. Fostering lifelong learners means supporting and cultivating individuals who are highly motivated and persistent, who are sensitive to relationships with others, and who are able to use group and private opportunities wisely in pursuit of desirable personal and societal goals. While not suggesting that incidental learning can or should be planned, individuals must be prepared to be open to it. Thus, learning is viewed from the perspective of a lifelong *natural* human function, but it is to be nurtured *extraordinarily*.

Experiences. The second component of the model is experiences. (See Figure 1.) Humans are involved in experiences and activities all the time. Some experiences are intentional, others accidental. The experiences from which learning results may be specially developed or occur fortuitously. For example, one might journey to Yellowstone Park or the Grand Tetons for aesthetic purposes, recreational purposes, scientific purposes, or political purposes. More or less might be learned in pursuit of any of these ends. Similar learnings might occur, but the specific learnings would be heavily dependent upon the learner's purpose(s).

The fact that the learner is involved in an experience is not the determining factor in whether or not learning is taking place. *The perception of the experience as important or significant to the learner is the critical element.* Intentional activities are sought, requested, arranged, even purchased by the learner; some are provided by institutions, others by individuals or groups. The experience itself may be short term or long term. It is in the realm of the paracurriculum identified by Shane that wider opportunities need to be developed by and recognized as valuable intentional learning.

For a geographer, the first drive from Indiana to Wyoming may reveal new insights into the topography, watersystems, populations, and productivity of the mid-American Grain Belt that previously had been inert facts. For a young child the same trip may be a nightmare of endless hours cooped up in a car "enjoying" travel games. For a teenager it may be an introduction to new soft drinks sampled at country gas stations, or to the task of being navigator or even pilot. For parents and children alike the trip may occasion learning skills of relating in order to survive in a small tent at a campsite while keeping down travel costs. What becomes clear is that the nature of the activity, its duration, or its source are not as important as how learners perceive it in terms of their purposes.

The *structure* of experiences or activities is another aspect of the components being described here. An excellent illustration of formal, controlled structure is a lesson. For example, a lesson may be designed for the young, designed to be purchased, or designed to be required. Formal education tends to be a series of lessons with a high degree of formal control and requirement. As long as the learner is a passive "receiver of lessons" the structure remains static, even oppressive. It is when learners become active, purposeful seekers that the structure must change to meet their demands. The lessons sought and directly paid for by adults tend to be considerably more responsive to learners' needs than lessons designed to meet some credentialing requirement. Seldom are such experiences recognized as lessons. But the traveler to the Grand Tetons whether artist, mechanic, housewife, student, or geographer creates or uses a structure critical to the realization of his or her intent.

In a similar way, *the locus of responsibility* has much to do with the learner's perception of the experience. There are laws, parents, traditions, unions, and schools requiring certain things to be learned. When the learner is immature, some requirements are a necessary part of the introduction to learning. But as learners mature they need an increasing amount of say in what responsibilities, desires, and needs they will fulfill and why. Such independence and personal judgment permits individuals to meet requirements for different reasons—the geographer gains professional knowledge, children respond to parental planning and direction, while teenagers pursue personal learning goals. In addition, individual growth and development cause individuals to relate to reasons for learning in changing ways at different times.

Resources. The third component is resources. (See Figure 1.) Often the experiences and resources are indistinct in that an experience may itself be the resource for certain learnings. (The automobile trip across the heartlands of the United States is at once an experience and a resource for other types of experiences.) We learn about resources, we experience them in the process of using them for other experiences with differing purposes. The learner may move to the resource in seeking fulfillment while trying to identify desirable experiences. For example, when planning an experience such as a trip it is not uncommon to seek out maps, travel guides, research reports, or other resources related to one's learning goals before determining the final form of the experience. Whatever the order or relationship, resources for learning are indispensable. In large measure the unavailability of adequate resources at the appropriate time is a major inhibitor in any effort to realize the lifelong learning potential of most of society. The resources used in lifelong learning are apt to be the same as those used in less extensive learning situations. The critical ingredient is learner intent.

Resources, whether books, films, informed persons, catalytic ideas or information, machinery or equipment, are inert without purposeful action or involvement of the learner and/or planner creating purposive involvement in an activity. Usable artifacts are all about us. But lifelong learning takes more than availability of some artifacts. Appropriate resources must be widely accessible and economically feasible. Today, resources are organized in places such as libraries, schools, stores, inquiry centers, and homes. In the future they may be organized not according to place, but according to topic or purpose in central storage centers with access through computer terminals in homes and businesses. While some of our current organizations and regulations make artifacts inaccessible to some at certain times and for different reasons, technology that bids to remove this obstacle is rapidly becoming available. But even when inaccessibility is no longer an obstacle, the learner must be aided to recognize needed resources and to develop ability to utilize diverse resources that are already available. Part of our learning must include being weaned away from dependence on others for supplying all resources and learning opportunities.

Authentication. During any learning experience or at its culmination comes a time of accounting or authentication of the value of the experience. This is the fourth major component of lifelong learning. In many ways it is the most critical because the popular practice of equating learning with the product of formal, instrumental certification of schooling has severely proscribed our vision of learning.

Attention only to formal, instrumental evaluation of experience fails to recognize the critical importance of personal authentication, both intrinsic in terms of personal feelings of success or failure and instrumental in terms of personal awareness of ability to perform up to one's self-set standards.

This is not to suggest that societally developed authentication of learning is not important. Given the interdependent nature of human relationships and the desire for a stable, just, social situation built on the highest standards of quality possible, accrediting and certifying mechanisms are indispensable. But they should not be permitted to limit our vision of learning.

The mode of authentication must vary according to the purpose of the learning. For example, continuing the analogy of a trip, we might embark upon a cross-country journey to test the efficiency of a vehicle's gas consumption. In such a case, quite elaborate and controlled authentication and certification procedures will be required. On the other hand, if the individual simply gets in a vehicle and takes off cross-country for his own pleasure or to get to a new location, simply arriving or supplying friends or relatives with snapshots taken enroute or an informal description of the trip may be adequate authentication (informal, external authentication). In some cases, only authentication of the activity is necessary, while learning is assumed.

Authentication of each and every aspect of lifelong learning is most immediately personal. Beyond personal authentication lies societal valuation and certification. Here too at least two types of social recognition result. On one level there is a recognition of completion of an increment of learning usually demonstrated through a graduation exercise, announcement of overcoming a hurdle, or awarding a certificate of completion. At another level for certain purposes groups or organizations award certificates or licenses which affirm completion of preparation or achievement of competence of instrumental value.

All manner of authentication must be recognized and more sophisticated record keeping systems must be developed to provide credibility for greater varieties of authentication, personal and societal, intrinsic, and instrumental, formal and informal. With the emphasis in lifelong learning on human fulfillment as a primary aim it suggests the need for wider recognition of personal intrinsic and informal forms of authentication to complement existing formal, social processes.

And So?

"Monday morning has arrived and I still don't know what I am to do," you protest. "How is such an analysis going to help?"

There are two responses. The model suggested as a tool for developing a comprehensive approach can be used to generate a series of questions—questions which will serve to focus the reflection and action of each learner or facilitator of learning. The questions arise in terms of learner, experiences, resources and authentication. You may ask, "What am I attempting to learn and what am I actually learning?" Or, "What am I trying to teach and what am I teaching?" "Am I going in the direction I wish to go?" Both inside and outside the existing structures we can begin to create or recreate new structures. Many of the questions will not be new. For example, we must ask, "What is the level of development of the learner?" "Is the time right for entry to or exit from a particular learning opportunity?" "What motivation is needed to engage the learner in a successful effort?" "What are the necessary resources?" "Can I make the necessary resources available?"

The second response is equally important and in many ways more difficult. We must face up to the fact that whether lifelong learner or facilitator of lifelong learning, we are all pilgrims in the human experience. The learning is personal—demanding commitment. Learning is not being a tourist in life's library, staring at covers of cultural records. There are no simple answers or surefire materials, methods, or curricula that will guarantee a learning society, that will permit us to be innoculated with wisdom.

"Then can we achieve a learning society?" The answer is yes, but the task will require commitment to a lifetime of involvement and cooperative seeking as travelers rather than as tourists. We must individually reflect on and grapple with the parables of life, the opportunities and temptations, as well as the principles that point the way. We must read and inquire, observe, and think, and grow. The educator and the learner are both travelers on the learning road, seeking to engage each other in an understanding, appreciation, and attainment of their mutual and personal interests and goals. As travelers, we join together to become creators of a learning society.

Those educational tourists seeking easy answers, instant, uniform learning, and unchallenged goals, may be on the same road as the traveler, but they see different things, and care little for the perspectives of others. They seek comfort and fuel at stations providing franchised familiarity, just like package tours. Whether teachers or students, they seek similar answers in the familiar educational institutions, regulations, and support systems that will provide information and degrees laid out in glossy catalogues and courses of study. The idea of a learning society extends beyond their immediate concerns and eludes them.

On the other hand, lifelong learners see themselves as pilgrims, traveling into unknown byways, seeking truth where it is, no matter what the form or how it may be packaged. As we set the goals as a learning society, we must seek to move from an educational system patterned after a common, industrial model to a more open, noncompetitive, self-selection model based on commitment rather than coercion. The best we can do on Monday morning is resolve to be travelers, pointing other travelers to some principles, utopian visions, and reformers' guidelines with the promise to join them on the journey. For those preferring to be tourists, they may turn to Colonel Sanders and Holiday Inn or their educational counterparts—teacher-proof curricula and Cousin Minnie Pearl's Franchised Nursery Schools.

ASCD 1978 Yearbook Committee Members

Norman V. Overly, Chairperson and Editor, Associate Professor of Education, Indiana University, Bloomington, Indiana

George D. Harris, President, Essex County College, Newark, New Jersey

Wilma S. Longstreet, Dean, School of Education, DePaul University, Chicago, Illinois

Edna Mitchell, Professor of Education, Mills College, Oakland, California

Carlos J. Ovando, Assistant Professor of Education, University of Southern California, Los Angeles, California

The Authors

Wilma S. Longstreet

Wilma S. Longstreet is the new Dean of the School of Education at DePaul University in Chicago. She received her Ph.D. degree in curriculum from Indiana University after living in Europe for an extended time, working as a foreign correspondent and as a teacher of English. She has taught in U.S. schools at both the elementary and secondary levels. Dr. Longstreet contributed to the 1978 Yearbook, and has pub-

lished several books and monographs, among them *Aspects of Ethnicity,
Beyond Jencks,* and *A Design for Social Education in the Open Curriculum* (with Shirley H. Engle). While at the University of Illinois she
developed and directed a pilot project, Teaching Ethnic Minorities,
which was based in the Chicago Public Schools. She continued working
in this area while at the University of Michigan-Flint, where she was
prior to going to DePaul. In addition to her chapter in Part III, Dr.
Longstreet wrote many of the literary pieces in Parts I and II of this
volume: Grandma's Search, p. 4; Sunday Feature 1990, p. 9; Helen
Keller's Search, p. 9; Seeing is not Enough, p. 10; News Feature 1995,
p. 17; A Commentary on the Intra-Generational Crisis, p. 23; A Teacher's
Lament, p. 32; Grandma and the Typewriter, p. 33; History through
Grandma's Eyes, p. 38; A Teacher's Musing, p. 52; A Professor Responds,
p. 53; Grandma's Wealth, p. 63; Newsflash 2006, p. 64; Committee Re-
flections on Remote Control, p. 65; Musings Circa 2010 A.D., p. 70; Italian
Reflection, p. 74; Round and Round, p. 85; Musings of a High School
Teacher, p. 92; Grandma Goes to School, p. 97; A Commentary on Edu-
cation, p. 98; Musings from a Master Teacher, p. 111; A Commentary on
Built-in Roadblocks to Change, p. 113; Musings of a Teacher, p. 117.

Virginia M. Macagnoni

Virginia M. Macagnoni is a professor in the Department of Curriculum and Supervision at the University of Georgia. A B.F.A. Art
graduate of Sophie Newcomb College with background in science, she
became a public school teacher and supervisor. She moved into the
generalist role because she believed that perspectives about the human
condition, including the aesthetic and the scientific, needed to be incorporated into the education of instructional leaders. She was invited
to contribute to the 1979 ASCD Yearbook because of ideas she had used
initially in a paper prepared for the 1977 World Conference of the World
Council for Curriculum and Instruction, "Lifelong Education in a World
Perspective," at Istanbul, Turkey. Two earlier publications projecting
her current interests are *Social Dimensions of the Self as an Open System:
A Curriculum Design* (Monograph, 1969) and *Democratization and Curriculum Renewal: An Exploratory Interdisciplinary Framework for Educational Planning.* Dr. Macagnoni contributed the Editorial, Watching a
Man Die, on p. 66, as well as the chapter in Part III.

Edna Mitchell

Edna Mitchell is Head of the Department and Professor of Education at Mills College, Oakland, California. She is a graduate of William Jewell College, Liberty, Missouri, and received her Ph.D. from the University of Missouri at Kansas City. Prior to joining the faculty at Mills College, she was a member of the faculty at Smith College, Northampton, Massachusetts and William Jewell College, and has taught preschool, elementary, and junior high levels. She served as an educational consultant to the Ministry of Education in Nepal for three summers, and has published articles on cross cultural educational issues related to Asia and Scandinavia. Her publications include articles on cross cultural patterns in toys and toy marketing practices, Danish play spaces, care of children in Scandinavian hospitals, women leaders in Nepal, career education for girls, sex roles in toys and books, and issues in teacher education. She is co-authoring a book, *From Folk Art to Modern Design,* which is an anthropological study of culture change in Denmark and Mexico. She also has research in progress examining children's friendship patterns during middle childhood. She has served on the publications committee for ASCD and as a Book Review Coordinator.

In addition to a chapter in Part III, Dr. Mitchell wrote Case Study of a Small Town, p. 15; Learning: Fun with Technology, p. 28; Ruth the "Zoomer," p. 48; Linda: Supermom, p. 79; Roundtable on the Hidden Curriculum, p. 88; and, A Commentary on A Break in the Walls of Time and Space, p. 119.

Carlos J. Ovando

Carlos J. Ovando is an Assistant Professor of Education at the University of Southern California. He received his Ph.D. in curriculum from Indiana University. His publications include *Factors Influencing High School Latino Students' Aspirations to Go to College: The Urban Midwest* (1977) and "Cultural Pluralism: Educational Concepts, Conflicts and Consequences," Special Edition of *Educational Research Quarterly* (1978). He recently addressed the Summer Institute of Chief State School Officers on "Political Issues in Bilingual/Bicultural Education," to be published under a grant from the U.S. Office of Education. Among his major interests are the development of pluralistic lifelong education and the analysis of bilingual and multicultural curricula. He is currently working on a bilingual education resource book for McGraw-Hill.

To Parts I and II Dr. Ovando contributed News Feature 1978, p. 25; 84 Year Old Receives M.S. in History, p. 28; A Commentary on the Role of Education, p. 30; George's Wife, p. 49; Steven's Dilemma, p. 74; Paulo, p. 91; A Commentary on Curriculum Voids and Institutional Violence, p. 94; Eunice and Camille, p. 100; Thoughts of an Inner City School Principal, p. 103; and, Scenes from a Staff Development Meeting, p. 114.

Norman V. Overly

Norman Overly, Chairperson of the ASCD 1979 Yearbook Committee and Editor of the Yearbook, is Associate Professor of Education and Chairman of the Department of Curriculum at Indiana University. He is a former elementary and high school teacher, educational missionary in Japan, Associate Secretary of ASCD, and Member at Large of the ASCD Board of Directors. He has edited and written a number of publications for ASCD, including *Global Studies: Problems and Promises for Elementary Teachers.* He has been active in the development of program and research for the World Council for Curriculum and Instruction and recently served as co-chairman of the Phi Delta Kappa Commission on Developing Curriculum Models for Lifelong Learning.

Dr. Overly wrote On Approaching the 1979 Yearbook, p. 1; The Learning Dream, p. 5; A Magnificent Twinkle, p. 8; Rico's Quest, p. 12; A Commentary on Determining the Basics, p. 13; Rico—Decision Maker, p. 35; A Commentary on Expanding the View of Learning, p. 36; The Price of a Ph.D. p. 40; Carol, p. 41; And Mike, p. 42; A Commentary on Lifelong Learning, p. 51; Dependence, p. 57; A Commentary on Global Values, p. 62; Parent's Lament, p. 67; Mac's Farm, p. 72; A Commentary on Stages of Morality, p. 75; Dave's Mid-life Christmas Card, p. 81; Rico: Justice, p. 95; Bakke Case Turmoil, p. 96; The Wizard of Menlo Park, p. 110; Universities and the Lifelong Learning Market, p. 122; A Commentary on Lifelong Learning: Conflicts of Purpose, p. 124; and the final chapter of the book.

ASCD
Board of Directors

Executive Council, 1978-79

President: DONALD R. FROST, Curriculum Director, Leyden High Schools, Franklin Park and Northlake, Illinois

President-Elect: BENJAMIN P. EBERSOLE, Assistant Superintendent, Curriculum and Instructional Services, Board of Education of Baltimore County, Towson, Maryland

Immediate Past President: ELIZABETH S. RANDOLPH, Associate Superintendent, Charlotte-Mecklenburg Schools, Charlotte, North Carolina

JULIANNA L. BOUDREAUX, Assistant Superintendent, Division of Instruction and Child Advocacy, New Orleans Public Schools, New Orleans, Louisiana

DOROTHY T. BRYANT, Coordinator of Instruction, Chicago Public Schools, Chicago, Illinois

GERALD BRYANT, Assistant Superintendent, Grand Island Public Schools, Grand Island, Nebraska

JOHN E. CODWELL, Education Consultant, Houston Independent School District, Houston, Texas

LAWRENCE S. FINKEL, Superintendent of Schools, Chester Township, Chester, New Jersey

DIANE GESS, Assistant Elementary Principal, East Ramapo School—Hillcrest School, Spring Valley, New York

EDWARD A. KARNS, Assistant Superintendent, Parma City Schools, Parma, Ohio

S. ELAINE KOHN, Consultant, National Middle School Resource Center, Indianapolis, Indiana

CHON LABRIER, Elementary Principal, Dulce Independent School, Dulce, New Mexico

DOLORES SILVA, Professor of Curriculum Theory and Development, Temple University, Philadelphia, Pennsylvania

Board Members Elected at Large

James A. Banks, University of Washington, Seattle (1980)

Marta M. Bequer, Dade County Public Schools, Miami, Florida (1982)

Gwyn Brownlee, Education Service Center, Region 10, Richardson, Texas (1979)

Reba Burnham, University of Georgia, Athens (1981)

Virgie Chattergy, University of Hawaii, Honolulu (1981)

Milly Cowles, University of Alabama, Birmingham (1982)

Mattie R. Crossley, Public Schools, Memphis, Tennessee (1982)

Theodore J. Czajkowski, Public Schools, Madison, Wisconsin (1980)

Ivan J. K. Dahl, University of North Dakota, Grand Forks (1979)

Lawrence S. Finkel, Chester Township Public Schools, Chester, New Jersey (1979)

Ben M. Harris, University of Texas, Austin, Texas (1980)

Ardelle Llewellyn, California State University, San Francisco (1981)

Blanche Martin, Public Schools, Rockford, Illinois (1982)

Marshall C. Perritt, Shelby County Schools, Memphis, Tennessee (1980)

Mary-Margaret Scobey, Educational Consultant, Eugene, Oregon (1979)

Ronald Stodghill, Public Schools, St. Louis, Missouri (1981)

Bob Taylor, University of Colorado, Boulder (1981)

William R. Thomas, Public Schools, Falls Church, Virginia (1982)

Georgia Williams, Unified School District, Berkeley, California (1980)

Mary J. Wood, Public Schools, Las Cruces, New Mexico (1979)

Unit Representatives to the Board of Directors

(Each Unit's President is listed first; others follow in alphabetical order.)

Alabama: M. Gardner McCollum, University of Alabama in Birmingham, University Station; James B. Condra, University of Alabama, Gadsden; Alvis Harthern, University of Montevallo, Montevallo

Alaska: Arlene Dey, Public Schools, Anchorage

Arizona: Dan Julien, Northern Arizona University, Flagstaff; Charles Fauset, Northern Arizona University, Flagstaff; Ben Furlong, Kyrene School District, Tempe

Arkansas: Harold E. Smith, Public Schools, El Dorado; James C. Williams, Geyer Springs Baptist Church, Little Rock

California (liaison) : William Georgiades, University of Southern California, Los Angeles; Leonard Herbst, Moreland School District, San Jose; Jessie Kobayashi, Whisman Elementary School District, Mountain View; David Martin, Mill Valley School District, Mill Valley

Colorado: Alex Reuter, Northglenn-Thornton School District, Denver; Dale F. Graham, Adams School District #14, Commerce City; P. L. Schmelzer, Poudre School District R-1, Fort Collins

Connecticut: Nelson W. Quinby III, Public Schools, Windsor; Edward Bourque, Public Schools, Fairfield; Joan D. Kerelejza, Public Schools, West Hartford

Delaware: Melville Warren, Capital School District, Dover; William J. Bailey, University of Delaware, Newark

District of Columbia: Mary Alexander, Public Schools, Washington; Phyllis J. Hobson, Public Schools, Washington; Andrea J. Irby, Public Schools, Washington

Florida: Charles Godwin, Palm Beach County Schools, West Palm Beach; Arthur J. Lewis, University of Florida, Gainesville; Patrick Mooney, Public Schools, Miami; Richard Stewart, Lee County Schools, Ft. Myers; Charlotte Eden Umholtz, Hillsborough County Schools, Tampa

Georgia: Ross Miller, West Georgia College, Carrolton; Martha Sue Jordan, University of Georgia, Athens; George W. Stansbury, Georgia State University, Atlanta

Hawaii: Ann Port, Hawaii Department of Education, Honolulu; Elaine Blitman, Punahou School, Honolulu

Idaho: Caroline Hulse, Nampa School District 131, Nampa; David A. Carroll, Public Schools, Boise

Illinois: Chester W. Dugger, Peoria School District 150, Peoria; Leone Bergfield, Litchfield Unit School District, Litchfield; Allan Dornseif, Matteson School District 162, Matteson; R. Kim Driggers, Centralia School District 135, Centralia; Mary Anne Elson, Public Schools, Springfield; Blanche Martin, Public Schools, Rockford; Lucille Werner, Peotone Unit District 207-U, Peotone

Indiana: Imogene Jones, Portage Township Schools, Portage; Georgia Bowman, Public Schools, Indianapolis; Donna Delph, Purdue University, Hammond; Charles Kline, Purdue University, West Lafayette

Iowa: Betty M. Atwood, Public Schools, Des Moines; Luther Kiser, Public Schools, Ames; Joe Lamberti, University of Northern Iowa, Cedar Falls

Kansas: Ruth Crossfield, Public Schools, Wichita; Paul Koehn, Unified School District 333, Concordia; Glenn Pyle, McPherson Unified Schools, McPherson

Kentucky: Hugh Cassell, Jefferson County Public Schools, Louisville; Ernest H. Garner, Public Schools, Bowling Green; Jack Neal, Western Kentucky University, Bowling Green

Louisiana: Lee Faucette, East Baton Rouge Parish Schools, Baton Rouge; Darryl W. Boudreaux, St. Mary Parish Schools, Patterson; Julianna Boudreaux, Public Schools, New Orleans; Edwin H. Friedrich, (retired) Public Schools, New Orleans

Maine: Richard Babb, Public Schools, Auburn; Kenneth E. Marks, Public Schools, Farmington

Maryland: Louise M. Berman, University of Maryland, College Park; Thelma Sparks, Anne Arundel County Public Schools, Annapolis; Janice Wickless, Maryland State Department of Education, Baltimore; Dennis Younger, Anne Arundel County Public Schools, Annapolis

Massachusetts: Paul V. Congdon, Springfield College, Springfield; Gilbert Bulley, Public Schools, Lynnfield; C. Louis Cedrone, Public Schools, Westwood; Armand LaSelva, Great Oak School, Danvers; Robert Munnelly, Public Schools, Reading

Michigan: Phil Robinson, Public Schools, River Rouge; LaBarbara Gragg, Wayne County Intermediate School District, Wayne; James L. Leary, Public Schools, Walled Lake; David Newbury, Public Schools, Hazel Park; Stuart Rankin, Public Schools, Detroit; Virginia Sorenson, Western Michigan University, Grand Rapids

Minnesota: Robert D. Ramsey, Public Schools, St. Louis Park; Richard Kimpston, University of Minnesota, Minneapolis; Thomas Myhra, Public Schools, Fridley

Mississippi: Mildred Williams, State Department of Education, Jackson; Norvel Burkett, Mississippi State University, State College

Missouri: Patricia Rocklage, Normandy School District, St. Louis; William Anthony, Public Schools, Jefferson City; Frank Morley, Ladue School District, St. Louis; Anne Price, Public Schools, St. Louis

Montana: Alice E. Hemphill, Public Schools, Great Falls; Donald R. Waldron, Public Schools, Libby

Nebraska: Mary Lou Novak, Public Schools, Waverly; Dorothy Hall, Public Schools, Omaha; Edgar A. Kelley, University of Nebraska, Lincoln

Nevada: Edward Howard, Nevada Department of Education, Carson City; Melvin Kirchner, Washoe County School District, Reno

New England: Jeanne M. Gardner, Rhode Island Department of Education, Providence

New Jersey: Charles J. Grippaldi, Township of Ocean Schools, Oakhurst; Mary Jane Diehl, Monmouth College, Witong Branch; Jean L. Greene, Public Schools, Moorestown; Frank Jaggard, Public Schools, Cinnaminson; Nicholas J. Sferrazza, Gloucester Township Public Schools, Blackwood; Arnold D. Tversky, Public Schools, Dover

New Mexico: Zella Hunter, Public Schools, Roswell; Patricia Christman, Public Schools, Albuquerque

New York: Thomas E. Curtis, State University of New York, Albany; James A. Beane, St. Bonaventure University, St. Bonaventure; Robert S. Brellis, Public Schools, Ronkonkoma; Frank Dunn, State University of New York College, Potsdam; Albert J. Eichel, Lawrence Public Schools, Cedarhurst; Helen Gerhardt, Public Schools, Rochester; Marcia Knoll, Public Schools, Forest Hills; Conrad Toepfer, Jr., State University of New York, Buffalo

North Carolina: J. Milford Clark, Western Carolina University, Cullowhee; Lucille Bazemore, Bertie County Public Schools, Windsor; Robert C. Hanes, Chapel Hill/Carrboro City Schools, Chapel Hill; Marcus C. Smith, Public Schools, Salisbury

ASCD
Review Council

ASCD
Headquarters Staff